The Artisan Republic
REVOLUTION, REACTION, AND
RESISTANCE IN LYON, 1848–1851

The Artisan Republic

Revolution, Reaction, and Resistance in Lyon 1848–1851

MARY LYNN STEWART-MCDOUGALL

McGill-Queen's University Press
Kingston and Montreal

Alan Sutton
Gloucester

© McGill-Queen's University Press 1984
ISBN 0-7735-0426-5
Legal deposit 3rd quarter 1984
Bibliothèque nationale du Québec
Printed in Canada

First published in Great Britain in 1984 by
Alan Sutton Publishing Company Limited
30 Brunswick Road
Gloucester GL1 1JJ
ISBN 0-86299-200-1

This book has been published with the help of a grant from
the Social Science Federation of Canada using funds provided by the Social Sciences and Humanities Research
Council of Canada.

Canadian Cataloguing in Publication Data

Stewart-McDougall, Mary Lynn.
The artisan republic: revolution, reaction, and
resistance in Lyon, 1848–1851
Includes index.
Bibliography: p.
ISBN 0-7735-0426-5
1. France–History–Second Republic, 1848–1852.
2. Lyon (France)–Politics and government.
3. Radicalism–France–Lyon–History–19th century.
I. Title.
DC801.L98S72 1984   944'.582307   C84-098465-0

For Mary C. Stewart

Contents

Tables

Acknowledgments

The late Mme Roche and other archivists at the Archives Départementales de Rhône and M. Hours at the Archives Municipales de Lyon initiated me in the pleasures of police, judicial, and local archival research; they gave generous, "insider" advice to "the foreign visitor who is always here," and I am very grateful for their suggestions about sources. Harvey Mitchell introduced me to the fields of labour and social history; Jeffrey Kaplow encouraged me to pursue local, urban studies; Robert Paxton and Isser Wolloch honed my analytical skills in the supervision of my dissertation on the workers' movement in Lyon. I thank them for their assistance and inspiration in the early stages of the long process of writing first a thesis, then a dissertation, and now a book on radicals in Lyon. Later, my colleagues, Rod Day, Anita Fellman, Bob Koepke, Bob Liebman, and an anonymous reader at the Social Science Federation of Canada made useful recommendations for revising first and second drafts of this book; their suggestions have been appreciated, even if not always accepted. Glen McDougall shared the joys – and sometimes isolation – of three of my trips to Lyon; he also assisted in very practical ways in the preparation of one version of the manuscript, for which I am most grateful. Bunnie Muter and Barbara Barnett patiently and efficiently typed and processed the manuscript, while Jenny Alexander helped with reproducing and mailing it at a critical juncture. The Social Sciences Research Council of the United States provided a generous Foreign Area Fellowship, Smith College offered Faculty Fellowships, and Simon Fraser University made President's Research Grants available to enable me to conduct nearly two years of research in Lyon. The Social Science Federation of Canada awarded a grant to facilitate publication of the manuscript. I thank all the above for essential contributions to this book. J.B. Noëllat's "Nouveau Plan Pittoresque et Historique de la Ville de Lyon" (1849) is reproduced by permission of the Bibliothèque Nationale, Paris.

Introduction

For too long, histories of the French Second Republic concentrated on the relationship between the national government and the Parisian crowd during the revolution of 1848 (February through June of 1848).[1] A reinterpretation of the revolution characterized it as a Parisian event overruled by the votes of the more traditional provincials in the April 1848 elections to the National Assembly and by the army, seconded by provincial militias, in the bloody repression of the Parisian revolt known as the June Days.[2] Yet a cursory reading of the dozens of books on the revolution in the departments published during the centennial corrects the vision of a radical capital awash in a sea of conservative provinces.[3] While the capital alone initiated the revolution, as one might expect in a centralized state, other major cities had "municipal revolutions," club movements, and economic experiments similar to the Parisian National Workshops. Too often the municipal revolutions were seen as products of the intervention of the Provisional Government commissioners. However, François Dutacq proved as early as 1910 that France's second city had an independent, almost federalist revolution, a radical club movement, and a variety of economic activities and organizations.[4] Justin Godart's centennial volume on the Voraces of Lyon added details on the only paramilitary unit to seize and hold fortifications in February 1848 and act as a semiofficial security force in subsequent months.[5]

Since the centennial, much more work has been done on revolutionary institutions and voluntary associations. Because most of the new institutional and social histories have also focused on Paris, this book attempts to redress the imbalance between the capital and the provinces by providing a modern institutional and social analysis of the Lyonnais revolution. Wherever possible, I have compared Lyonnais clubs, National Workshops, and Voraces not only to the current knowledge of their Parisian counterparts but to the available information on other provincial cities and towns. This social and comparative approach confirms Dutacq's basic insight about a uniquely radical yet peaceful revolution, but attributes less responsibility to the Provisional Government commissioners and more to the independent club movement. In addition to revealing a surprisingly sophisticated provincial club movement, the early chapters of this book posit a correlation between a popular radical tradition and a peaceful radical revolution.

Under the Provisional Government that governed France from February through April of 1848, the characteristic political response to the proclamation of manhood suffrage was to form clubs to prepare the urban electorate for the April elections to a National Assembly. Recently Peter Amann has studied the Parisian clubs as forerunners of modern mass political parties. His study shows that secret societies founded the clubs, that these clubs attracted mainly artisans and workers, and that clubs aimed to indoctrinate the electorate and elect democratic-socialists to the National Assembly. He argues that clubs rarely instigated the revolutionary *journées*, including the June Days, and that they elected few democratic-socialists because democratic procedures and concessions to occupational organizations (*corporations*) delayed the selection of a slate.[6] Economically, the Provisional Government promised the "organization of work" but did little more than divert radical theorists and *corporations* into the Luxemburg Commission, which was set up to consider work issues and which created public works in the guise of National Workshops. Remi Gossez, who scrutinized the *corporations* in the Luxemburg Commission, contends that the *corporations* merged into a single working-class political agent in the Luxemburg.[7] Amann and Gossez both believe the June Days revolt originated in the National Workshops rather than the clubs or *corporations*.

By comparing Lyonnais clubs, *corporations*, and National Workshops to the new interpretations of their Parisian counterparts, we can assess the broader significance of these interpretations. For instance, the Lyonnais club movement, which was smaller, more proletarian, and more pragmatic than the Parisian networks, was correspondingly less susceptible to extraneous (nonelectoral) demonstrations, more closely aligned with the *corporations*, and better able to avoid mistakes in the elections to the National Assembly. Consequently the Rhône, not the Seine, elected more democratic-socialist workers than any other department. Similarly, the club movement used its merger with the *corporations* and close ties to the National Workshops to restrain *corporations* from mass demonstrations and workshops from class warfare in June 1848. Although the clubs were seconded in their peace-keeping mission by sympathetic Provisional Government commissioners, these commissioners would not have been appointed, or responsive in turbulent situations, without a strong radical presence before and during the revolution.

Simply contrasting Parisian and Lyonnais clubs and *corporations* did not adequately account for the democratic-socialist yet peaceful quality of the Lyonnais revolution – or for the stubborn persistence of club networks and the flourishing of cooperatives after the revolution. Although Amann and others claim that secret societies established the clubs, no one has traced any but the club leaders back to the secret societies of the July Monarchy (1830–48).[8] The older histories of secret societies under the Second Republic pay equally little attention to the prototypes of the monarchy.[9] Three recent exceptions to this tendency have examined a less radical city (Toulon),[10] communists who were apolitical under the republic (Icarians),[11] and transitional workers' organizations (*compagnonnages* etc.).[12] In some radical cities, the oversight may reflect a lack of evidence. However, Lyon's Municipal and Departmental Archives contain fifteen years of daily police reports, files on political "criminals" and suspects, several cartons of Special Police investigations of secret societies, and dozens of dossiers on suspects and societies in the military court records of 1849–51.[13] Moreover, two members of secret societies under the monarchy left memoirs which help historians fill in the blanks in the police and judicial archives.[14]

These rich records yielded data on hundreds of radicals' initiation into and passage through radical circles. While many, as suspected, entered radical-republican conspiratorial groups, more belonged to communist propaganda societies and a minority began in friendly societies, proto-unions, or cooperatives. These patterns of recruitment explain why Lyonnais radicals were able to take advantage of manhood suffrage and avoid violent confrontations during the revolution. More specifically, a radical working-class leadership already had a constituency in the working-class community and an organization suitable for a political machine. Second, the leadership had already abandoned conspiratorial for evolutionary change through propaganda. Third, many remained on good terms with economic associations, which facilitated the links with the *corporations* during the revolution and with the cooperatives after the revolution. Finally, their prerevolutionary experimentation with clandestine networks and cooperatives helped them survive the repressive phase of the Second Republic. More attention to the prehistory of revolutionary associations in other radical cities may adjust the view of the revolution as *the* mobilizing event for workers and explain the flowering of voluntary associations under the Second Republic.

Modern scholarship and copious records also prompted a revaluation of the metamorphosis of the Voraces from a drinking society under the monarchy to a paramilitary unit in the revolution and then to a secret society and instigator of insurrection in 1849. To understand the initial revolutionary conversion, I relied on Natalie Zemon Davis's anthropological interpretations of traditional recreational groups as outlets for a variety of emotions, for the Voraces initially expressed rage about military installations directed at their community and then reorganized themselves as a paramilitary unit. However, research revealed prerevolutionary contacts with communists, who had also infiltrated a reformed *compagnonnage* (journeymen's association) known as the Union. Here, Agulhon's work on the assimilation of progressive politics into customary forms of sociability[15] and Robert Bezucha's article on "masks for revolution"[16] clarified the analysis by contrast with the Lyonnais situation. The Voraces and all the previously nonpolitical organizations that became radical during the Second Republic were newer, more urban, more formal, and ultimately, in the case of the Voraces, more consciously political than the *carnavals* and popular recreations of peasant villages. In Lyon, progressive politicians stood aloof from traditional recreation. More positively, the sections on the Voraces suggest historians might profitably examine the Republican Guard in Paris to understand the vital link between hostility toward the army as the main agent of government repression and distrust of all governments, including republican governments.

Plentiful police and judicial records provided information on over 1,500 alleged radicals; to compensate for the biases in these sources, the 1,500 names were cross-checked against references in the workers' and democratic-socialist press, the two inside accounts mentioned above, and a collection of electoral posters and pamphlets in the Fonds Coste of the Municipal Library; this procedure reduced the file to 1,206 individuals with reliable biographical data. Following the method of analysis introduced by George Rudé and refined by more quantitative historians of the working class,[17] I transferred the information to computer cards and submitted the file to the frequency and crosstab procedures of the Statistical Package for the Social Sciences. The statistical and tabular output helped me draw an enonomic, social, and demographic profile of the militants, which revealed much about the motivations and character of Lyonnais radicalism.

The most striking, and predictable, socioeconomic feature of this militant population was the predominance of silk workers. Since the seventeenth century, Lyon had been, in effect, a single-industry city producing a luxury good subject to a highly elastic demand. In the eighteenth century, the silk industry, or the *fabrique*, had become a capitalistic putting-out system with a few hundred merchants commissioning a few thousand master weavers to produce the silk. Masters' dependence on merchants' hiring and piece-rate (or wage) practices forged a bond of solidarity between masters and their "employees" or journeymen. One consequence was a tradition of economic militance. As early as 1709, silk weavers boycotted merchants to get higher piece-rates; in 1786 and again in 1789 and 1790, they struck for a general piece-rate agreement. Even under the ancien régime, silk workers had perceived the importance of concerted action, although they still depended upon paternalistic government officials to set piece-rates.[18] The Great Revolution (1789–94) had an ambiguous effect. On the one hand, the Constituent Assembly (1789–91) suppressed workers' *corporations* and outlawed all intervention, including, in theory, government intervention, in the labour market. On the other hand, the Jacobins introduced some workers to the concept of a right to work and to organized political activity. Yet bitter memories of the gruesome "terror" inflicted on Lyonnais counterrevolutionaries in 1793 outlasted the contradictory heritage of "liberal" economics and "social" politics.[19] Silk workers and local authorities returned to the ancien régime concept of collective contracts guaranteed by the government in 1807, 1811, 1817–19, and 1822. Moreover, silk workers formed authorized voluntary versions of their old *corporations* and used these mutual aid (benevolent or provident) societies as covers to organize strikes.[20]

After a severe depression, Lyonnais workers followed local liberals in welcoming the July Monarchy in 1830.[21] Yet a year and a half later, a master weavers' Mutualist Society united with a journeymen's group known as the Rhône Volunteers to force the prefect to grant a *tarif*, or contract. When the prefect hedged, they called a general or industry-wide strike which erupted into fighting. The Rhône Volunteers, who had been assembled by the conspiratorial Carbonari to reunite Savoy to France, withstood the infantry and governed the city for thirteen days before the insurrection was crushed by the army. Fernand Rude's influential *thèse* on the Mutualists and the insurrection of 1831 discerned in mutualism the seeds of syndicalism, in the Rhône Volunteers the germ of working-class political organization, and in the insurrection a demonstration of "the political capacity of the Lyon working class, the French working class." A subsequent interpretation characterized the insurrection as the birth of "working class consciousness of its unity."[22] In the next two years, the Mutualists enlarged and reorganized on craft (specialized) lines, while the journeymen founded a more purely occupational organization known as the Ferrandiniers. In 1834, the two societies asked merchants, *not* the authorities, for a *tarif*, then called a second general strike. When the government tried to suppress voluntary associations a few months later, the Mutualists pushed the small local radical-republican society into a second working-class insurrection. As Robert Bezucha shows in his study of the revolt, a monarchy recently established by revolution and consequently paranoid about republican rebellions reacted by bombarding the rebel suburb of Croix-Rousse and indicting eighty-seven alleged insurgents.[23] To deter future revolts, the army enclosed Croix-Rousse with armed fortifications. To prevent future mutualist associations, the civil authorities appointed a Special Police commissioner to monitor secret societies.[24]

Just as Bezucha's social analysis of the insurgents of 1834 went beyond Rude's more impressionistic emphasis on master silk weavers by noting the presence of immigrants and prominence of suburban insurgents, so the present analysis delves deeper into the nature of Lyonnais working-class culture and, more specifically, into the economic, social, and political sources of the radical movement of 1834 through 1851. Examining the industries and communities of the 1,206 radicals about whom we have sufficient data confirms and combines some earlier theses on the roots of working-class militance. Chapter 1 indicates that the movement recruited silk and other semi-artisanal workers in manufactures that were growing and innovating without industrializing; this corroborates Peter Stearns's hypothesis about the (economic) leadership of artisans in expansive but erratic industries and Christopher Johnson's conclusion about the Icarian communists' base in manufactures undergoing nonmechanical but capitalistic change.[25] Similarly, militants followed a pattern of migration from silk-weaving rural communes (or urban *quartiers*) to silk-weaving suburban communes. This pattern replicates and consolidates Agulhon's findings about a geographic break with tradition, Sewell's findings about trades receptive to outsiders, and Joan Scott's findings about the establishing of a permanent residence[26] as essential ingredients in the making of a working-class movement.

This analysis also suggests why and how workers became politically militant. Because most radicals were mobilized in the early adult years, when they were married and supporting young children, the pressures on the family economy at this stage of the family cycle radicalized workers. Their interest in mutual credit (savings and loan) institutions and consumer cooperatives argues for more attention to the pressures on workers as consumers. Second, the location of the radical societies, clubs, and cooperatives in suburban communes, and the social homogeneity and political independence of these communes, show the influence of working-class suburbs in engendering working-class consciousness and facilitating political experience.

Accounts of the repression of the second Lyonnais insurrection enabled me to examine the relationship between repression and resistance before as well as during the Second Republic; this examination refined the theories of a simple interaction between central government agents and local radicals. Clearly, the harsh sanctions and police surveillance of the mid-1830s made workers suspicious of government, susceptible to radical critiques, and adept at avoiding detection of their secret societies before (and after) the revolution. Similarly, the fortified wall around Croix-Rousse, as a constant reminder of the hostility of the government, was subversive of the politics of deference. However, another interest group intervened between government and radicals. Unlike local elites in more conservative cities,[27] Lyonnais "society" did not alleviate the effects of public policies by the practice of adequate private charity. Throughout this period, the fundamental antagonism was between merchants and workers. Although government policy shaped how and when radicals organized, local class conflict was the motor of working-class organization. All government officials, and especially the new republican officials, had to operate in the context of local social relations.

Earlier histories of the postrevolutionary phase of the Republic stressed the imposition of repressive measures by General Cavaignac (president from June through December 1848) and the erection of a virtual police state by Louis Napoleon Bonaparte (president from December 1848 to December 1852).[28] Since then, scholars have looked beyond the central state apparatus to inquire into the postrevolutionary acceptance of the Second Republic in rural regions. In particular, Philippe Vigier uncovered the socioeconomic bases of the indoctrination of peasants in many eastern departments by the time of the elections to the Legislative Assembly (1849).[29] Ted Margadent's systematic analysis of the sources of the peasant revolt against Napoleon's coup d'état of December 1851 suggests the catalytic role played by proto-urban towns integrated into a wider, often international market.[30]

This kind of research has enriched our understanding of the socioeconomic and geographic foundations of a radical movement in the countryside. It has sensitized historians to the "cultural diffusion" of republican ideas from urban to rural areas. Nevertheless, synthesizing the regional interpretations has been difficult, because one link in the causal chain has not been examined. Although Vigier, and Leo Loubère in his study of the radical transformation in the south of France,[31] ascribe a key role to provincial *urban* radicals, no one except Maurice Agulhon and John Merriman has inquired into radical organizations in provincial cities. Most surprisingly, the city Vigier labelled "the real capital of red France"[32] has not been investigated in the light of the new regional studies. The middle sections of this book, which carry on where Dutacq and Godart left off, are intended to rectify this obvious oversight by describing the survival of the democratic-socialist movement in Lyon after June 1848. In Lyon democratic-socialists were able to form electoral alliances appealing to peasants and capable of winning elections – as in the

April 1849 elections – and to maintain the clandestine network on which the electoral machine depended. Chapter 5 also assesses the responsibility of the secret societies, and the government, in provoking the Lyon insurrection of June 1849. The theme of these chapters is the durability of the democratic-socialist movement in the face of the first blasts of the repression; one implication is the need to take the secret societies of the republic seriously.

Another new approach to the postrevolutionary republic has been to study the dynamic between repression and radicalism from June of 1848 through the coup d'état of December 1851. John Merriman documented the series of blows directed at democratic-socialist associations, periodicals, and personnel and their cumulative effect of annihilating urban movements before the coup d'état.[33] Ted Margadent's complementary consideration of the rural revolts against the coup d'état as a crisis in political modernization disclosed a correlation between the sporadic coercion of government officials and armed forces and the creation of a democratic-socialist infrastructure in the countryside. Most recently, Thomas Forstenzer has looked at the often-ignored intentions of the government bureaucrats who implemented massive preventive strikes against radicals. He concluded that they were motivated by an exaggerated but not entirely unrealistic "social fear" of radicals who threatened an overthrow of the hierarchical social order.[34]

Taken together, these three works provide a comprehensive overview of the regional and, to a lesser extent, the local variations in the dynamic between governmental repression and radical resistance. This book adds a microcosmic view of the parallel growth of government sanctions and radical opposition before and during the Second Republic, a more precise identification of the cut-off point, when the imposition of martial law finally stunted the development of democratic-socialism, and finally, an assessment of the bureaucrats' perception of the "problem" of democratic-socialism in a particular local context. The final chapter explains why the insurrectionary city and its immediate hinterland did not resist the coup d'état and indirectly explicates the strange rebellion in much of the rest of the southeast.

The book is arranged, as much as possible, on both chronological and topical lines. The narrative sections reflect the author's belief that the revolution and the prolonged struggle between the reactionary governments and the democratic-socialist machine after June 1848 ought to be appreciated as an epic confrontation. The analytical sections try to link the drama to the larger themes of Second Republic history and, more generally, to the reception of democratic-socialism in a traditional world. Thus the first chapter, which examines the social, economic, and political bases of radicalism in the July Monarchy, contributes to the body of scholarship on the socioeconomic construction of revolution. Chapter 2 describes the autonomous and radical inception of the revolution in Lyon, and addresses the central question about the radical response to the republic: why did they forgo the use of force against the moderate republic? Chapter 3 charts the reciprocal relationship between a Provisional Government commissioner and the Voraces, the unemployed, and the clubs, and contends that both the commissioner's sensitive handling of an explosive situation and the clubs' sensible dedication to electoral politics account for the radical success in the National Assembly elections and the nonviolent experience of the revolution in Lyon. Conversely, chapter 4 attributes the conservative resurgence of May–June 1848 to the clubs' complacency after the National Assembly elections, and the peaceful resolution of the National Workshop crisis of June–July 1848 to the clubs' reawakening for another election, as well as the diplomatic conduct of another government commissioner.

The final three chapters discuss the dialectic of repression and resistance after June 1848 and describe the birth of the police state and death of the democratic-socialist movement in this radical city. Chapter 5 demonstrates how democratic-socialists entered cooperatives as a concrete expression of their commitment to a more egalitarian order and formed electoral alliances to withstand the reactionary assaults on their clubs; chapter 6 shows how the government's restrictions on open political activity drove seasoned radicals back into clandestine networks and recently politicized radicals into triggering the insurrection of June 1849. The final chapter reveals how the unrelenting pressure of martial law, military trials, and army surveillance ultimately broke the resistance in the city – and how the authorities' preoccupation with the city permitted democratic-socialist organizations to flourish in the country.

The Artisan Republic

Lyon and its suburbs in 1849

CHAPTER ONE

Ready for Revolution

When Parisians proclaimed the Second Republic in February 1848, the Lyonnais populace was prepared for a democratic revolution. In a few short weeks radicals, most of them workers, organized a club movement and elected more democratic-socialist workers to the National Assembly than any other department. As we shall see, the explanation for their prompt resort to electoral politics may be found in the structural factors promoting politicization under the July Monarchy. Both geography and demography had fostered functionally and socially distinct communities within the metropolis. By the 1840s the commercial city was already physically and politically separate from its industrial suburbs, in which workers lived as well as worked, developing class consciousness and a political leadership before the revolution. An economy dominated by a capricious silk market and social relations shaped by abiding antagonism between silk merchants and their labour force meant constant social tension. The first two working-class insurrections, provoked by the contentious state of the silk industry, attracted radical theorists to Lyon; moreover, repression of the insurrections alienated Lyonnais workers from the July Monarchy and interested a minority in radical critiques of the regime. Although this minority considered every current democratic, socialist, and communist theory, they rejected conspiracy to concentrate on propaganda. By 1848, they were able to capture the Lyonnais revolution, assuring its peaceful, democratic-socialist character.

GEOGRAPHIC AND DEMOGRAPHIC FACTORS

Although Lyon's radical reputation clearly owed much to its status as a major metropolis, the radical movement developed in the suburbs. The agglomeration drew people from much of southeastern France, with most immigrants settling in new industrial suburbs. Despite growth by immigration, the suburbs were stable and homogeneous enough to coalesce into working-class communities. Residents in these communities had to deal with serious economic and social problems. Since the suburbs were independent communes, working-class inhabitants had the opportunity to develop an indigenous political leadership to address these problems.

While Lyon was France's second largest metropolis, topography divided the city from its suburbs. The two great rivers that come to a confluence there carve a V-shaped peninsula tapering from north to south. In 1848, most of the city was confined to the peninsula between the Rhône and Saône rivers south of the steep slopes of Mount St Sebastien. On the opposite banks of the two rivers and on the northern plateau lay independent suburban communes. Physical and political divisions had encouraged functional differentiation into a commercial core enclosed within industrial quarters and suburbs.[1]

The peninsula contained a new industrial quarter, residential districts, administrative sections, and the banking and commercial firms for which Lyon was famous. At the southern tip of the peninsula developers were constructing an industrial quarter, Perrache, around the terminus for the second French railroad (and, businessmen and politicians hoped, for the proposed Paris-Marseilles lines).[2] Perrache also contained the main barracks for the huge army stationed in Lyon. Just north came Bellecour, a large square restored under Napoleon. In its imposing buildings lived the few aristocrats residing in Lyon and the wealthier bankers and silk merchants. Further north were the Renaissance-style administrative and political centres. The Prefecture and Hôtel de ville would be the destination of many demonstrations during the Second Republic. To reach them, however, the demonstrators had to snake through narrow, winding streets overshadowed by five- or six-storied tenements full of silk weavers.

Some of these streets ascended Mount St Sebastien to a fortified wall on the ridge of the hill. The hill and wall, installed after the insurrection of 1834, created a physical and psychological barrier between Lyon and its closest suburb, Croix-Rousse. This independent commune of thirty thousand inhabitants sheltered most of the weavers of fancy silk in the metropolis. Because Croix-Rousse weavers owned and operated the big, new Jacquart looms, they rented and lived in large rooms in apartment blocks built since 1808 to accommodate the looms. The streets were wider and sunnier than in the weaving quarters of the city.[3] These relatively fortunate weavers had led the insurrection of 1834 and would lead the insurrection of 1849. More constructively, they would create and maintain the democratic-socialist movement of the monarchy and the republic.

To the west, the old parishes of St Jean, St Paul, and St Georges were crushed between the Saône River and the precipitous cliffs of Fourvières. From St Jean Cathedral to St Georges Church, tall Renaissance houses towered over dark, damp streets. Here thousands of plain silk weavers crowded into tiny rooms, where they strained to see the fine threads on their looms and coughed up silk dust. Medical authorities considered the old quarters one of the unhealthiest districts in Europe.[4] Few of these unfortunate weavers participated in the radical movement. The plateau of Fourvières, overlooking the old quarters, was dominated by convents and charitable institutions, notably the Houses of Providence that taught indigent youngsters how to weave. Silk weavers resented the Providences, whose low prices undercut their piece-rates. On the first evening of the republic, crowds from Croix-Rousse would smash looms in these and other charity workshops throughout the region. Crowds would also devastate the few mechanized workshops located in the suburb of Vaise, to the north of the old quarters.[5]

In the east, the largest suburb spread out from the Rhône River onto the plains. Compared to Croix-Rousse, the commune of Guillotière had a disparate socioeconomic base. A small section known as Brotteaux served as an elegant residential district, but most of the area was covered with humble new apartment buildings housing textile and clothing workers. Docks, shipyards, and an infant chemical industry had appeared along the river.[6] During the republic, Guillotière would become a democratic-socialist stronghold and fight a long battle for lay control of elementary education.

In the first half of the nineteenth century, Lyon's growth rate of 1.62 (to 177,190 inhabitants) hardly compared with the virtual doubling of factory town populations. But suburban growth was explosive: the population of Croix-Rousse quadrupled to 28,711, and the inhabitants of Guillotière multiplied seven-fold to 41,528.[7] As in other metropolitan centres, growth was not primarily "natural," for two-thirds to three-quarters of the new residents were immigrants. Because mid-nineteenth-century social statisticians assumed that mass immigrations meant "floating" populations, census-takers categorized people as householders or lodgers. The 1839 census recorded six householders for every lodger in Lyon.[8]

Social historians like Rudé and the Tillys have challenged the connections made by contemporaries and Louis Chevalier between uprooted urban male populations on the one hand, and rising crime and revolution, on the other.[9] The Lyonnais data confirm a correlation between immigration, increased crime, and revolution. For instance, almost two-thirds of the largely male criminal defendants, whose numbers tripled, were not native to Lyon. Similarly, immigrants accounted for 68 per cent of the known participants in the radical societies

TABLE 1

Changes in the Incidence of Apolitical and Political "Crimes," 1845–47

Type of Crime Date	Begging and Vagrancy	Theft	Other Apolitical	Political and Union Offences
1st semester 1845	239	227	337	45
1st semester 1847	404	355	477	33
% change 1845–7	+69	+56	+41	−27

Source: ADR, U, Tribunal Correctionel, January–July 1845 and 1847.

of 1834 through 1851 and 58 per cent of the convicted insurgents of 1849.[10] However, an 1841 survey of men eligible for the Croix-Rousse National Guard (twenty-five to thirty-five years of age) found that 74 per cent of these suburbanites had not been born in the Lyonnais agglomeration.[11] Apparently, immigrants were not overrepresented among common criminals, radicals, and insurgents. Furthermore, the causal relationships between immigration, criminality, and revolution are dubious. Thus the Lyonnais population declined slightly in the mid-1840s, while the number of criminal prosecutions rose by over 40 per cent. Since emigration was more characteristic of these difficult years, immigration hardly swelled the crime wave. Rather mass unemployment prompted both crime and emigration as the destitute either resorted to begging or left the city to survive. More to the point, soaring crime rates should not be related to political militance or revolution. In the three years preceding the revolution, begging, vagrancy, and other apolitical crimes increased, but political trials decreased.

Further analysis reveals that common criminals and militants were quite different people. Only a handful of common criminals had been prosecuted for political or union offences; equally few political or union defendants had committed felonies.[12] Table 2 indicates that the largest occupational category in Lyon, silk workers, was underrepresented in the criminal population but overrepresented in the radical movement, while artisanal workers were more prevalent in criminal than radical circles. Table 3 shows that far more of the criminal defendants fell in the difficult sixteen to twenty-five years cohort, when young single men moved around to find work and learn a trade. Conversely, the bulk of the insurgents and radicals were in the twenty-six to thirty-five years cohort, when men tended to settle down, marry, and start a family. Silk weavers especially were "carried by vocation and character" to marriage, usually between twenty-four and twenty-seven years of age. As soon as they could afford two looms, they married silk workers and most couples

TABLE 2

Occupational Analysis of Common Criminals, Recidivists, and Radicals

	Common Criminals, 1st semesters, 1838 and 1845	Recidivists, 1834–8	Radicals, 1834–51
Percentage of silk workers	14	19	43
Percentage of artisans	33	42	26
Number of cases	1,477	1,074	1,150

Sources: AN BB³⁰ 1287–8, Etat des individus jugés pendant l'année 1834 (–1838) et précédemment condamnés pour crimes, délits ou contraventions; ADR, U, Tribunal Correctionnel, 1834–51; AML, I², Police générale.

TABLE 3

Age Profile of Common Criminals, Insurgents, and Radicals

Population: Cohorts	Criminals, 1st half of 1838	Insurgents, June 1849	Radicals, 1834–51
16–25	33%	21.5%	18%
26–35	29%	52%	40%
36–45	18%	16%	29%
46 and older	19%	10.5%	12.5%
Total	637	56	614

Source (Insurgents): ADR, U, Conseil de Guerre, Dossiers individuels, Insurrection de 1849.

raised two or three children. This stage in the family cycle, when young children were a drain on family income, put added strain on already precarious family economies and this must have radicalized many weavers and induced them to join consumer cooperatives.[13] Finally, most criminals lived in the cheaper, overcrowded old quarters, with their concentration of single men, but half the militants resided in the suburbs, which had lower population densities and higher proportions of married men.[14]

Clearly, immigration had mixed effects on Lyon. Middle-aged, married immigrants who found work in the silk industry and settled in the suburbs often engaged in political or professional activities. Younger immigrants practising other (usually less skilled) trades and living in the city were more likely to commit crimes. Social scientists visiting Lyon certainly paid more attention to its radical, working-class movement than to its crime rate. When they did comment on Lyonnais crime, they contrasted it with the rampant criminality in Paris and the factory towns. They also noticed fewer signs of the alcoholism and family breakdown that they associated with large immigrant populations.[15]

Lyon probably suffered less social disruption than Paris because of its immigrants' origins and options. Unlike the capital, which attracted people from all over France, Lyon drew peasants from adjacent and nearby departments, particularly the overpopulated mountainous departments which had traditionally sent their excess population to Lyon.[16] Short- and medium-distance migration to a city inhabited by fellow countrymen must have alleviated individual alienation and hence a good deal of social malaise. Since many migrants came from villages with cottage silk industries, their work experience helped them find employment in Lyon. Having a job facilitated integration into a new community.[17]

Lyonnais immigration also nurtured militance. As table 4 illustrates, more Lyonnais militants had been born in other regions of the Rhône or in contiguous departments than had been born in the metropolis. Also, nearly half of the radical weavers came from the same outlying districts. These migrants did not import revolutionary ideas from their natal villages.[18] Although a third of the radical migrants had left departments that would resist the coup d'état of 1851, only twenty-two can be traced to the actual centres of resistance.[19] The decisive factors for Lyonnais migrants, as for the radicals Agulhon and Scott studied, were the break with tradition and the move to the metropolis.

Residential patterns also discouraged social disorder and encouraged political activism. Two-thirds of the new inhabitants established their residence in the suburbs, which had lower taxes than the city and better housing than the old quarters.[20] Although a majority of suburbanites were immigrants, a significant minority had "moved up" from the city to the suburbs. Whether they came from the countryside or the city, they generally married just before or after moving to the suburb and setting up in a trade.[21] The suburbs, though growing by immigration, were inhabited by stable families.[22] Table 5 reveals that more radical migrants lived in the suburbs than in the city and nearly half of the native militants resided in the suburbs. The statistics suggest that radicals, like their neighbours, tried to improve their living conditions by moving to the cheaper yet healthier suburbs.

Two examples will clarify how immigration and immigrant communities fostered radicalism. One individual illustrates the break with tradition; the largest "foreign" group illustrates how immigrants coalesced to help one another. Joseph Benoit was born into a peasant family in the Ain, but he was sent first to a friend of his father in Geneva, and then to a school in Lyon for an education. His break with tradition was accentuated by his unusual educational opportunity, especially since his

TABLE 4
Birthplaces of Radicals

Birthplaces	All radicals	Radical Silk Weavers	Radical Migrants
Lyonnais metropolis	30%	36%	
Rhône and contiguous departments	36.5%	47%	52%
Noncontiguous departments	27%	14%	39%
Foreign countries	6%	3%	9%
Total	665	265	463

TABLE 5
Radicals' Residential Communities

	Communities				
Radical Groups	Lyon	Croix-Rousse	Guillotière	Other Suburbs	Elsewhere
370 silk workers	38%	38%	7%	9%	8%
358 migrants	47%	19%	12%	18%	4%
191 short-distance migrants	39%	26%	11%	17%	7%
161 native Lyonnais	52%	24%	11%	12%	1%

first teacher was a former revolutionary who steeped him in democratic and egalitarian theories. However, his formal education ended prematurely when family reverses threw him on the mercies of two former peasants from his natal village. He found work as a weaver and eventually became a *chef*, married, and moved to Croix-Rousse, where he and a group of friends began the communist propaganda which culminated in his (and several radical weavers') election to the National and Legislative assemblies.[23]

The Savoyards, who had been French until 1815, continued to migrate in large numbers to Lyon. Most Savoyard householders in the census books had lodgers, often apprentices, from Savoy. Presumably the householders were assisting more recent arrivals by providing lodging and employment.[24] Like other foreign communities in Lyon, the Savoyards founded mutual aid societies to help one another in times of sickness or death.[25] Unemployed Savoyards also joined the Rhone Volunteers organized by the Carbonari in 1831 to reunite Savoy to France; others would form a legion to "liberate" their homeland in 1848.

Probably their habit of associating for self-help spilled over to organizing for political purposes.

The suburbs themselves inspired class consciousness. Excluding
Brotteaux, the suburbs were socially homogeneous. Three-quarters of
the economically active Croix-Rousseans worked in the silk industry,
while nearly half of the nonagricultural population of Guillotière were
textile or clothing workers. Almost every apartment in sections of these
communes housed textile workers.[26] Because these workers wove at
home, they spent most of their lives in their neighbourhoods. If they did
not share a communal workplace like a factory, they did work, play, and
live in close proximity. Indeed, these communities enhanced the narrow
occupational base of class consciousness by making workers aware of
their common predicament as consumers as well as producers.[27]

Moreover, these working-class suburbs became, by default, centres of
working-class political life. In the absence of a significant aristocratic or
bourgeois presence, except in Brotteaux,[28] workers developed an indigenous political elite. Because the suburbs were beyond the Central Police
commissioner's jurisdiction, radical politicians eluded serious police
surveillance. Radicals simply met in the surburban cafes and posted a
sentry to watch for the four or five local agents, whom they knew. When
an agent approached, the political gathering switched into a social
occasion.[29]

In sum, the experience of short-distance migration and residence in the
suburbs left many Lyonnais receptive to new social and political theories.
Suburbs full of immigrant workers awakened class consciousness, while
isolation from bourgeois elites and police surveillance permitted working-
class political expression. Yet demography and geography only provided
the recruits and locale for radicalism; economic and social tensions
mobilized the movement.

ECONOMIC AND SOCIAL CONFLICT

Lyon's industrial and commercial base subjected the populace to constant
economic fluctuations unrelieved by adequate employment or welfare
policies. The luxury good industry which dominated the economy
depended upon a peculiarly unstable overseas market. The silk merchants
tried to protect themselves by passing on the costs of slumps to the master
silk weavers, who consistently resisted the cutbacks and wage reductions.
Their proto-unions and strikes mobilized and radicalized workers. In
July Monarchy Lyon, no traditional elite existed to mitigate this stark
class conflict by paternalistic policies. Disillusioned by frequent crises
and unresponsive elites, many workers abandoned the politics of

deference and accepted radical critiques of the economic and social system even before the revolution of 1848.

The silk industry overshadowed all other industry and commerce in the metropolis. It produced almost one-third of the city's annual income, while its closest competitor, banking, earned less than a fifth. Silk weaving, the final stage of production, employed nearly a third of the economically active population. In the silk-weaving suburb, Croix-Rousse, there was one loom for every two residents.[30] A Croix-Rousse weavers' newspaper referred to the *fabrique* as the "soul" of the commune.[31]

In the first half of the nineteenth century, silk merchants had introduced lighter fabrics and cheaper labour, which had lowered costs and nearly doubled sales in three decades.[32] Because the lighter, simpler fabrics could be woven by less skilled workers, merchants had relied more and more on female and rural labour. They had accelerated the process of decentralization after the depression of the late 1820s and the insurrections of the early 1830s, which taught them to appreciate the cheaper and more docile rural labour force.[33] The number of looms in the metropolis increased by only 25 per cent between 1835 and 1848, while the number in the five surrounding departments almost doubled to 22,000 (almost two-thirds as many as in the metropolis).[34] Lyonnais weavers realized that ruralization intensified proletarianization and complained bitterly about it.[35] But this was a distant threat compared to the immediate problems of job and wage uncertainties.

In the 1840s about 550 Lyonnais merchants participated in the silk market. They had cornered a segment of the high fashion market by catering to every fanciful whim. Since fashion was fickle, merchants who specialized in novelty fabrics were ruined when their fabric lost favour. As a result, two or three firms would file for bankruptcy in generally buoyant years. Other firms soon replaced them, for the average firm required only a relatively modest initial capital outlay. Two or three merchants formed a partnership, rented a shop, hired a designer to create patterns, purchased silk thread, and put it out, on commission, to master weavers.[36] Because they did not have to maintain expensive plants or machinery, they could cut their commissions during the recurring crises. These cutbacks hurt the master weavers, who had often hired a "mounter" to attach the threads to the looms – a process which could take a month for fancy silks. Cutbacks without compensation for mounting looms were a constant source of irritation between merchants and masters.[37]

As a luxury good and an export commodity, silk was subject to tremendous shifts in demand. Three-fifths of the finished product was exported, principally to Great Britain and the United States.[38] Unfortunately, the foreign market was an unstable foundation for expansion, since British and American demand fluctuated wildly. Once a decade these countries experienced serious financial crashes and their buyers slashed their orders for luxury silks. French buyers, equally responsive to international financial crises, also restricted their purchases. Faced with a drastic drop in demand – and a scarcity of specie or credit – dozens of marginal silk firms declared bankruptcy.[39] Even solid firms limited production, for few merchants could afford to stockpile expensive silks during slumps. The silk market affected every industry in the metropolis. "When it prospers, everything around it prospers; when it declines, everything declines equally."[40]

Although merchants had few contacts with production, they had sponsored technical advances. The Jacquart device which mechanized the apparatus guiding the pattern halved the time needed to mount looms, eliminated the weaver's helper, and quadrupled productivity. When merchants introduced Jacquart looms in 1807, weavers' helpers rioted and destroyed the new looms. When merchants persisted, masters learned to attach the device to old looms and, if they could afford five hundred francs, bought it.[41] By 1846 almost one-third of the looms in the metropolis had Jacquarts.[42] Efforts to encourage further mechanization mainly subsidized inventions that adapted the Jacquart to complicated fabrics. Few merchants imported power looms from England because the fragile silk thread broke on the rickety wooden looms.[43] In 1848, the only fully mechanized looms were ribbon looms, which would be the only privately owned looms demolished in the first days of the revolution.

Technical advances without full mechanization had not resulted in concentration of production, so most silk workers laboured in their own or someone else's homes. Ten thousand master weavers set up two or three or, more rarely, four to six looms in their apartments.[44] Most masters took charge of one loom, had their wife operate the second, and hired journeymen for any others. The masters, called *chefs d'atelier*, were not independent artisans but domestic workers who received orders, raw materials, and piece-rates for the finished product from merchants. Often they borrowed from merchants to buy or mount a loom. The *fabrique* had even devised a special *livret d'acquit*, which required a master to work for a merchant until the loan was repaid.[45] The *livret* bound masters to merchants much as the truck system trapped workers in factories, but masters had less job security than factory workers, since masters rarely worked through recessions.

Thirty thousand journeymen worked for about half the masters' piece-rates.[46] Half were men, and many of them specialized in fancy silks. In the busy summer season, they earned enough to wear bourgeois attire. Because they were hired for particular pieces and then released, they were underemployed in the slow winter season, when they regularly pawned their good clothing. Only 2,000 *compagnons* accumulated enough money to open new workshops between 1834 and 1846. The women concentrated in simple silks and received lower wages. Conversely, they had more security, for demand was steadier for simple silks and masters usually lodged *compagnonnes*. Masters also lodged apprentices. As they learned their trade, they received a percentage of the piece-rate which rose with their proficiency. But a growing number of orphans and indigent children served long, virtually unpaid apprenticeships in Providences.[47] Abuse of apprenticeship was another cause of friction, in this case between weavers and the religious orders.

The market and merchants' labour policies made silk weaving an uncertain occupation which called out for rational organization. During the depression years of 1837 and 1845–6, as well as the winters of 1839 and 1842, up to three-quarters of the silk weavers were underemployed.[48] Merchants who continued to commission silk lowered piece-rates. After the *fabrique* revived, merchants were reluctant to return to the old rates before they recouped losses incurred during the recessions. Weavers realized they could not resist rate reductions during downturns but could strike for better pay during upturns of the business cycle. Under the July Monarchy, they developed the tactic, familiar later in the century,[49] of waiting until full employment to withhold their services. Working-class political activity also ebbed and flowed with the business cycle, albeit in a less direct, reverse manner: political activism frequently peaked in the economic troughs.

In 1830, as silk orders picked up following a depression, master weavers converted their "Mutual Assistance Society" into a resistance society. Once the *fabrique* reached full employment in 1831, the Mutualists approached the prefect for a *tarif* (guaranteed piece-rates). After the prefect reneged on his promise to grant a *tarif*, the Mutualists lost confidence in government intervention and called an industry-wide general strike. When they lost control of the situation, the first working-class insurrection began. Although they gained little from this insurrection, they learned two valuable lessons: do not rely on government officials and be prepared to control strikes. Accordingly their second general strike, three years later, began as a partial, progressive boycott of merchants paying below average rates and this time they prevented any significant outbreak of violence. The second insurrection erupted two months later, in reaction to government repression, notably an association act outlawing large associations like the Mutualists.[50] Government policy toward voluntary societies became another determining factor in the evolution of working-class organization.

After the insurrection of 1834, the new Special Police commissioner investigated any large aggregation of workers with broad occupational concerns, especially if they tried to circumvent the law by means of tiny local sections linked by delegates to a central committee. He arrested *chefs* who tried to form legal producers' cooperatives for replicating "all the elements of Mutualism" or, more specifically, for organizing a large number of shareholders in small branches. When the Mutualists reassembled in 1839 or 1840, they were very secretive and circumspect. Thus they formed "workshops" of twenty members who reported, through representatives, to the "*patrons* of the *fabrique*"; they screened aspiring members for "morality" and subjected them to initiations like traditional secret societies, and they avoided strikes and, until 1846, cooperative schemes. The Mutualists would stay out of politics during the revolution because they believed the "era of liberty" would solve economic problems, but some of the "new Mutualists" of 1846 would contribute to the democratic-socialist campaign for the Legislative Assembly in 1849. Meanwhile, their system of local sections coordinated by a central committee served the club movement well in 1848 and their provisions for secrecy helped political societies survive the repression of the monarchy and the later years of the republic.[51]

Moreover, *chefs* developed new and more efficient organizational modes for strikes. In 1843, when the *fabrique* revived and a new prefect decided to temper the police pressure on voluntary societies by authorizing occupational "circles," eight hundred *chefs* applied for authorization for six circles. Whereas previous circles had functioned as social/cultural associations, these circles, which represented weavers of specific silks, collected strike funds. In the booming economy of 1844, four circles blacklisted those merchants paying below rates set by the circles and three circles wrested concessions from merchants.[52] These smaller, craft-like unions represented a useful specialization, as indicated by their decision to remain craft unions in 1848, when previously unorganized silk workers tried to form industry-wide associations. In 1848, these proto-unions also waited before abandoning the tactic of striking in full employment.

Strikes and insurrections could lead to political radicalization. Table 6 reveals that twenty-seven men first involved in strikes were next implicated in the insurrections of the 1830s, while forty-three strikers proceeded directly to radical political activities. Similarly, twelve men first implicated in the insurrections of the 1830s moved on to the radical societies of the monarchy and thence to clubs and committees under the republic. The most famous example is another self-educated immigrant weaver, Louis Greppo, who wet his feet in the strikes and insurrections of the early 1830s, plunged into communist propaganda in the late 1830s and early 1840s, and emerged as a municipal councillor and a deputy in 1848 and 1849.

TABLE 6
Some patterns of mobilization into radicalism

First Activity	Second Activity		
	Insurrections of the 1830s	Radical Societies of the Monarchy	Radical Politics under the Republic
Unions or strikes under the monarchy	27	11	32
Insurrections of the 1830s	5	12	1
Radical societies of the monarchy		9	54

Sources: see tables 2 and 3; AN BB[30] 294, ADR, M, Police générale; ADR, R, Conseil de Guerre, Sociétés secrétes.

Strikes were only the most dramatic clashes between merchants and masters. As early as 1806, the national government established one of the new industrial relations boards known as the *Conseil des Prud'hommes* representing the two parties. Forty per cent of the nearly 6,000 conflicts referred to the *Conseil des Prud'hommes* in 1846 concerned masters and merchants. Usually masters charged merchants with arbitrarily cutting commissions after masters had paid to mount looms in expectation of commissions large enough to cover the costs of mounting. While the council did order merchants to reimburse masters, it could not enforce these orders. Throughout the July Monarchy, *chefs* tried to translate favourable decisions into precedents to introduce some certainty into this chaotic industry.[53] Under the republic, they would turn to other agencies to institutionalize "workers' rights."

Master-journeymen disputes filled less than a quarter of the council's calendar – a low proportion given their numerical preponderance and close contacts. In most instances, masters initiated proceedings against journeymen who left without finishing pieces. Although journeymen contested deductions in pay for poor workmanship, they did not challenge *chefs* about piece-rates, for they realized that merchants set the rates. Their *compagnonnage*, called the Ferrandiniers, supported the two general strikes in the 1830s and the smaller job actions in the 1840s.[54] Solidarity between *chefs* and *compagnons* would also be the keynote during the republic.

Most of the remaining cases and half the disputes adjudicated by small panels of Prud'hommes pitted a master against an apprentice. The large number of apprentices leaving before their contract stipulated implies that they did not need three years to learn silk weaving. A few egregious cases involved apprentices spending up to seven unpaid years in Providences. An 1840 case came to the attention of a Croix-Rousse newspaper and prompted a campaign against the unfair competition of the charity workshops. Seven years later the local republican newspaper, together with republican newspapers throughout France, renewed the campaign. Six months before the revolution a scandal in a Croix-Rousse Providence provoked violent attacks on the Providence and petitions demanding that charitable shops be subjected to Prud'hommes' regulations on the length of apprenticeship and pay scales. When the prefect accepted only the first suggestion, he left the weavers dissatisfied.[55]

In addition to textiles, Lyon had a clothing industry employing over 3,000 in 1847.[56] Like the *fabrique*, the clothing industries were putting-out industries undergoing nonmechanical change in a capitalistic direction. Adapting the silk workers' model to their own situations, tailors' and shoemakers' workers formed resistance societies and held industry-wide, then selective strikes in the 1830s. The tailors' society was part of a regional federation of friendly societies, while the shoemakers' society was a coalition of three rival *compagnonnages*.[57] The leader, Castel, and two members of the repressed tailors' society went on to radical politics in the 1840s; the more provisional shoemakers' society reassembled and struck in 1848. In general, clothing workers provided the second-largest contingent of militants under the republic.

As befits a city on two rivers, Lyon had transport industries. Since 1831 steam-powered boats had reduced travel time and attracted passengers and cargo. After a few incidents, other transport workers tolerated the steamers, but in 1848, luddites would hit steamship construction yards. Despite this, the eleven steamship companies would thrive and the busy steamboat builders, like other construction workers, would strike for the ten-hour day under the republic. While steam navigation enjoyed a golden age, Lyonnais railways endured hard times. The glowing promises of the 1830s, when Marc Seguin built France's first locomotives, flickered out in the 1840s, as workshop after workshop closed. The railway workers, so active in revolutionary Paris, would be absent from Lyon. Meanwhile, Lyonnais entrepreneurs caught "railway mania." In the 1840s, over a hundred local firms raised millions of francs for lines from Paris to Marseilles, promoted these ventures, and were represented on the boards of the companies that received the concessions. Unfortunately, the financial crash of 1845 burst the speculative bubble and sent railroad stocks tumbling down. The Lyon-Avignon Company was liquidated in 1847; the Paris-Lyon Company would be nationalized in August 1848.[58]

Thus the promises and problems of an expansive but erratic economy, exacerbated by laissez-faire wage and employment policies, evoked working-class organizations (craft-like unions) and tactics (selective strikes in full employment) to combat wage reductions. But the dilemma of unemployment remained unresolved when the revolution shattered the fragile economy and intensified demands to mend it.

Although Lyon had aristocrats and paupers, citizens could be – and were – categorized as either bourgeois or working-class. Clear-cut class lines limited the scope of paternalism and deference, which mediated social tensions and deflected protest in other provincial centres.[59] Instead of calming class conflicts, the elite's efforts to ameliorate the workers' plight angered many workers.

The top of the social hierarchy, measured by the size of the average estate transmitted by inheritance, was still the preserve of large landlords, bankers, and merchants. Large, often noble landlords, bankers, and wealthy merchants owned huge tracts of rural land as far away as the Beaujolais; they also held up to 64 per cent of the property in the cantons surrounding the city. Nevertheless, the old elite was more commercial than elsewhere, for even the nobles were descended from banking and mercantile families. On the second rung of the socioeconomic ladder, with fortunes of 500,000 to 1,000,000 francs, came industrialists.[60] The old elite had lost its antipathy to industrialists as the former invested in industry and the latter bought land. All outside observers agreed that a proclivity for "making money, doing business" marked Lyon's high society.[61] Businessmen also dominate the 10,000 to 500,000 francs bracket. Although officials, officers, professionals, and prominent clerics did accumulate fortunes of this magnitude, most shared the merchants' outlook because merchants placed their younger sons in the bureaucracy, the professions, and the church hierarchy.[62]

Lyon had experienced an early revival of the church after the Great Revolution. Under the July Monarchy, all the religious orders returned to the city and multiplied their charitable works, including the notorious Providences. The Brothers of the Christian Doctrine and the Sisters of St Joseph, who staffed many religious schools and Houses of Providence, would be assailed for their zeal in 1848. But few Lyonnais were anticlerical. In the assaults on Providences, no one would hurt the monks and nuns or desecrate a church. Part of the credit must go to Archbishop de Bonald, who not only supported an independent legitimist newspaper, *La Gazette de Lyon*, but tolerated Social Catholicism among the lower clergy. Frederick Ozanam, founder of the St Vincent de Paul Conferences, taught in Lyon and influenced important lay groups. But it would be wrong to use the trite phrase, "city of faith." Women outnumbered men at mass and few Lyonnais left legacies to religious institutions. Lamartine shrewdly characterized the average Lyonnais as more devoted to "work, economy, and probity" than religion.[63]

These essentially bourgeois values encouraged charitable foundations. In 1822, a young *bourgeoise*, Pauline Jaricot, had founded the famous Propagation of the Faith to collect money for foreign missions. The four other foundations of this period served more practical, local needs. More lay people made donations to the health and welfare institutions administered by the municipality. During every depression, the elite, like other urban elites, held charity balls and collections.[64] However, their efforts did not foster dependence and deference, as, for instance, legitimist charity did in Toulouse,[65] because their impersonal gifts did not eliminate hostility toward merchants who were blamed for unemployment. Nor did their donations fill the needs of the unemployed.

A chasm separated bourgeois society from the next socioeconomic category, composed of shopkeepers, small proprietors, and artisans. The average value of estates plummeted from 45,000 francs for merchants, industrialists, and professionals, to 8,677 for shopkeepers, 2,694 for artisans, and 1,539 for some *chefs d'ateliers*. Since the seventeenth century, few had bridged the gap by marriage.[66] Most members of the petty bourgeoisie were attached to the working class, since most serviced working-class communities. The few master weavers in this economic bracket were pivotal. Owning four or more looms, they alone had the privilege of electing weavers' representatives to the *Conseil des Prud'-hommes*. The cafés they frequented were not those of other *chefs*; their wives snubbed wives of two-loom masters.[67] Nevertheless, these *chefs* were as interested as other weavers in the level of piece-rates; they had transformed the Mutualist Society and initiated the workers' movement in Lyon.[68]

Most Lyonnais were workers, and most of them left behind nothing of monetary value.[69] Workers lived on wages which varied considerably. A fortunate few, like steamboat-builders, received over four francs a day and did not endure seasonal unemployment.[70] Most weavers were underpaid *and* underemployed. Experts calculated that *chefs* averaged one and a half francs (for simple silks) to three francs (for fancy silks) a day. Given slow seasons, most master weavers could net only 600 francs a year. Journeymen earned 400 francs for luxury silks, 200 francs for simple silks.[71] Because of the predominance of silk workers with their meagre incomes, the average daily wage was lower than in other major cities.[72]

Conversely, the cost of living was high, sometimes higher than in Paris. The reasons for this were high duties on goods entering the city and exorbitant rents. In the old quarters, a room large enough for two looms absorbed up to a tenth of the *gross* revenue from two looms.[73] Inflationary price trends for basic necessities compounded the problem.[74] Since most weavers had stationary incomes,[75] they reduced their standard of living by eating less meat and drinking less wine. Some moved to the suburbs, where duties were lower and living conditions better. Weavers of luxury silks flocked to the suburbs.[76]

The economic squeeze predisposed workers toward consumer co-operatives. Over 200 workers subscribed to the first French consumer cooperative, established by a Lyonnais silk merchant influenced by Fourier's ideas about an association of labour and capital. From 1835 through 1837, the *Commerce Veridique* set up seven shops in workers' neighbourhoods; the shops served more than 1,400 people. The cooperative's bankruptcy was due to rapid expansion during the depression of 1837, not to lack of customers.[77] When food prices skyrocketed in 1846, other Fourierists opened two cooperative bakeries. Cooperation was the concept Lyonnais workers assimilated from the bourgeois Fourierists who propagandized in their midst. Until the Fourierists began to publish a less expensive newspaper in 1845, few workers could afford their publications; only 130 people attended their moderately expensive banquets commemorating Fourier's birth. The workers' press publicized their cooperative ideas but criticized their insistence on an association of labour, capital, and "talent" and on the division of profits. The workers' press, and most workers, preferred producers' cooperatives without the participation of "capital" or the payment of dividends.[78] Nevertheless, under the Second Republic four worker-shareholders of the *Commerce Veridique* would direct consumer cooperatives which resembled the prototype of the 1830s. Nine more would join democratic-socialist clubs and committees. Clearly consumer cooperatives also mobilized radicals for the republic.

In addition to household expenses, masters had to purchase looms costing 80 to 400 francs, depending on the size of the loom. In periods of high demand, merchants extended credit to masters to buy looms and pay up to 600 francs to mount looms. Even in boom years, *chefs* were in debt.[79] Then during slowdowns, when many needed loans to survive, merchants cut off credit. After 1834, the government had instituted a bank to make small loans to master weavers at 5 per cent interest in crises. But after 1837, the bank never had more than 2,000 borrowers; far more pawned tools, furniture, and clothing at the government pawnshop which charged 12 per cent interest. Similarly, a bank to encourage savings – and "moralize" the poor – only benefited a tiny minority.[80] The problem was not the weavers' profligacy but their poverty and insecurity: few could set aside enough to see them through repeated recessions. Since 1825, 1,100 *chefs* had formed fourteen friendly societies to save for sick benefits and widows' pensions, but these societies could not offer unemployment insurance because they could not accumulate enough to see members through recessions.[81] *Chefs* were acutely aware of their need for credit and, as early as 1832, had conceived of mutual credit (savings and loan) banks. In 1848, they would treat Proudhon's credit ideas seriously.

When the *fabrique* ground to a halt, most weavers had to apply for welfare. City officials investigated to determine indigence and distributed relief in kind. At the depth of the depression of 1837, one-quarter of the population had been on relief. The recessions of the early 1840s saw one-eighth of the population on welfare – still one of the highest ratios in Europe.[82] In the disastrous winters of the late 1830s and early 1840s, the city also created jobs for 1,500 to 2,000 workers, most of them silk workers.[83] But when the depression of 1845–7 shocked other cities into opening public work projects, the indebted city council merely raised its allocation to the Welfare Bureau and subsidized bakers to soften the blows of the two bad harvests. The council did not even regulate river shipping rates for grain until companies quadrupled the rates and the price of the staple brown bread nearly doubled.[84] If food prices were still less exorbitant than in northern France, unemployment was more pervasive.[85]

Economic hardship coupled with political inaction produced the greatest distress in July Monarchy Lyon. For the first time in decades weavers reverted to their old, demeaning habit of singing for handouts. In the past they had criticized the Welfare Bureau for its humiliating investigations for indigence and the public works programs for providing only dirty, hard unskilled jobs. By late 1846 these proud weavers were voicing open hostility toward merchants, speculators, and authorities. Early in the new year the police worried about impending revolt. However, all that happened was the attack on the scandal-ridden Providence,[86] for Lyonnais revolts did not occur during depressions.

Despite economic pressures, weavers were not demoralized. Since they could not see to weave the fine silk in the dark, their evenings were free. As sociable as the peasants Agulhon studied, they were nevertheless urban and hence more attracted to circles and cafés than to the rural *chambrées*.[87] Traditional Carnival societies still arranged parades in working class suburbs[88] and the transitional *compagnonnages* held their annual balls and battled with "renegade" or nonaffiliated workers.[89] The authorized friendly societies had more formal constitutions and, beginning in 1840, professional and literary circles were formed.[90] Much of this rich associational life centred on the dozens of suburban cafés which were the despair of the police.[91]

In Lyon, the more traditional the popular recreation the more remote it was from radicalism. Thus only the café owners among the members of the Carnival societies would be identified with democratic-socialist clubs or committees. Unlike peasant villages, Lyon did not infuse carnival with political content.[92] One reason for the distance between traditional recreation and progressive politics was strict police surveillance of all large, potentially explosive gatherings. Another reason was the radicals' disdain for the excesses of Mardi Gras, expressed most openly when the democratic-socialist committee governing Croix-Rousse during the revolution forbade Mardi Gras because of its "immoral disguises."[93] Moreover, other "masks" were available for radicalism. For instance, eight Mutualists and twelve men prosecuted as insurgents of 1834 took cover in the legal *Commerce Veridique*.[94] The cooperatives formed after the revolution would also function as fronts for political meetings in the reactionary phase of the Second Republic.

If the popular culture retained traditional elements like the *charivaris* Natalie Davis discovered in sixteenth-century Lyon,[95] there were more signs of change, improvement, and modernity. Although pulmonary diseases remained a problem among weavers, the Jacquart had eliminated the job that had made contorted spines a hallmark of the *canuts* or silk weavers of Lyon. Free vaccinations reduced the incidence of smallpox and, after 1831, surveillance spared Lyon the cholera epidemics that afflicted other urban populations.[96] Both the church and the local Mutual Education Society established free elementary schools, which the *chefs*, who had to be literate to understand their silk contracts, filled with their children. Some of the eighty-four schools provided adult education, which was almost as popular. For those who wanted to go beyond rudimentary instruction, there were republican and communist study groups, as well as less ideological lending libraries and literary circles.[97] Observers began to contrast the "old *canuts*," whom they stigmatized as "misshapen," ignorant, and "submissive," to the "new *canuts*," whom they praised as "the most sober, laborious, and intelligent workers." Conservatives had misgivings about the *chefs'* pride: "They consider themselves the first, the only important element in the silk industry ... "; "they have the pretension to be responsible only to themselves ... "[98]

Under Louis Philippe, these literate, proud, and independent weavers supported seven workers' newspapers – the only French workers' papers funded and run without the assistance of bourgeois ideologues.[99] These papers were overtly class-conscious. Although they catered to *chefs*, they addressed all workers. On the few occasions when difficulties arose between *chefs* and *compagnons*, the papers emphasized the need for solidarity. When they recognized differences between masters and journeymen in other trades, they identified with the latter.[100] They took umbrage when bourgeois papers ridiculed *canuts* (a word that conjured up images of "old *canuts*"). They censured silk merchants for everything from their humiliating practice of keeping masters waiting for orders, to depressing piece-rates. More remarkably, they transcended their particular grievances by excoriating laissez-faire capitalism for the "cupidity," "divisions," and "egoism" of French society.[101]

This critical attitude was closely linked to a belief in progress and amelioration. At an individual level, the papers championed education and, secondarily, a most bourgeois propriety.[102] On a legal plane, they exhorted the *Conseil des Prud'hommes* to adopt a workers' code and when the council did not comply, they campaigned to democratize it.[103] A few newspapers called for a "social revolution" or "radical reconstruction of society" without condoning violent overthrow. More constructively, the papers advocated associations to overcome competition in the entire economy. The associations ran the gamut from mutual aid societies and mutual credit (savings and loans) banks, to producers' cooperatives and social workshops. In general, the papers shifted their support from private, voluntary associations to public organization of work.[104] The shift reflected the politicization of workers.

POLITICIZATION

The revolution of 1848 precipitated a political struggle which transformed Lyon from an apparently conservative centre under the July Monarchy to a radical stronghold. The triumph of the Left can be explained by the facts that sociopolitical factions had emerged and workers had adopted and advocated radical theories before the revolution. The proclamation of the republic prompted dramatic political change because working-class radicals had a following among the disenfranchised before the advent of universal manhood suffrage.

The insurrections of 1831 and 1834 first crystallized sociopolitical divisions. On the one hand, the insurrections frightened legitimist opponents of the new regime into the fold of the new government. When workers held much of the metropolis captive for thirteen days in 1831, men of property had to turn to the national government and army for protection. When the nervous government misrepresented the second revolt as a republican rising, they generated more fear – and support – among the elite.[105] On the other hand, the spectacle of working-class solidarity inspired radicals to proselytize among Lyonnais workers. Following the first revolt and the Parisian "massacre of the rue Transnonian," republicans concentrated their efforts on Lyon until it became the most republican city in France.[106] About the same time, Fourierist "missions" converted the editors of the first working-class newspaper to association or cooperation. One editor, Marius Chastaing, publicized association in four subsequent workers' papers and his own democratic organ, *La Tribune Lyonnaise* (1845–51).[107] In the 1840s, most major socialist and communist theorists visited and spoke to Lyonnais workers.[108] The eclectic and pragmatic workers' press discussed all the current theories and praised practical elements in each one of them. The state socialist Louis Blanc did not visit Lyon; one consequence was the common misconception of his social workshops as public workshops for the unemployed. The press made it clear that they preferred government-sponsored but worker-run producers' cooperatives.[109]

Repression of the second revolt accentuated sociopolitical differences. The army retook the rebel suburb of Croix-Rousse with mobile artillery, and then, to deter future rebellions, implanted cannon in military installations around the suburb. The government prosecuted eighty-seven insurgents and, to prevent agitation, added a Special Police commissioner to monitor secret societies.[110] Such a forceful response relieved bourgeois anxieties about a regime imposed by revolution.[111] But workers resented the indiscriminate bombardment of their neighbourhoods and the ring of fortifications; a Croix-Rousse society known as the Voraces would seize the forts and cannon on the first night of the republic. Meanwhile, workers hindered the prosecution of insurgents by refusing to testify and ostracizing the few witnesses who did testify.[112]

Other government policies widened the gap between bourgeois and working-class politics. While the commitment to an unregulated labour market delighted merchants,[113] it annoyed workers who wanted collective contracts guaranteed by the government. In the 1840s, the regime irritated workers with three restrictive labour laws: the child labour law of 1841, the licensing law of 1845, and the *livret* law of 1846.[114]

The Lyonnais, who elected a majority of Orleanists until the end of the monarchy, had really registered a shift to the left of the political spectrum under the surface of electoral politics. Whereas the legitimist right-wing had principles without practical sense, the Orleanist centre had only peace and prosperity for policies and pragmatism for tactics. On the moderate Left, the liberals, who stood for a limited expansion of the electorate, were gaining in the polls and the republicans, who wanted a more democratic franchise, had an influential newspaper. But it was the plethora of popular radical societies that distinguished the Lyonnais political scene. These working-class radicals were democratic in their political theory and egalitarian (mainly communist) in their economic program. However revolutionary in theory, their strategy in the 1840s was peaceful education and organization of the working class. Despite the usual ideological and tactical splits, democrats, socialists, and communists had a history of working together which would facilitate the emergence of a single democratic-socialist club movement in 1848. Their experience in secret societies would also help them sustain the democratic-socialist alliance in the reactionary phase of the republic.

By the 1840s, Lyon's legitimists had dwindled to the point of being inconsequential.[115] Their *Gazette de Lyon* accepted the regime as a guarantor of order but complained about its indifference to Catholic schools.[116] In the 1846 national elections, their two candidates (for five constituencies) were trounced. The *Gazette*'s post-mortem suggested an alliance with liberals around a platform of "educational and religious freedom" and suffrage reform. In a January 1848 by-election, the marquis de Mortemart made an arrangement, endorsed reform, and won on the third ballot.[117] Mortemart's flexibility and popularity as a local notable in his home constituency of Villefranche account for his election then and under the Second Republic. However, he would be the only local legitimist to win a national election, for most legitimists would not make electoral arrangements.

January 1848 saw the first slip in the Orleanists' stranglehold on the Rhône delegation to the Chamber of Deputies. Even when other major cities had returned opposition candidates, as in 1840, Lyon's 5,000 electors had stood by ministerial candidates.[118] The Orleanist organ, *Le Courrier de Lyon*, had the largest circulation of the Lyonnais newspapers (1,120 subscribers in 1841). *Le Courrier* praised the government as the restorer of peace and prosperity and warned that opposition would "revive revolutionary instincts." In the 1846 election, it recommended the incumbents on the expedient grounds that they voted with the government and operated well in the Chamber.[119]

The Orleanists also controlled the City Council, though they did have to deal with opposition members. They were so confident of their position that in the 1846 municipal elections, they endorsed one of the legitimist incumbents. *La Gazette*, enraged, railed against authorities who "designate ... the competitors upon whom they will confer the honour of overseeing their administration." Even when Liberals took one-third of the seats, *La Gazette* blamed Orleanists for "excluding men of the right."[120] It would take the radical committee governing Lyon during the revolution to forge an alliance between legitimists and Orleanists. In the reaction, their coalition party would recapture the Hôtel de ville.

After 1840 Orleanists ran against liberal candidates, whom they portrayed as "auxiliaries of a violent party," referring to their ties to the republicans. Municipal voters were less easily manipulated than the narrower national electorate: as of 1842, there were three liberal councillors and as of 1846, seven.[121] In January 1848 the liberal Committee of the Quai de Retz ran candidates in by-elections for the Chamber of Deputies and the General Council (a departmental advisory committee usually dominated by local notables). A popular notary and long-time city councillor, Démophile Laforest, withdrew from the Chamber race only after Mortemart supported suffrage reform. Laforest won a seat on the General Council while another veteran councillor, Joseph Bergier, lost the other seat by one vote on a second ballot.[122] On 25 February, the official mayor would relinquish power to Laforest, who would appoint Bergier and four other liberal councillors to a revolutionary committee. Laforest would also represent the Rhône in the National and Legislative assemblies.

Lyon had active and articulate republicans from the beginning of the

July Monarchy. Even before the July Revolution, Carbonari had
plotted against the Restoration. Immediately after the July Days, more
moderate republicans took over *Le Précurseur*, a liberal newspaper edited
by Petetin, one of the best provincial journalists. Two years later, radical
republicans established another newspaper and two propaganda societies, including the plebian Rights of Man. After the second insurrection,
heavy fines and sentences silenced both newspapers and dismantled the
more elitist of the two societies.[123] However, republicans promptly
founded a new paper, *Le Censeur*, and hired another talented journalist,
Rittiez. His critique of every repressive measure in the postinsurrectionary period brought the paper before the courts five times in as many years
and built a circulation second only to that of *Le Courrier* (760 subscribers
in 1841).[124]

Once past the severe repression of the mid-1830s and into the
depression of 1837, members of the Rights of Man regrouped in tiny
conspiratorial democratic and even socialist societies. Their elaborate
screening procedures, oaths, and initiations to assure secrecy and loyalty
resembled the *compagnonnages'* occult ceremonies and appealed to
Lyonnais workers' love of the mysterious.[125] But police surveillance soon
destroyed the societies and drove members into more constitutional
activities. The local branch of the "Family," a loose network dedicated to
overthrowing the monarchy, broke up after the failure of the Parisian
branch's coup in 1839; another society foundered after the arrest of
members accused of plotting to kill the king in 1840. Some members,
including Castel of the tailors' union, joined *Le Censeur's* legal
petition-and-banquet campaign for suffrage reform.[126] In 1840, a recently
amnestied leader of the Rights of Man reactivated the society to protest
Thier's foreign policy. Although the protests merely consisted of crowds
singing the "Marseillaise," they and the society were suppressed. Many
ex-agitators drifted over to *Le Censeur's* Reform Committee; many
workers radicalized by the demonstrations formed study groups to learn
more about democratic and socialist theory. Sebastien Commissaire,
another immigrant weaver, came to political consciousness in the course
of the demonstrations, then entered communist study groups. As a
democratic-socialist, he would represent the Rhône in the Legislative
Assembly of 1849.[127] The Rights of Man would help elect him, for the
society was reconstituted as a secret society in the waning days of the
revolution and, thanks to its clandestine nature, kept the democratic-
socialist alliance alive in the repressive phase of the Second Republic.

Le Censeur coordinated local republicans, much as *Le National*
coordinated Parisian republicans. Initially *Le Censeur* assumed a more
democratic stance than *Le National*. In 1838, it amended a Parisian
petition for a modest expansion of the electorate to ask for manhood

suffrage, workers' eligibility for office, and payment of deputies. With the assistance of working-class leaders, the paper gathered 11,526 signatures for their petition. Two years later the Reform Committee held a huge "Democratic Banquet" for a similar petition. The 6,000 diners heard speeches from communist weavers and shoemakers as well as the more familiar republican journalists, professionals, and merchants. The bourgeois republicans broke with the working-class communists after the communists hosted a smaller banquet and made very revolutionary toasts. When *Le Censeur* sponsored a third reform petition, they gathered fewer signatures and did not present the petition to the Chamber. Thereafter *Le Censeur* moved closer to the respectable liberals. By 1847, the republicans and liberals collaborated on a reform banquet, and, to propitiate the liberals, Rittiez moderated republican demands by proposing a "transitional" reduction of the tax required of electors. Very few of the 1,600 diners – one of the largest audiences in the second banquet campaign – objected.[128]

The banquet was not disrupted because few working-class radicals were present. *Le Censeur* had tried to appeal to them. As early as 1839 (when the first contingent of radical republicans joined *Le Censeur*), it advocated social reforms such as cooperatives and "the right to work, that is, the constant organization of work for able men whom circumstances leave unemployed." Bourgeois republicans even brought workers into the banquet committee, only to alienate them by charging too much and scheduling the event for a workday. The workers resigned to plan a workers' banquet, which they were still arranging when news of the revolution arrived.[129] The rift between bourgeois republicans and working-class radicals meant that republicans would appoint themselves to the revolutionary committees in Febuary 1848. Only one working-class ally, the typesetter Doutre, would be "elected" by the crowd.

By January 1848 liberals felt that they had to invite humble radicals to their electoral organization, known as the Committee of the Quai de Retz. Joseph Benoit and four other communists accepted in order to act as a Vigilance Committee. Their distrust would be vindicated in the early hours of the republic, when the Committee of the Quai de Retz would consider excluding workers from the National Guard. At that point the Vigilance Committee would "rouse the populace" to impose radicals on the revolutionary committee composed of liberals and republicans.[130]

Reformers made overtures to working-class radicals because of the advances radicalism had made among workers. The trials after the second insurrection eliminated the Carbonari's bourgeois leaders but left behind the humbler rank and file. Workers flowed into the clandestine society when it regrouped. Although the Carbonari had disintegrated in 1837–8, a segment based in Croux-Rousse perpetuated the useful network of a central committee and cells, which helped them survive two police raids on specific cells. The Reformed Carbonari retained the arcane rituals and democratic ideology of the original body, but added an interest in communism. The 300 Reformed Carbonari were symptomatic of two trends: workers' entry into political societies and their acceptance of early communist ideas.[131] The Reformed Carbonari would act as a civil guard and a club in the revolution. .

Another secret society that predated the insurrections and persisted through the 1840s also reflected the trends toward working-class participation and more radical, in this case socialist, theory. While the Freemasons were overwhelmingly bourgeois, twenty adopted Fourierist ideas and seceded in 1843. The Fourierist lodge relocated in Croix-Rousse and, shortly before the revolution, lowered its dues and welcomed workers from Croix-Rousse and Guillotière. During the revolution five of its fifty members would sit on municipal committees and, in 1849, two would run cooperatives.[132]

The postinsurrectionary societies were working-class in composition and communist in ideology from their inception. In the wake of the insurrections, Joseph Benoit and a few other weavers read Buonarotti's account of Babeuf's 1796 plot and adopted Babouvist concepts, such as equal property and equal wages. By 1837 they had a *chambrée*, a tiny private society, to disseminate their conspiratorial and egalitarian message. Their code names were the names of flowers and they met in the woods outside the city limits. That same year a silk designer formed a Reading Society of twenty-seven people to distribute pamphlets by the utopian communist, Etienne Cabet. Police and judicial harassment wrecked the Babouvist and Cabetian *chambrées*, but Benoit and two other weavers, Grinand and Perret, reconstituted themselves as a Committee of Equals. After a brief interlude, they broke with the local Family over the latter's predilection for coups. Instead, they elaborated and coordinated a network of cells of seven people studying all communist theories. In 1840, the committee coopted the founder of the Cabetian Reading Society and another immigrant weaver living in Croix-Rousse, Louis Greppo. Like Benoit, Greppo would be a member of the revolutionary municipal committee and a representative to the National and subsequently the Legislative Assembly.[133]

The early 1840s saw Babouvists and Cabetians cooperating in a purely propagandistic campaign. After the break with republicans, Babouvists contacted bourgeois communists like the notary Felix Blanc and the silk merchant Edant, Edant, who travelled to Paris on business, provided links to Parisian communists, which broadened the Babouvists' outlook but undermined their dominance over local communists. Benoit explained: "Poor workers began the social work in Lyon … But precisely because they came from the womb of the people ... there were prejudices against them ... when Cabet, Pierre Leroux, Louis Blanc, or Proudhon spoke, these foreign voices immediately acquired a great superiority. Cabet especially, with qualifications as a former deputy and attorney-general, ... detached a good many followers from us, but invariably they returned, repelled by his dictatorial attitudes and and exclusivism." The rush to Cabet, who published *Voyage en Icarie* in 1839, commenced in 1841, when one group offered to handle Icarian propaganda and another asked his assistance on a newspaper. Unlike Icarian committees elsewhere, the Lyonnais committee consisted solely of workers, including Perret of the Committee of Equals. Lyonnais Icarians were also unusually independent.[134] For instance, their eclectic newspaper wrote favourably about Babouvism and Fourierism. When the newspaper succumbed to massive court fines,[135] the editorial board – and two more Equals, Greppo and Grinand – entered the Icarian Committee.

In the mid-1840s the communists divided over tactics. The Babouvists revolted against Cabetian elitism and pacifism, turning to a class-conscious, activist communism which became known as neobabouvism. In 1842, Equals on the Icarian Committee refused to publicize the polemic between Cabet and the materialist communist, Dézamy. Instead these irrepressible autodidacts wrote to the two theorists to suggest a more constructive dialogue. True to their egalitarian and conspiratorial origins, they criticized Cabet's dictatorial tendencies, reliance on the bourgeoisie, and commitment to nonviolence, as well as Dézamy's determinism. Their letters laid out a uniquely *ouvrierist* interpretation of communism, one which accepted the need for education but did not deny the possibility of revolution.[136] Their interpretation bears some resemblance to the revolutionary syndicalism of the late nineteenth century. After sending the letters, about 130 neobabouvists ceased corresponding with Cabet. Soon others criticized Cabet's refusal to use force to establish Icarie. In 1843, he had to come to Lyon and concede that, if his system could not triumph by "reason," it might be necessary to resort to force. The following year, when the Parisian committee ordered them to adopt the name Icarian to distinguish themselves from Babouvists, Poncet, the local correspondent, and fourteen other workers rejected attempts to divide the communists. Another visit by Cabet, and furious politicking on his part, partly restored the Icarian infrastructure.[137]

Although loyal Icarians remained the largest communist sect in Lyon, like Icarians elsewhere, they were diverted into a futile immigration scheme. Unlike Parisian Icarians, they would be apolitical throughout the republic. The neobabouvists and dissident Icarians were different. As Proudhon, then a shipping clerk in Lyon, reported in 1844: "Should there arrive a moment favourable to the revolutionary spirit, people will

... see the masses of Jacobinized proletarians rise everywhere ... I personally know in Lyon and the suburbs more than 200 of these apostles who evangelize while working. It is a more enlightened and tenacious fanatacism than I have ever known. In 1838 there was not a single socialist in Lyon; ... today there are more than 10,000."[138] Arrested militants and police used similar figures. Indeed, the authorities cracked down on secret societies and sent six members of an armed group and ten dissident Icarians to jail.[139] But the militants survived and remained political. Greppo and several other Equals weathered the storm in a legal cooperative venture; Benoit and eleven other neobabouvists regrouped as the Communist Workers of Lyon, an organization which published articles on communism. They now advocated peaceful change through education but condemned Cabet's immigration scheme. Dissident Icarians joined public political committees like the Workers' Banquet Committee.[140] These neobabouvists and dissident Icarians, who had cooperated in the early 1840s, would create the Central Democratic Club in 1848 and sustain the democratic-socialist alliance throughout the republic.

Militants also took shelter in associations which were unauthorized but tolerated by the authorities. The Voraces, so known because they drank wine by the cheaper, larger litre bottle, were similar to a traditional recreational group. Like the neighbourhood-based youth groups of sixteenth-century Lyon studied by Natalie Davis,[141] the Voraces were almost exclusively Croix-Rousse journeymen under thirty-five years of age who met informally to socialize. Several Voraces had been or still were in *compagnonnages*, most likely the Ferrandiniers. Surprisingly, given the preponderance of immigrants in this community and this cohort, three-fifths of the known Voraces were natives of the metropolis. Their long residence and memories of 1834, *not* prior organization as a secret political society, explain why they would take the initiative in seizing the Croix-Rousse fortifications in 1848. It was precisely because the Voraces were simply drinking buddies and were perceived by the authorities to be "incorrigible drunkards," that militants could take cover in their café meetings in periods of political debate, notably in January 1848.[142] Their contacts with militants had political consequences only in the revolution, when, for instance, they would collaborate with clubs in demonstrations.

Neobabouvists also infiltrated and influenced the Union, a nineteenth-century coalition of *compagnonnages* which omitted the humiliating initiations of most *compagnonnages* and tried to heal the divisions between rival occupational groups. Although the Union headquarters were in Lyon, it had begun in Toulon and spread to other cities. At least three communists joined the Union in 1846, the year that fifteen Union

TABLE 7
Voraces' Domiciles, Birthplaces, Occupations, and Cohorts

Domiciles	Croix-Rousse 78% (15 of 19)	Lyon 22% (4 of 19)	
Birthplaces	Lyon 44% (10 of 23)	Suburbs 17% (4 of 23)	Elsewhere 39% (9 of 23)
Occupations	Silk workers 64% (14 of 22)	Other journeymen 18% (4 of 22)	Others[1] 18% (4 of 22)
Cohorts	16–25 7% (2 of 27)	26–35 60% (16 of 27)	36–52[2] 33% (9 of 27)

Source: ADR, R, 2me Conseil de Guerre, 1850, Société dit les Voraces, and Dossiers individuels.
1 Three were café operators; the fourth was a chef d'atelier.
2 The three oldest were café operators.

members were arrested at a communist lecture. The following year the Union adopted a more democratic constitution, which they did not submit to the police. This oversight resulted in a court order dissolving the Union early in 1848. Nevertheless, at least one Union member, the shoemaker Vincent Guillermin, who had collaborated with Greppo in the cooperative venture, became a club and cooperative leader in 1848 and 1849.[143]

When the future commander of the Parisian Republican Guard, Marc Caussidière, conferred with local communists in October 1847, posters called the Lyonnais to revolt. By January 1848 the police reported that the communists were gaining support and workers only awaited the order to arise. Twice in February, the "seditious posters" reappeared, causing the authorities to double the army posts and provision the forts. More and more workers sat around cafes, especially in Croix-Rousse, awaiting news from the capital that would change their social situation.[144] On the 25th that news came, and the workers who had already developed an indigenous, informed, and experienced leadership were ready for revolution.

Only by surveying the geography of the Lyonnais metropolis, with its physically and politically separate segments coinciding with socially distinct communities, can we understand the radical suburban movement of the Second Republic. Similarly, the repudiation of the politics of deference in the first hours of the republic was rooted in the silk weavers' antagonism toward merchants who passed on the risks of an erratic market to their dependent workers. Impersonal charity did not compensate for their irresponsible treatment of their labour force. Finally, the rapid adoption of democratic political forms and practices owed much to the Lyonnais workers' susceptibility to democratic, socialist, and communist propaganda after the first two insurrections. Radicalized workers already had organizational models and a network of personal contacts to rely on in the early days of the revolution – and in the renewed repression after the revolution. Moreover, they had abandoned conspiracy for the longer-term educational and organizational effort essential in a newly enfranchised electorate. Their dedication to electoral politics helps to explain the peculiarly radical yet peaceful character of the Lyonnais revolution and the democratic-socialist triumph in the Legislative Assembly elections of 1849.

CHAPTER TWO

The Red Flag,
25–28 February 1848

The proclamation of the republic, which stupefied most provincials,[1] galvanized Lyonnais radicals, who as we shall see promptly intervened in the municipal revolution and subsequently lost control of the new municipal committee. When moderates tried to appropriate the Prefecture, Hôtel de ville, and National Guard, communists mobilized the crowd, which imposed more radicals and workers on the new municipal committee than would be found on any other revolutionary council. The Central Committee governed Lyon until the arrival of the provisional Government commissioner on 28 February. Because moderates outnumbered and outmanoeuvred radicals on the committee, democrats, socialists, and communists formed a Democratic Society or club to act as a watchdog. The creation of the Central Committee and Democratic Club transformed the political scene.

In the same short interval Lyonnais workers made two other dramatic moves. On the first night of the republic, Voraces rushed the fortifications surrounding Croix-Rousse. Since the commander of the armed forces in Lyon did not relish a confrontation, he ordered the troops to abandon the forts. Before the Provisional Government commissioner appeared, the Voraces controlled a major component of the city's defence system and an independent paramilitary unit, another leading participant in Lyon's revolutionary spectacle, was looming in the wings. While Voraces besieged military installations, other workers launched more typical attacks on the machines.[2] By 29 February, luddism stopped and a more calculated and constructive effort – unionization – began.

Faced with a political, military, and economic assault, the authorities capitulated. Wealthy citizens poured out of Lyon in a veritable exodus – one of the few in 1848.[3] In the absence of conservative elements, the radicals dismantled much of the old order and tried to erect a democratic-socialist regime. Paradoxically, they quickly contained the crowds which had elevated them to power and thereby stemmed the revolutionary impulse. But the paradox was only apparent, for these radicals had long ago abandoned a strategy of violent overthrow for the more "modern," long-term tactics of indoctrination and organization. These tactics presupposed some degree of order, which, in turn, dictated some compromise with moderate republicans. The commitment to order and the politics of compromise contributed to a relatively peaceful and moderate changeover.

THE MUNICIPAL REVOLUTION

On the morning of 25 February, the prefect of the Rhône released a communiqué about Louis Philippe's resignation in favour of a regency. The people who had been expecting important news reacted swiftly. By afternoon, republicans had gathered in the office of Le Censeur; liberals were meeting at the Electoral Committee headquarters on the Quai de Retz, and workers jammed the main squares. Although the crowds merely roared "Vive la Réforme!" their positive response activated the republicans. They hurried to the Quai de Retz, then, finding the liberals irresolute, sent their own delegation to the Prefecture. Editor-in-chief Rittiez and other leading republicans called on the prefect and insisted on a restoration of the National Guard as the "best guarantee of order and liberty." The embarrassed prefect claimed he would have to wire the capital for authorization. He was stalling, postponing the announcement of the republic to gain time to burn the Special Police commissioner's files.[4]

While the republicans waited on the prefect, the radicals were busy. The communist Vigilance Committee heard the Electoral Committee entertain a motion to exclude journeymen and masters of small workshops from the National Guard. When the indecisive Electoral Committee did not reject or adopt the motion, the communists decided "to organize a popular movement." Joseph Benoit, Felix Blanc, and the three other neobabouvists proceeded to the suburban squares where they joined radicals already addressing the crowds, whom they persuaded to march in orderly fashion to Bellecour. By late afternoon, a column of 5,000 people descended from Croix-Rousse; smaller contingents came from the other suburbs. Ten to fifteen thousand people crammed into the central square, Bellecour, and then surged toward Terreaux square in front of the Hôtel de ville.[5]

Before they reached their destination, the prefect contacted Le Censeur and relinquished his position to Rittiez. Republicans appointed a Prefectural Committee and dispatched twenty-one delegates to the Hôtel de ville. Simultaneously, the acting mayor had mandated his power to the popular liberal, Laforest, who had convoked five prominent liberals. As the throng in Terreaux square began stoning the Hôtel de ville, the gendarmes assigned to protect the building summoned Laforest. The new mayor met the *Censeur* delegates on the way to Terreaux and agreed to "take" the Hôtel de ville with them. Between eight and nine o'clock that evening, Laforest mounted the balcony and spoke to the demonstrators, who applauded his proclamation of the republic, temporary assumption of the mayoralty, and appointment of a Central Committee composed of five liberals and twenty-one republicans.[6]

At this point, the municipal revolution resembled the change of regime in many provincial cities. Then the Lyonnais took an exceptional step. Dozens of demonstrators had trailed Laforest and his appointees into the council room. When the committee began coopting other liberals and republicans, the "observers" imposed twenty-five members of radical secret societies and occupational groups on it. Hundreds more took possession of the main hall and nominated at least as many more, including Benoit, Blanc, and three other neobabouvists. Their list was communicated to the committee, which incorporated the nominees. The next day other political societies and workers' *corporations* presented themselves and remained until their leaders were absorbed into the committee. In twenty-four hours, the Central Committee had acquired ninety-four members, over half of whom belonged to previously illegal associations.[7] As table 8 shows, thirty-two came from radical societies and seventeen represented unions; table 9 indicates that thirty-seven were workers.

To appreciate the novelty of this sequence of events, let us glance at what happened elsewhere. In cities like Bordeaux, Toulon, and Toulouse, not to mention most smaller places, crowds had little say in the selection of new officials.[8] In Paris and Rouen, where crowds had some influence, the new city councils included few socialists and no workers, while the Provisional Government had only Louis Blanc and a token worker, Albert. Even in Avignon and Reims, where city councils did respond to popular pressure by admitting democratic-socialist workers, they were few in number (four and six, respectively).[9] Only in Lyon were lower-class radicals sufficiently well known and numerous to mould the populace into an effective political agent and to participate in government on a grand scale.

By midnight, most demonstrators had departed and the mood of the few hundred remaining around the Hôtel de ville shifted from the ebullience of the early hours to apprehension. Except for the Central Police commissioner, who had read the riot act before the invasion of the Hôtel de ville, the civil authorities had not opposed the takeover. Although the soldiers posted around City Hall had not tried to contain the crowd, the army's position was unclear since the local commander

TABLE 8
Political Affiliations of Central Committee Members

Liberals	12	Moderates
Censeur Republicans	24	36
Radical Republicans[1]	14	Radicals
Neobabouvists[2]	13	32
Fourierists	3	
Social Democrats	2	
Carlists and Bonapartists	2	
Democrats from the unions	17	

Principal source: F. Blanc, "Le Comité éxécutif de Lyon en 1848," *Révolution de 1848* 9–10 (1912–13): 342–66.
1 Blanc refers to them as Carbonari, but many can be traced to the Rights of Man and its offshoots.
2 Blanc calls them communists, but most were neobabouvist communists.

TABLE 9
Social Composition of the Central Committee

Class		Occupation	
Bourgeois	30	Merchants	9
		Lawyers	7
		Journalists	6
		Others	10
Petty bourgeois	16	Shopkeepers, etc.	8
		Employees	8
Workers	37	Master silk weavers	20
		Other silk workers	6
		Artisans	11
Unidentifiable			9

Source: see table 8.

had issued no statement on the republic. Fearing that the garrison of 8,000 men would be deployed against the Central Committee in the morning, the demonstrators demanded arms to defend the committee. Some republican and radical committee members sent emissaries to the local commander to requisition enough guns "to arm the people and the National Guard." The emissaries argued with General de Perron until he raised his original offer of two or three hundred to eight hundred rifles. A few dozen were delivered at daybreak.[10]

While the clamour for weapons was almost universal on the first day of the republic, the Lyonnais, employed their weapons and strong position in a manner that was unusual at this early stage of the regime. The first men armed marched to the Central Committee's chambers, assumed battle formation, loaded their rifles, and in that menacing atmosphere, their radical leader warned committee members that they "would certainly be shot if they betrayed the people's cause."[11] Simultaneously, the men from Croix-Rousse who had guarded the Hôtel de ville greeted the day – and the army's apparent acquiescence – jubilantly. They raised the red flag over the seat of the municipal government, where it flew until the advent of the Provisional Government commissioner.[12] In Paris, Lamartine had talked the crowd out of adopting the red flag; the Provisional Government's only compromise was to place red rosettes above the tricolour on flag poles.[13]

These attempts to steer the Central Committee onto a radical track were not isolated acts, for many people distrusted the committee. Later that morning, Provisional Mayor Laforest independently named a republican of 1830 who had rallied to the monarchy "Commander of the National Guard." This maladroit move provoked a large crowd into surrounding the Hôtel de ville and part of the crowd into invading the council room and intimidating committee members. Although the nominee was hastily replaced by Dr Lortet, a popular but absent republican, the invaders refused to disperse until their leaders were admitted to the committee. The same day, workers who had naïvely believed that the republic would promptly resolve economic and social problems accused the committee of inaction. Various groups rushed the council chambers, presented their grievances, and demanded retribution. The committee could only, in Joseph Benoit's words, "calm and appease" them with promises.[14] After the 26th, incursions into the Hôtel de ville tapered off due to disappointing results and better protection for the committee.

Between interruptions, the Central Committee worked incessantly. After a night trying to fill the demand for firearms, they tackled the pressing problem of how to govern effectively, given their numbers. The solution was to subdivide into four commissions of nine to fifteen members. Three specialized commissions reflected their priorities: a War and Police Commission was responsible for security; a Provisions Commission would furnish food to the needy, and a Finance Commission would deal with the disastrous monetary situation. To coordinate and implement policies, they set up an Executive Commission. Organized in this manner, the Central Committee was capable of administering Lyon until the Provisional Government commissioner came.[15]

Membership on the commissions mirrored the factionalism of the Central Committee. The moderates ensured the election of liberals and *Censeur* republicans to all positions on the Executive and most positions on the Finance Commission. Consequently, moderates could hamper extreme measures by exploiting the Executive's right to ignore the other commissions' proposals and by exercising the Finance Commission's control over the purse strings. Because they had not excluded radicals from government, as most moderates had, they had to use these more subtle methods of limiting the Left. Radical republicans – former members of conspiratorial societies like the Carbonari – took over the War and Police Commission. Their determination to democratize the security forces dictated constant clashes with the police and National Guard. Communists and socialists dominated the Provisions Commission because the bourgeois communists, Felix Blanc and Edant, convinced the twelve other neobabouvists to congregate in one agency, claiming they could accomplish more as a "compact body." Blanc also made the extremely materialist argument that "when you are master of provisions, you have the population at your disposal." However, all the communists except Edant soon became disillusioned and left the commission.[16]

Socially, the commissions reflected class biases. Merchants, lawyers, and clerks predominated on the Executive, Finance, and Police commissions, while four of the six workers elected to the commissions sat on the Provisions Commission and the other two joined the Police Commission.[17] The middle-class majority may not have been solely responsible for this social division of labour, for workers probably deferred to the political and financial expertise of lawyers and merchants.

The War and Police Commission wasted no time and spared few sensibilities. Without soliciting the Executive's approval, the commissioners placarded the city, reassured the populace that they would provide weapons, and requested all armed men to report to them. The placards implied general armament and subverted any lingering hopes of restricting access to the National Guard. The commissioners tried to honour their promise, going so far as to empty the arsenals and expropiate rifles in a private warehouse. They also tried to dissuade bands of workers from stealing arms by distributing guns through the National Guard. This diversionary tactic had little effect because the Guard was leaderless and disorganized. Dr Lortet, the man entrusted with the enormous task of organizing a militia, had stolen away from Lyon, so the Police Commission, and the Executive, asked the citizens to form companies to protect the republic.[18] Hundreds of men from all social classes responded to their plea. One example stands out. On 26 February, a mechanic who had fought on the barricades in 1830 and 1831 volunteered and was advised to gather and arm enough men to patrol his neighbourhood in the industrial quarter, Perrache. By evening he had mustered eighty neighbours, distributed rifles, and arranged for patrols throughout the quarter. For a week, his company of the National Guard maintained order in Perrache;[19] they required assistance only to suppress the largest outbreak of luddism.

The commission had less support and success in its effort to republicanize the police. Instead of appealing to the people, it followed the procedure laid down by the Central Committee: it sent a recommendation to the Executive Commission to replace the police with a Republican Guard similar to the Republican Guard Caussidière was creating in the capital. Since liberals on the Executive Commission had no intention of dismantling the police or establishing an independent, radical guard, they simply did not act on the advice. Laforest did agree to formalize the status of the workers protecting the Hôtel de ville, but only by naming Felix Blanc "Commander of the Civil Guard."[20] Despite Blanc's efforts, the Civil Guard received little support and was never equivalent to the Republican Guard.

The War and Police Commission took both parts of its name seriously. The first day it summoned General de Perron, "under the protection of the Civil Guard," to inquire if he adhered to the republic. A wary de Perron sent a note informing the commission of his appointment as provisional commander, pledging allegiance to the republic, and offering his cooperation to restore order, but continued to release rifles very slowly. Since his personal appearance at the Hôtel de ville and open cooperation were necessary to pacify the crowd, the Central Committee dismissed de Perron and promoted one of his subordinates, General Neumayer, to a new post as commander of the General Forces of Lyon. When de Perron did not protest this arrogation of sovereign power, Neumayer accepted his irregular commission and swore an oath to the republic on the balcony of the Hôtel de ville. As early as 29 February, the Provisional Government sanctioned the change in leadership, but emphasized that this kind of decision was a prerogative of the national government by retiring de Perron and naming Neumayer commander of the Rhône.[21]

The commission also overstepped jurisdictional boundaries by dispatching radicals to set up revolutionary councils in the suburbs. There the monarchical councils, reduced in size by resignations, had called in local liberals, republicans, and, by the second day, a few radical workers. Following the Central Committee's lead, they formed four commissions and democratized the National Guard. When Greppo, Grinand, and their comrades returned to their communes on the 27th or 28th, they were absorbed into the councils as delegates from the Central Committee. The Provisional Government later reconstituted these councils but incorporated many of the delegates.[22] The Lyonnais penchant for a loose federalism based on communes always surfaced in revolutionary situations. In 1848 the War and Police Commission was the main exponent of local autonomy.

The Provisions Commission was so busy that it was less bold. Edant and a couple of workers, one a former Ferrandinier, worked night and day trying to meet the need for food. As unemployment skyrocketed, requests for assistance reached staggering proportions. Even people with savings had trouble buying bread because bakers, fearful of the crowds, closed their shops. Accordingly, the commission placed bakeries "under the protection of the Republic," printed bread vouchers, and ordered bakers to open their shops and accept the vouchers (which they could redeem for cash). Members of the commission took turns issuing vouchers at the Hôtel de ville. Their makeshift operation prevented food riots but could not screen applicants, so the commission soon decided to reestablish welfare boards in each quarter to ascertain real need. Workers who had opposed the verification of indigence were mollified by the inclusion of workers on the new boards.[23]

With the active members like Edant devoting themselves to the relief effort and inactive members like Blanc dissipating their energy on police affairs, the Provisions Committee had little opportunity to remedy the fundamental problem, unemployment. Its one proposal, that the men in the new security forces be paid, was neither original nor comprehensive. The committee did not proclaim the "organization of work"[24] because it expected the central government to do this. (Indeed, the Provisional Government had already done so, but the Lyonnais did not know about this, or anything else happening in the capital, until the 28th.)

The Finance Commission was even more conventional. Chairman Bergier and the other businessmen were more preoccupied with the monetary than with the fiscal crisis. After consulting the Commercial Court and the Chamber of Commerce they put the usual revolutionary moratorium on bills maturing between 25 February and 15 March, to help merchants caught in the financial crash. They found funds in the city's general receipts to reimburse the government Savings Bank, which faced a drain on its reserves. Despite the escalating cost of welfare, they did not supplement the budget until 1 March. Even then, they did not respond inventively, let alone adequately, for they merely revived the old standby, a public subscription, after private citizens sent in unsolicited donations.[25]

The Executive Commission chaired by Laforest concentrated on restoring peace and public services without arousing suspicion. Rather than demanding the return of several hundred stolen rifles, it offered a reward for any rifle "misplaced in the inevitable confusion." It appealed to republican sentiments by labelling all who destroyed property "enemies of the Republic." Privately, the commission retained the old regime police; publicly, it tried to regulate the sprawling National Guard. On 28 February, it advised courts, schools, and all public facilities to resume normal operations.[26]

On the same day the Executive Commission received a reinforcement in the person of the Provisional Government commissioner. Emmanuel Arago, son of the astronomer, began by backing the commission's effort to remove the red flag. His speech to the crowd outside the Hôtel de ville echoed Lamartine's words to the Parisian crowd three days before, save for a special point linking the flag to the Convention, which had a bad reputation because it had imposed a horrible "terror" on Lyon. After a few tense moments, the crowd consented to the lowering of the red flag.[27] Lowering it symbolized the end of the Central Committee's potentially radical phase; raising the tricolour signalled the restitution of central authority.

Central Committee meetings soon lost their original vitality, since the general assembly now referred substantive issues to other agencies. In the early, daily sessions, the committee received many deputations but passed requests on to Arago or the commissions. Although a motion to pay members two francs each time they attended stirred up some debate, it passed with only one nay vote. Unhappily, payments did not begin until April, when Arago found the needed funds, and in the interval, working-class attendance had dropped.[28]

Increasingly, Commissioner Arago and the more moderate commissions administered the city. For instance, Arago implemented the committee's suggestion of a paid security force. He established a Mobile Guard for the same reasons that the Provisional Government had done so in Paris: he hoped to provide "a useful diversion" for the energies of the unemployed and "to prepare an active, devoted revolutionary force in the country."[29] However, the Mobile Guard did not fulfil anyone's expectations. The paid militia never enrolled more than 1,400 men, or one-tenth the manpower of their counterpart in the capital.[30] While this helped, it hardly made an impression on the unemployment rate. Moreover, the Mobile Guards were undisciplined. After they tried taking a fort on 11 April, inquiries found 126 unfit recruits and unsanitary conditions in their barracks. Arago removed the unfit, arranged for new quarters, hastened the delivery of uniforms, and generally encouraged military behaviour. He also installed a disciplinary council which handed down seventy penalties in its first two weeks. Although these measures improved morale, the damage had been done: the minister of war cut off funding and the minister of the interior only partly filled the gap.[31]

Similarly, the War and Police Commission failed to democratize the National Guard, in large part because of distrust between bourgeois and working-class Guards. Despite the commission's guidelines, intended to ensure a democratic election of officers early in March, enumerators drawn from the old National Guard refused to canvass upper stories of tenements and thereby excluded eligible workers. The exclusions angered enrolled workers and so many boycotted the election that balloting had to be rescheduled in some working-class quarters. Even before middle-class moderates swept the elections, radicals and workers protested to Arago. On 8 March, he responded by summarily removing control of the militia from the factious commission. After denouncing his arbitrary interference, the Central Committee capitulated and changed the War and Police Commission into the Police Commission. The most radical members realized that the new commission would not be permitted to run the police and quit.[32]

In fact, the Central Committee had accomplished nothing particularly radical while it was the sole authority in Lyon. Its hierarchical structure, with the most conservative members in the Executive Commission, partly explains its moderate record. The provisional mayor also played an important role. Laforest used his popularity and his office, especially his obligation to countersign ordinances to make them official, to hinder drastic measures. Considering the committee an extension of the overthrown council, he packed it with liberal councillors, other liberals, and his old allies, the *Censeur* republicans. The thirty-six liberals and moderate republicans proved a fairly solid voting block. Familiar with parliamentary politics, they exploited the rivalries among the fourteen radical republicans, thirteen communists, and five socialists.[33]

The radicals themselves contributed to the Central Committee's moderation. Some of the most revolutionary leaders refused to partici-pate in the committee, probably because they believed that basic changes would require national attention. These and other abstentions assured that the effective strength of the committee was never more than seventy-four. Moreover, radicals like Blanc who did join the committee became so engrossed in protecting it by organizing the National or Civil Guard that they found little time to shape its policies.[34]

Most radicals, doubtful about the committee, preferred to act as a pressure group. As early as 26 February, Benoit, another early Babouv-ist, Grangy, and a dozen Croix-Rousseans decided that an extragovern-mental body was necessary to "resist reaction" and "educate" workers in their rights and duties. Almost two weeks before other provincials,[35] they founded a society to sit in emergency session until the republic was safe, and then to discuss political issues, "especially social reorganization." On the evening of the 26th, the Democratic Society drew hundreds to its first meeting in Croix-Rousse. The assembly adopted a motion by a neobabouvist, Gabriel Charavey, to march on Paris "to reinforce the revolution if it was triumphant" or "to rouse the country against the monarchy if it had been restored." When Charavey brought this proposal to the Croix-Rousse Municipal Council, members of noncommunist secret societies vehemently opposed it, arguing it would leave Lyon vulnerable to reactionary forces. Charavey had to flee the council room in defeat.[36] This disappointing beginning taught the Democratic Society a lesson: henceforth *they* would demonstrate to influence the government.

Another neobabouvist, Felix Blanc, later accused the political crowd of squandering the revolutionary potential of the first three days. He felt that the demonstrators who had modified the political and social composition of the Central Committee could have continued intervening to radicalize its program. Instead they looked to the national government for major reforms and to the local government only for arms to safeguard the republic. In practice, safeguarding the republic meant restraining the crowds so that a reaction would not develop. "The people," he wrote, "were furious for order."[37] Though suggestive, Blanc's critique underestimated the realism of the crowds' instinctive realization that the central government would have to implement basic changes. His indictment also ignored the radicals' unconscious complicity. He himself had rallied the crowd on the 25th, and then had commanded the Civil Guard that dispersed crowds after the 26th. Others organized the National Guard, which would quell the luddite riots. Already he and other Lyonnais radicals had resolved the central dilemma of radicals in 1848, whether it was legitimate to use force against a republican government, with a resounding negative. They took less time to do so than the Parisian radicals[38] because they had long ago rejected conspiracy and violent overthrow in favour of indoctrinating and organizing the disenfranchised. Now that their constituency had the vote, it is hardly surprising that they chose to emphasize election campaigns and change through democratic processes.

VORACES AND LUDDITES

While the political crowd influenced the municipal revolution, smaller bands of workers threatened the detested fortifications around Croix-Rousse and the Providences. The Voraces' frontal attack on the forts was the most singular event of the revolution in Lyon, though the assaults on the Providences were more destructive. In the military and economic arenas, as in the political sphere, workers took the initiative. Militarily and economically, if not politically, they dominated the first three days.

Shortly after the initial invasion of the Hôtel de ville, several hundred workers from Croix-Rousse hastened to the smaller installations on the line of fortifications around their suburb. Their daring march surprised the army and hence they encountered little opposition: only one installation responded with gunfire, killing two attackers. Since most small posts received no instructions, soldiers neither abandoned nor defended their posts. By the morning of 26 February, workers had scaled the walls of small posts, disarmed many soldiers, and massed outside the Bernardines' barracks and the largest fort, St John. When General de Perron ordered the garrison to fall back to their base in Perrache, the troops obeyed so promptly that they left behind heavy artillery and ammunition. Workers entered the fort and manned the cannon. Soon they sent out raiding parties to seize convoys of small munitions. By the time Arago arrived, armed workers were ensconced in the fortifications.[39]

The new occupants of the forts subsequently identified themselves as Voraces and demanded that the fortifications girding their suburb be dismantled.[40] Most Croix-Rousseans realized that the military facilities had been designed to discourage insurrections and that the fixed cannon could inflict more damage on their neighbourhoods than the mobile artillery had in 1834. Only the Voraces had the numerical strength and inclination to take a long string of military installations. Radical political societies, which might have done so, favoured using the civilian arm of government to control the army. Later, radicals on the municipal councils would persuade the Voraces to leave the forts. The Voraces had less faith in the civilian authorities, at least regarding the forts.

In contrast to the Voraces with their single-minded approach, the military command vacillated. The acting commander, de Perron, was a career officer who had served in Napoleon's Grand Army and briefly in the Restoration forces. In Lyon during the second insurrection, he had appealed to residents of Croux-Rousse to lay down their arms, but his humane and futile gesture apparently left him uncertain about how to deal with the Voraces. Although he wanted to avoid armed confrontation, he refused to be embroiled in the political strife and he let two subordinates, Brigadier-Generals Neumayer and Rey, make all the decisions. Unfortunately his subordinates took quite different postures: Neumayer opportunistically accepted the republic, while Rey played a Machiavellian game. Rey, a Polytechnician discharged for criticizing the Restoration during the Hundred Days, did not intend to lose his commission in another change of regime. He posed as a guardian of order by proposing the retreat to Perrache, which he presented as a gathering of forces, and by visiting the Bernardines' barracks to recover the artillery. Of course, the retreat turned into a rout; he did not recover the artillery, nor did he stop pillaging from arsenals.[41] Divided and confused leadership resulted in a complete eclipse of military authority.

As Voraces hurried to the forts late on the 25th, other workers filed down from the main square in Croix-Rousse, crossed the Saône, and climbed up Fouvières to the Chartreaux enclosure sheltering several Providences, where they dismantled looms and burned the wooden parts and fabrics. Returning to the old quarters, they stopped at a religious boarding-school singled out by *Le Censeur* in its campaign against charity workshops. Here they wrecked the principal's library as well as students' looms. In the early morning, the crowd clustered around St Jean Cathedral and cheered as a delegate hoisted a red flag over the adjacent Archbishop's Palace. They did not physically harm the cathedral or palace.[42]

Another column had left Croix-Rousse for Caluire, the commune immediately to the north. At Abbé Collet's orphanage, they pulled looms apart, piled the wooden pieces, patterns, and fabrics into a pyre, then sang and danced around the bonfire. The next morning, other groups burned looms to the accompaniment of song and dance at Croix-Rousse charity shops. Adolescents besieging the Providence which had been implicated in the scandal six months previously let the building catch on fire. Flames consumed the premises, property worth over 100,000 francs.[43]

On the 27th, luddism spread to other workshops and communes. Partly armed silk and ribbon weavers assailed five "so-called religious workshops" in Croix-Rousse and Lyon, then spilled over to five noncharitable workshops in the same neighbourhoods. They picked private shops that contained mechanized trim looms or over fifty silk looms. In some large establishments, charitable and private, they ruined furniture and tools; in the small private establishments they demolished only mechanical looms.[44] Other groups attacked a steamboat construction yard in Vaise and two mechanized mills in Guillotière. At the boat yard, men hammered a steam engine until parts fell off or were warped beyond repair, then dumped the loose parts into the Saône. Residents of Guillotière were more protective of their property. A boiler-maker located beside a beleaguered lumber mill took his rifle, clambered onto his roof, and ordered the aggressors to burn the debris in the street. At the other mill, National Guards prevented any damage.[45]

By the 28th, luddites met resistance in the city. Two ribbon weavers tried to defend their master's shop from fifteen to twenty invaders; two joiners, also employees, explained that destroying the steam engine would deprive them of work. Though their bravery did not save the machines, they gave others time to assemble the National Guard, which arrested the ringleaders and dispersed the rest of the troublemakers. In Perrache, where over 400 workers were smashing machines at the state-run tobacco factory, Guards and soldiers quelled the riot.[46]

Once the city deployed the militia and the troops, machine-breakers fanned out into surrounding communes. The same day, a column originating in Croix-Rousse and augmented while passing through Vaise burned tools and furniture at two convents outside the latter commune. For the first time in the tumult, some participants raided the wine cellars and stole money. A worker from Vaise led other participants back to a lumber mill where he had worked and directed the demolition of the steam-powered saw which had deprived him of a job. Other residents of Vaise converged on two local factories and a shipyard. The match factory escaped devastation because the assailants, learning that the workers were incurably ill from sulphur poisoning, spared their jobs. The shipyard emerged unscathed due to the construction workers' defence. Late in the afternoon, a company of the Lyonnais National Guard swept through the suburb, scattering the marauders.[47]

Meanwhile, machine-breakers struck three rural communes. One group went to nearby St Genis-Laval and St Foy-les-Lyons, where they set looms in two convents on fire. The St Foy Municipal Council asked the Lyonnais authorities for assistance, and when that was refused, the councillors, gendarmes, and private citizens ended the disturbance. Lyon did dispatch National Guards and troops to a third village, Oullins, but the militia and infantry did not interfere until the 29th, when a second detachment of infantry arrived. About 200 men, women, and children had followed a red flag and drummer from the metropolis to the Oullins orphanage. Fifteen to twenty flourished guns; others brandished sticks. Although half left after burning looms or sinking them in the Rhône, they were replaced by local workers, who entered the private quarters and threw furniture out the windows to the bonfire. Others broke into the cellar and drank the wine, then ripped out cupboards and fed the shelves into the furnace. Inevitably, flames engulfed the building, which blazed all night. Courts later awarded the abbé who founded the orphanage 398,699 francs damages.[48]

On 29 February and 1 March, the National Guard halted the last two sorties into the countryside before anything was harmed. Luddism ceased after the destruction of property worth over 750,000 francs. Over three-quarters of the losses were suffered at church-run charities.[49]

An explosion so specific in its targets expresses long-standing antipathies. But the crowds were not anticlerical, nor opposed to all charities. In the commotion, no one injured a priest, hurt the monks and nuns running charity shops, or violated a church. The clergy's accommodating attitude and the orders' refusal to defend their shops may have obviated any need for physical force against churchmen.[50] Churches were never in danger, for the crowds aimed squarely at charity *workshops* (and secondarily at mechanized workshops) whose cheap labour (and labour-saving devices) imperilled their livelihoods. At most of the shops, they left everything but looms, machinery, and tools intact. Only two thefts occurred, probably committed by isolated individuals. The fires did not involve deliberate arson, for adolescents accidentally ignited the Croix-Rousse Providence, while drunken rural labourers touched off the Oullins conflagration. Since only two dozen arrest or trial records have been preserved, meaningful statistical analysis of the luddites is pre-cluded. However, observers and judicial officials agreed that adult Lyonnais played little part in senseless destruction.[51]

The red flag on the Archbishop's Palace can be construed as evidence of anticlericalism, but only in relation to church policies toward the charity shops. The flag symbolized the assailants' belief that the republic would rid France of the shops; the location signified a loss of confidence in Archbishop de Bonald's handling of the shops. In 1841, workers had petitioned the new archbishop to shut down the shops and welcomed his promise to authorize no new shops in the city. When the promise, faithfully executed, had merely encouraged new shops outside city limits, many workers had lost faith in the archbishop.[52]

Even their victims agreed that the Lyonnais luddites had purely economic objectives. At the trial of the luddites arrested on 27 and 28 February, the prosecutor argued that workers from Croix-Rousse came to wreck machines, hoping "to free themselves of the implements that offer their industry crushing competition, suppressing work. Not only did they want nothing else; they were determined to resist all other disorders." While some hit workers who resisted them, the same men prevented a gratuitous attack on a master's wife. The attorney-general's report concluded that "people were respected." Finally, most luddites frowned on looting. At Oullins, a ring leader cautioned the crowd that "everything must be burned and nothing stolen." One member of the Central Committee gave sweeping testimony to the workers' probity in this regard: "If you abandon heaps of gold and diamonds on a public road, we assure you the workers will not touch them."[53]

As elsewhere, most machine-breakers believed that their actions were just – believed, in a phrase, in the old moral economy.[54] Others thought their devastations were legal under the new regime – a more modern note. The indictment recognized this: "The rumour that one result of the Revolution would be the suppression of all looms operating in religious and lay communities, as well as machines and steam engines, spread in Croix-Rousse … Many apparently accepted in good faith that this was a natural, legitimate consequence of events." A weaver apprehended at Oullins "seemed surprised that we arrested him for what he regarded as the free exercise of a right." A cooper refused an order to leave Oullins with the remarks: "We will stay; we will drink; we are in a republic; everything belongs to us. You citizen military men have no power over us." A doubtful weaver reasoned thus: "We have already done it and no one did anything, so I think it is permitted … I do not think I am doing wrong."[55]

Comments like these, coupled with the crowds' methodical behav-iour, caused talk of conspiracy. Noting that the machine-breakers "seemed subject to some sort of discipline," observers suggested that they were "the instruments of a plot" by *Le Censeur*, communists, or simply "outsiders."[56] Of course, *Le Censeur* and the workers' press had criticized charity shops, sympathized with workers displaced by new technology, and urged lenience for previous luddites.[57] Unsophisticated readers might have interpreted their position as a licence to wreck machines, but this had not been the newspapers' intent. Conspiracy theories ignored *Le Censeur*'s attempt to stop luddism by reassuring workers that the republic would officially close charity shops, as well as the communists' disavowal of industrial sabotage.[58] By June, the prosecutor accepted that the only "outsiders" were rural labourers and that they were the most unruly. The silk and ribbon weavers were disciplined,[59] but only because they shared an occupational problem and community ties.

When conservatives recovered enough to counterattack, they charged the Central Committee with directing or at least facilitating the machine-breaking. Since the only evidence that the committee masterminded luddism was an oblique reference to written instructions,[60] *de jure* complicity seems unlikely. *De facto* complicity is a more complicated question. The committee did little to protect property until after the Oullins disaster and later courts ordered the municipality to indemnify victims. In their appeal, the city's lawyers argued rather convincingly that the committee *could* do little until it had organized a reliable security force. We have seen that, even among radicals, organizing a police force was a priority. However, the judge ruled against the city (and suburbs) on the ground that the law required communes to safeguard property whether or not a republican militia existed.[61] By emphasizing the establishment of the National Guard, the committee misled workers into thinking that luddism would not be opposed. Quite unwittingly, the committee encouraged luddism.

The equivocal conduct of the army, militia, and private citizens did not clarify the situation. Commander Neumayer gave few orders, probably because he could not count on the troops' loyalty as long as the Provisional Government did not confirm his appointment, and Rey refused to obey an "irregularly invested" commander. Lacking guidance, only two officers acted unilaterally and forcefully (in Perrache and Oullins).[62] The National Guard did not act until luddites threatened individually owned eatablishments, and then it showed more solicitude for these establishments than for the charitable workshops.[63] The remote location of many charitable shops and their operators' hesitation about calling the militia may account for the militia's late response to the threats. The unpopularity of the Providences explains the Guards' discrimination once they did respond. Dislike of the charitable shops and fear of the crowd encouraged citizen apathy; fear for their personal safety even caused masters to desert their own workshops, leaving workers to defend them.

After the tumult died down, the Provisional Government regulated work in charitable communities such "that it will not create troublesome competition for free industry."[64] The decree merely extended the prefect's prerevolutionary ordinance to the rest of France. Repression and the minimal results of luddism persuaded Lyonnais workers to forgo this kind of conduct. They would lash out in this spontaneous and destructive way only once more during the revolution. Instead many workers would take a more calculated and constructive approach: they would form unions and formulate demands. By the end of February, unionization was already under way.[65]

Characteristically, the Lyonnais workers' initial response to the news of the revolution was their most "modern." From the very start of the Second Republic, they rejected the old politics of deference in favour of the new politics of mass participation, not only in acclaiming the new authorities, as other workers did, but in the more meaningful sense of entering the new government. Even more shrewdly, radical weavers set up extragovernmental agencies to monitor the still heavily bourgeois and moderate "representative" governments. These innovative features of the first days would mature in the months and years to come. The more transitional element of the early days, the semitraditional Voraces, would also institutionalize and last for a few months. Only the most primitive response to revolution, luddism, would fade away after February.

CHAPTER THREE

The Provisional Government, March–April 1848

To assert the new republican government's authority over the largely conservative local elites throughout France, the Provisional Government sent commissioners to every department. The commissioner to the Rhône had special problems, for he had to impose central control and a moderate republic upon an autonomous and radical Lyonnais revolution. First, he had to regulate the popular paramilitary force and, alone among commissioners, recover military property of the magnitude of forts. With the Voraces' mistrust of the government and a humiliated army seeking vindication, this task was fraught with danger. Second, he had to revive the collapsed economy, an assignment complicated by a devastated silk market and organized, militant workers. Politically, he had to work with self-constituted local governments and prepare for national elections in competition with the largest and most independent provincial club movement.

For the demanding post of commissioner to the Rhône, the Provisional Government had chosen Emmanuel Arago, a lawyer who had defended radical republicans in the conspiracy trial of 1839 and in other political and press trials. More recently, he had demanded a provisional government in the Assembly before the arrival of the crowds.[1] After the revolution, conservatives would criticize the Provisional Government for appointing a man sympathetic to conspirators, a man without administrative experience or local ties. They would accuse Arago of surrendering to the Voraces, encouraging demonstrations, and exceeding his authority by instituting an extraordinary tax and misappropriating funds.[2] Arago, who denied all charges, would justify negotiations with the Voraces, concessions to the crowd, and heavy spending to create jobs as means of avoiding class conflict in this volatile city. Government approval of his expenditures on the National Workshops bolstered his case.[3]

Without Arago's correspondence during his brief, hectic tenure, it is hard to assess his intentions and competence.[4] The public record suggests that his political affiliation and lack of contacts in the community inhibited acceptance by the elite. However, such acceptance might not have promoted a peaceful transition to the republic, as it did in conservative provincial cities.[5] Lyon, with its tradition of insurrection and radicalism, required a commissioner sensitive to social tensions and capable of negotiating with radicals. Although Arago's conciliatory approach to agitators probably prolonged unrest, it also reduced violence. Only in the strange episode of the Savoy expedition can he be faulted for provoking violence. Rather than attributing his failure to restrain the Voraces, restore military property, provide employment, and elect moderate republicans to personal shortcomings, we shall find a more convincing explanation in the strength of the new paramilitary unit and the radical club movement, not to mention the stubborn depression in the silk industry. Moreover, it should be remembered that the Parisian authorities had trouble regulating their paramilitary force (the Republican Guard) and few commissioners were able to stimulate the economy and swing an election in two months.[6]

Similarly, much of the credit for the peaceful transition to a republic can be assigned to the radicals. Arago dislodged the Voraces from the forts without a fight and defused a series of explosive situations only with the help of radicals on the suburban and central committees. The Central Democratic Club limited and controlled its demonstrations; at a point when other radical cities erupted into riots, the clubs calmed an angry crowd and disciplined its expression of frustration. The radicals' devotion to orderly change derived from their prerevolutionary disavowal of violent overthrow and the early revolutionary decision to support the republic, facilitated by their strong position, which assured successes without resort to fighting. The Voraces kept the army out of the forts and operated as an independent security force, while the Central Democratic Club built an extensive club network and elected more democratic-socialists to the National Assembly than any other radical organization. If the democratic-socialist republic was not established, it was not defeated either. The confrontation between moderate and radical republicans had been postponed.

THE VORACES, MARCH – APRIL 1848

The Voraces were the most obvious menace to order and central authority in Lyon. When theatened with the loss of their food vouchers, they did leave the forts but intimidated the government commissioner into transferring the forts and artillery to the National Guard. To keep the essential vouchers, they offered to act as a security force and Arago accepted in order to supervise them. However, Arago never exercised as much authority over the Voraces as the minister of the interior, Ledru-Rollin, did over the Republican Guard. In addition to joining one of the three armed legions that attacked other countries, the Voraces abetted the most serious mutiny in revolutionary France. Although they acquired a fearful reputation as vagabonds and conspirators, they were simply a Croix-Rousse journeymen's society transformed into a paramilitary unit.

The pressing problem greeting the Provisional Government commissioner was the civilian occupation of the Croix-Rousse military facilities. Fearing that a display of force would trigger a battle, Arago decided to negotiate.[7] After touring the occupied facilities, he addressed the Croix-Rousse City Council, conceded that the posts "seemed" to be directed against the suburb, and promised to advise the government to destroy them. The suspicious Voraces refused to depart until the government made it official; meanwhile, they began razing small posts. On 5 March, they learned that the government had decreed the dismantling of all installations around Croix-Rousse except Fort St John, which, the authorities claimed, was needed for external defence. The Voraces ignored the army engineers sent to supervise the project and continued their self-directed demolition work.[8]

The new and more bellicose divisional commander, General Le Pays de Bourjolly, advocated seizing the large installations by a "show of strength." Fortunately, the Provisional Government commissioner had precedence in matters of internal security and overruled him.[9] Arago asked the Croix-Rousse City Council, which had been in regular communication with the forts since it had agreed to provide food vouchers to the occupants, to intercede. Council emissaries, two of whom were radical weavers, returned with the Voraces' explanation that they had appropriated military property for the National Guard. With Arago's approval, the council offered to transfer the property to the Guard. When the Voraces hedged about relinquishing the forts, the council suspended the food vouchers and the outmanoeuvred Voraces quickly arranged for a transfer.[10] Two-and-a-half weeks after entering the forts, they left peacefully.

Peace was soon jeopardized by the army's demand for the posts and artillery. While the Croix-Rousse council rejected proposals to return the posts, they did authorize the release of some cannon on condition that the rest remain in the commune. Next the army approached the mayor, a holdover from the monarchy, with a request for their munitions. When the mayor and a detachment of troops went to get the munitions on 23

March, a large crowd blocked their path, then sent forty armed delegates to force the council to give the magazine keys to a National Guard officer. The following day, Arago pleaded with councillors, militia officers, and Vorace delegates to exchange cannon and cannon balls for light ammunition. The Voraces, alone, refused the compromise. As Arago emerged from the Hôtel de ville, hundreds of people surrounded and jostled him. He postponed recovery of the military equipment.[11]

In the course of razing the small forts, the Voraces abandoned their amorphous recreational format for a democratic military structure. They subdivided into units, elected leaders, and soon were presenting arms to a "commander." When they transferred the forts to the National Guard, they insisted on a changing of the guard ceremony. Afterward, they set up patrols and offered to serve as a security force, not only to remain together but to retain their precious food vouchers.[12] The authorities accepted the offer because they wanted to supervise paramilitary corps. For two months, the Voraces functioned as an irregular corps similar to Caussidière's Republican Guard but more independent of government.[13]

Their first official duties involved crowd control. On 26 March, Mayor Laforest dispatched Voraces to disarm members of a National Workshop who had seized thirty cases of carbines from a steamboat. Their leader, Perret *dit Sans Rancune*, exchanged some rifles for the carbines. Three days later, Perret stopped a National Workshop from sinking a steamer which seemed to be flying the royalist flag. Without consulting the government commissioner, he circulated a rumour that the state was nationalizing the offending vessel. Arago confirmed the rumour to disperse the crowd. To prevent a recurrence, he had Perret assign details to protect the "nationalized" vessel and search the boats. Perret, a shrewd man, selected men from the workshop implicated in the incident and persuaded the boatowner to pay the guards. A month later, the boatowner reclaimed his property and billed the city for the guards' wages.[14] On these occasions, Perret had exceeded his instructions in the interests of order. In subsequent disturbances, the Voraces accentuated the disorder.

Like other depressed areas with foreign communities, Lyon tried to oust foreign workers.[15] First *Le Censeur* initiated a campaign to that end and the government commissioner advised them to go home; then local workers met to discuss competion from foreigners and, in many cases, to demand more decisive action. The Prefectural Committee composed of *Censeur* republicans responded by providing financial assistance to foreigners leaving France. Learning that a few people who had accepted travel expenses had not left, *Le Censeur* urged expulsion and four days later (28 March) gangs of workers sacked shops employing foreigners. The Voraces helped the National Guard halt the pillage.[16] Although everyone condemned these acts of aggression, the authorities still "invited" foreign workers to go home and the Voraces offered the departing workers protection. Three hundred Germans declared that they were going to "liberate" their country. On the 29th, they were escorted out of town by clubs and Voraces to the music of the "Marseillaise." Other nationalities departed in the same festive way.[17]

The largest ethnic minority, from the closest foreign country, actually formed a "liberation army." At a meeting of several hundred Savoyards on 27 March, speakers called for volunteers to go to Savoy, liberate it from Piedmont, and reunite it to France. Thousands attended an organizational meeting the following day. Emboldened by letters from the capital of Savoy saying that the populace favoured union and the garrison was away, many signed up. When 1,300 volunteers assembled on the 30th, a deputation from the Central Committee praised their devotion and presented them with a republican flag. The deputation, club delegates, and National Guards accompanied them out of the city. On the outskirts, 200 Voraces joined the expedition.[18]

The expedition encountered no obstacles on their four-day march to the capital. In Chambéry, a "French party" promoted annexation, the militia announced that it would not resist, and the governor general withdrew. On 3 April, 1,100 poorly armed men easily occupied the Hôtel de ville, disarmed the militia, and proclaimed the republic. Yet on the following day priests rallied the peasantry and recaptured the city for the Piedmontese monarchy. Only five invaders were killed, but over 800 were imprisoned. When news of the outcome stirred the clubs, Voraces, and Savoyards still in Lyon into talk of revenging their "brothers," Arago averted a second invasion by sending an envoy who secured the prisoners' release. The leaders returned as heroes.[19]

Just before the Savoy incursion, Germans and Belgians in Paris and Lille set up similar "legions" and, encouraged by officials, left to "liberate" their homelands. They encountered troops, who killed more than thirty and captured over 400, including about 100 Frenchmen.[20] These incursions neither inspired nor deterred the Savoyards, who knew nothing about them. Like the Germans and Belgians, they responded to the high unemployment, xenophobia, and republican fervour of their surroundings. In all three cities, local officials' desire to dispose of a problem and radical republican hopes of expanding the republic contributed to the débâcles. But several features distinguished the Savoy expedition. The idea was not new, for the Carbonari had recruited unemployed Savoyards to reconquer Savoy in 1831.[21] Former Carbonari on Le Censeur now promoted, and perhaps helped organize, a similar venture. Second, Italy was in the throes of indigenous revolutions and the Piedmontese, in particular, were distracted by external warfare. Letters from the French party in Chambéry encouraged volunteers who were aware that small armed groups had instigated urban revolutions else-where in Italy. Finally, the representative of the central government hardly discouraged the Savoyards or Voraces. Unlike Ledru-Rollin, who vetoed Caussidière's plan to dispatch the Republican Guard to Bel-gium,[22] Arago met the organizers, implied he would supply arms, and secretly supplied travel documents and funds. His later claim that he was powerless to intervene seems insincere, for he could have refused travel assistance.[23] His closest allies, the *Censeur* republicans, openly sympath-ized; they too bear responsibility for this sorry episode.

While some Voraces interfered in external affairs, others meddled in military matters. After weeks of radical propaganda directed at soldiers stationed in Lyon, General Le Pays de Bourjolly had confined the men to quarters and prohibited "dangerous" literature. His attempt to keep the army above democratic politics failed. The by now numerous political clubs and noncommissioned officers protested to Arago, who pressured the commander until he reluctantly agreed to lift the restrictions.[24] Just then a Sergeant Gigou, who had been making speeches in clubs against "the abuses which made a soldier a machine, a blind supporter, a praetorian in the service of the Monarchy," wrote a letter to the *Censeur* advocating that soldiers participate in political life. Gigou and a Corporal Beauvoir signed the letter "a group of noncommissioned officers" and thereby implicated their peers in public criticism of military policy. When other noncommissioned officers read the letter in the 28 March edition, they denounced the authors. In the resulting altercation, Gigou insulted superior officers. The colonel in charge got Gigou out of the barracks on a pretext, then had him spirited away to a Grenoble prison in the dark of night.[25]

The next morning (30 March), Corporal Beauvoir appealed to the Voraces and the Central Democratic Club to find his friend. The Voraces and the Central Club mounted a demonstration at the barracks to demand Gigou's release, a demonstration which mushroomed as people who had accompanied the Savoyards out of town converged on the military compound. After a group broke into the guardhouse and emerged empty-handed, General Neumeyer tried to calm the disappoin-ted crowd; even after they knocked him off his horse, he offered to be their spokesman before the divisional commander. Thousands trailed him to Divisional Headquarters and threatened to break down the doors; when the doors opened, hundreds surged into the commander's apart-ment. Once inside, though, they waited patiently for three hours while Neumeyer, Laforest, and other members of the Central Committee pleaded with Le Pays de Bourjolly. The commander finally relented after contacting Arago, who intimated he ought to free Gigou to avoid worse disturbances. Many demonstrators spent the night in Bellecour square north of the barracks, waiting for Gigou. In the morning, they welcomed him with a triumphal march to the prefecture, where Arago promised to free all soldiers detained for simple infractions and Gigou spoke to the crowd of the need for military discipline![26]

A more serious check to military discipline coincided with the Gigou affair. On the evening of Gigou's arrest, soldiers from two other regiments gathered in their canteen, reproached nonrepublican officers, and proposed electing officers from the ranks. When the canteen was closed and the ringleaders jailed, the mutineers released them. On 30 March, they took part in the procession for the Savoyards and the demonstration at the barracks. Transfer orders came for their regiments, so the mutineers asked the Voraces and the Central Democratic Club to delay their departure. At 10 P.M. on the 30th, Voraces and clubs surrounded the Prefecture and persuaded Arago to grant a postponement. (The demonstration kept Arago at the Prefecture during the crisis at Divisional Headquarters.) The next day, most of the mutineers welcomed Gigou, then returned to their barracks.[27]

These eventful days were almost as tumultuous as the last days of February. They resembled the 17 March *journée* in Paris only in so far as the tumult reflected tensions between radicals and the military. On the 17th, Parisian clubs demonstrated for the removal of the regular army;[28] on the 30th, Lyonnais clubs demonstrated to retain two regiments whom they had indoctrinated. Nor did 17 March prompt the Lyonnais outbreak, for the conflict between the clubs and the military command was already brewing my the time that local newspapers reported the *journée*.[29] When Voraces resumed confrontation with the army on 23 March, they were expressing fears about the fortifications around Croix-Rousse. Until they felt secure about the forts and cannon, they tried to oust soldiers from Croix-Rousse. After they received assurances about the fortifications and artillery on the 24th, they collaborated with the clubs in a more constructive approach to the troops. In short, the Voraces' new confidence and the clubs' gathering strength explain the timing of the Lyonnais outbreak.

Lyon's military revolt was far more serious than the mutinies elsewhere in revolutionary France. Democratic-socialist propaganda rendered the Lyonnais mutineers more political and persistent than other insubordinate soldiers.[30] The divisional commander's determination to restore discipline also prolonged the revolt. Whereas commanders in eastern France quickly acquiesced to demands and thereby curtailed disorders,[31] General Le Pays de Bourjolly made concessions only at the insistence of the Provisional Government commissioner and the mayor of Lyon.

After March, military insubordination ceased. Arago obtained leaves for Sergeant Gigou and Corporal Beauvoir; the army ordered one of the mutinous regiments to the eastern frontier. On 11 April, the regiment departed without protest, though the civilians and Mobile Guards accompanying them out of town tried forcing their way into the fort. The other "mutinous" regiment assisted in the forceful military response to this final assault on the forts. On this occasion, Arago could not convince an intransigent Bourjolly to yield. Immediately after, the new minister of war, François Arago, replaced Le Pays de Bourjolly with a republican general, Gemeau.[32] This change alone lowered the level of tension between the military command and the clubs. For their part, the Voraces stopped interfering in internal army affairs. They had not participated in the 11 April incident[33] because Arago had sent many of them to Grenoble to protect a shipment of arms.[34]

All through April, the authorities tried to occupy the Voraces with police work, notably guarding the Hôtel de ville during the national elections (an assignment they shared with the National Guard, Mobile Guard, Carbonari, and Ferrandiniers). Although the authorities praised their performance during the elections,[35] they discontinued the food vouchers, their sole remuneration, and ordered half the 400 Voraces to merge with the National Guard at the end of April. The other 200 were to remain a special corps.[36] These measures reflected the changing political situation, but also annoyance with the Voraces' disruption of daily routine. Day after day, the Voraces had searched private homes and religious establishments for arms. They claimed that they conducted their searches with scrupulous respect for people and property and some "victims" confirmed these claims. Nevertheless, they were blamed for the few unruly searches.[37]

During the revolution, the Voraces acquired a reputation as fearful vagabonds and vandals.[38] The police and judicial files tell a different tale. The thirty-five Voraces named in the files were predominantly journeymen silk weavers. Compared to the general population in Croix-Rousse, or to a the profile of radicals in the metropolis, an unusually high proportion were native Lyonnais. None had a criminal record.[39] A Croix-Rousse newspaper denying charges that the Voraces were "common pillagers" reported that "everyone in Croix-Rousse laughs at the fear the Voraces inspire."[40]

A self-proclaimed Vorace contributed to their false reputation by publishing a pamphlet tracing their origins to two fantastic, apparently imaginary prerevolutionary secret societies.[41] In fact, the Voraces society had been politicized and organized along formal lines during the revolution. Seizing the forts manifested the generalized hatred of the forts in Croix-Rousse and, only by extension, of the government which had erected them. Keeping the forts after the Provisional Government promised to dismantle them represented a more explicit distrust of the new national government. Finally, their behaviour as a security force had obvious political overtones, for the March Days revealed that they would collaborate with the clubs to pressure the government on military issues. Here their prerevolutionary contacts with the neobabouvists who had used their meetings as a cover for political discussions played a role. However, the Voraces shed their loose, social-club structure for a military format only to facilitate their demolition and police work; they did not become a secret society until after the revolution. During the revolution, they represented the popular impulse to defend their suburb, more than a larger, modern commitment to defend a republic they did not fully trust. One year later, they would take the broader, national overview.

ORGANIZATION OF WORK

Like urban workers throughout France, Lyonnais workers expected the new republic to solve economic problems, especially unemployment. Unlike their counterparts in other provincial cities, they also took matters into their own hands. First, they tried to raise wages and reduce hours through strikes and, with the assistance of a new government agency, devised a promising system of labour negotiations. Realizing that no contract could ensure full employment, they welcomed Arago's attempt to implement the organization of work. Though they were disappointed when the National Workshops did only conventional public works, the program was more successful than in other cities. To avoid conflict over this essential program, Arago allowed a relatively high rate of pay and refused to limit the program as expenses mounted. Furthermore, he recognized that weavers wanted meaningful, skilled work and obtained a government contract for silk flags. By insisting that the flags be woven in private workshops, he ensured that thousands of the often disruptive weavers were employed in their homes, where they were less likely to coalesce into angry crowds.

Because the *fabrique* was a seasonal luxury industry, the revolution had a more devastating effect on Lyon than other textile cities.[42] By 25 February, the modest autumn orders were almost completed and spring buyers were expected; after the 25th, concern about continuing political unrest and uncertainty about delivery of orders kept most buyers away. Merchants could not fill orders they did receive due to the financial crisis which spread rapidly from Paris and dried up credit. Runs on banks forced banks to stop payment in specie, yet many clients refused bank notes. Even silk merchants who could raise money did not stockpile the expensive, easily outmoded silks.[43] For the first time in decades, up to three-quarters of the looms lay idle in the usually lively spring and summer seasons.[44]

Reversing their previous pattern, workers became professionally as well as politically active in a period of high unemployment. In contrast to most provincial cities, organized workers met from the start of the revolution. As in the capital, the hard-hit construction workers led the way.[45] Rival *compagnonnages* sat down together and formulated demands for raises of fifty centimes to a franc a day and for a ten-hour day. Delegates approached the masters and local authorities, often accompanied by the *compagnonnage* in parade. A few hitherto unorganized trades followed their lead. Most notable were the silk spinners, for, as women, they were a new element in job actions.[46] After 5 March, the trades active under the July Monarchy – silk weavers, tailors, shoemakers – launched more conventional strikes.[47] These workers probably hesitated before abandoning their tried and true tactics of no strikes in high unemployment and no reliance on government officials. The creation of a Committee to Organize Work empowered to mediate industrial disputes evidently reassured them of the government's good will, for at least sixteen trades held job actions in March.[48] In less than three weeks, the Committee to Organize Work settled grievances in seven *corporations* and persuaded the shoemakers to adjourn their discussions until after the national elections. In April, there were virtually no strikes, in large part because many workers had received some satisfaction through the Committee to Organize Work. The master weavers of simple silks, for instance, won an unusually favourable contract, including an unprecedented agreement on a controversial issue, thread supplements to cover losses due to breakage during weaving.[49]

During the strike period, entire *corporations* met together and delegates of the masters and journeymen conducted negotiations; after the strike, the two interest groups met separately. A few *corporations* founded parallel societies to monitor the application of contracts. As early as 6 March, the painters and plasterers had a settlement which prohibited hiring outside the *corporation* and prescribed enforcement procedures. Both masters and journeymen were to establish formal societies and elect commissions to impose fines and exclusions.[50] Journeymen established a society immediately, but the masters dawdled until July. Although the masters' constitution alluded to a collective contract and a commission to enforce it, most of the clauses dealt with a price-fixing arrangement. The society either did not include all masters or did not bind members, for within weeks of its foundation, many masters were paying less than the contract stipulated. Workers blacklisted these masters and maintained their boycott for three months. Despite this conflict, masters and journeymen cooperated to bid on painting flag poles.[51]

The joiners began the shift to producers' cooperatives. At a strike meeting late in February, a master joiner urged staying on the job and using part of their wages to fund an association. He described the reaction: "at the single word, Association, outcries arose from all over the immense amphitheatre. 'Down with the communist,' they yelled." With neobabouvists like Greppo promoting cooperatives, the confusion is understandable. The master joiner did interest twelve joiners who formed the nucleus of a club concerned solely with "social organization." Three months later, forty of the several hundred members took a proposal for a cooperative to the Committee to Organize Work. On 1 August, the committee approved an amended constitution and, one month later, a workshop opened.[52] In general, the workers of Lyon turned to cooperation after the national elections and especially after the revolution.

Government officials and mercantile interests also tried old and new ways of resuscitating the economy. As always, they tried to restore confidence and credit; predictable, given the political turbulence and the wariness of the silk merchants, these efforts met with little success. After sustaining the Savings Bank until the end of the moratorium on bills, the Finance Commission appealed to bankers for funds, but by mid-March, bankers had no specie, creditors were refusing bank notes, and merchants were transporting coin out of the city. Arago gave orders to stop all export of silver and gold (save small sums authorized by the Prefecture) and to accept Bank of Lyon notes. The decrees slowed the export of precious metals and bolstered the bank notes.[53] Soon 150 local merchants formed a discount bank and, when the Provisional Government promised a branch of its discount bank, the Chamber of Commerce contributed generously. Unfortunately, the agitation at the end of March interrupted the tentative recovery of confidence.[54]

Arago's appointment of radicals, merchants, and workers to a Committee to Organize Work charged with considering how to provide work (and secondarily, mediating strikes) seemed a more promising response to the mass unemployment of 1848. Although twenty of the twenty-seven appointees were bourgeois, four of them were Fourierists and four, neobabouvists. The ubiquitous Joseph Benoit and one other weaver completed the neobabouvist contingent. In ten days, the committee coopted seven more bourgeois and six more working-class members. The Fourierists now numbered five, the neobabouvists thirteen. The Executive Board reflected the social and ideological imbalance: a Fourierist lawyer, Alphonse Morellet, became president and Benoit, vice-president; another Fourierist and three bourgeois neobabouvists took the other seats.[55]

Although the organization of work was the key slogan of the revolution, few knew exactly what the phrase meant and the committee's attempt to define it, as well as its own mandate, evoked bitter and divisive ideological debate. While the neobabouvists, taking the broadest possible interpretation, proposed immediate, permanent solutions to unemployment, the rest of the committee preferred stop-gap measures while they pondered long-term measures. On 8 March, the neobabouvists recommended suppressing charitable workshops, placing the orphans under the protection of the state, and assigning municipal work to cooperatives under the direction of the city. When the committee ignored these relatively feasible proposals, the neobabouvists ceased presenting practical projects. Two days later, Joseph Benoit called for nationalization of all royal and nonproductive land, government purchase of mines, canals, and bridges, state assistance for cooperatives, a progressive income tax, and free, equal education. He was clearly outlining a general political platform and the noncommunists responded in kind.[56]

Although the committee shunned neobabouvist schemes, it carefully considered a Proudhonian Central and Fraternal Workers' Bank. The bank would raise capital by payments of five sous a day for each worker (a fund-raising innovation of the Propagation of the Faith) and would function as a loan bank and an insurance and pension plan. Based on payments which would have to be suspended during depressions, when the need for loans was greatest, the bank was a shaky proposition. However, the concepts of mutual credit and mutual aid had been popular long before 1848. Ennemond Brosse, a former master and Mutualist leader, expressed many workers' sentiments: "Who will furnish capital to cooperatives? Will the State? No, the treasury is empty. Will a capitalist? But he requires security ... and the worker has only his arms, intelligence, and good will. If the worker counts on himself first of all, if by daily payments ... he funds the Workers' Bank, he will end misery, he will be through with the leper, usury; even more, he will assure the future of society."[57]

The most radical members of the committee decided that the Fourierists "wished to concentrate discussion of social questions in an official body and have the initiative there." Benoit and four other neobabouvists retired and "left the field free for the Fourierists." If Arago had appointed Benoit and his comrades to divert them from politics (as the Provisional Government had sent Louis Blanc to the Luxemburg Commission), he failed. Thereafter, the neobabouvists devoted their considerable energies to the club movement. On the other hand, the deradicalized committee never became a political machine or fomented a revolutionary *journée*, whereas the Luxemburg Commission did.[58] Instead the committee became a sounding board for cooperative schemes.

Meanwhile, the temporary response to unemployment aroused little opposition. The neobabouvists, realizing that they could hardly veto public works in the desperate economic situation, resolved "to draw some profit for the Republic by making them an organized force." Within three days, the committee recommended fifteen to thirty workshops of 500 men apiece to expand the overtaxed water system. The Central Committee adopted a more modest version of the recommendation. Although the Committee to Organize Work discussed other useful projects, the Central Committee rejected all but roadwork for budgetary reasons. Before the departure of five of its members, the neobabouvists ensured the appointment of Felix Blanc as director of the workshops.[59] In his brief tenure as director and longer term as a workshop spokesman, Blanc established a liaison between the workshops and the clubs that encouraged minor disturbances in April but discouraged a major conflagration in June, when the workshop program was modified.

By 26 March, the Committee to Organize Work had opened two workshops employing over 500 men at one franc seventy-five centimes (and a food voucher) a day.[60] Since workshops attracted the unemployed from the surrounding communes, and this intensified the campaign against foreign workers,[61] the solution increased the problem. The committee tripled the number employed in the first two weeks, only to have its meeting invaded by hundreds of people demanding work. Disheartened, the committee stopped administering the program. Although Arago continued to open workshops, he could not keep pace with enrolment in the program. By May, when 2,252 Croix-Rousseans were in the workshops, another 4,127 citizens of that commune were enrolled but not employed.[62]

In their haste, the Committee to Organize Work, the Central Committee, and the government commissioners showed poor judgment. All twelve workshops did earthwork, some of which was counterproductive. The Perrache workshop, for instance, took gravel from an embankment on the river bed to build a dike upstream, leaving a gap to be refilled. The committees and commissioners got very little help from the civil engineers, who procrastinated while the economic situation deteriorated. The government officials, in turn, gave few guidelines or resources to the engineer who soon replaced the overextended Blanc as director.[63] Unpleasant and often unproductive work, combined with lax supervision, induced workers to march off the job at the slightest provocation. Usually they "appropriated" arms being shipped through Lyon or joined demonstrations in progress. When the Perrache workshop thought a steamboat was flying the royalist flag, they boarded it, thrashed the captain, and threatened to sink it. This potentially explosive situation was, of course, defused by Perret and the Voraces.[64]

In addition to these problems, the workshops were expensive. The "patriotic collection" raised only enough money to cover the cost of food relief for a few weeks;[65] when the Committee to Organize Work proposed workshops, the normally moderate Finance Commission debated a "forced loan" from capitalists, before reverting to form and deciding to wait for the national government to bail it out of the financial débâcle. At this point, Arago announced the opening of "vast national workshops" and prodded the Central Committee into voting a surtax on the rich and an extraordinary tax equal to the ordinary direct taxes for 1848. On 19 March, Arago imposed the extraordinary tax.[66]

Introducing taxes clearly exceeded a commissioner's mandate. To complicate matters, the Provisional Government had just raised property taxes by 45 per cent. When the government heard of Arago's unilateral action, they rescinded all financial measures initiated by commissioners and ordered them to submit such measures to the central government for "prior approval." Then, acknowledging the need for supplementary revenue, the government authorized the City of Lyon and the Department of the Rhône to levy an extraordinary tax of fifty-five centimes, to be collected with the forty-five centimes tax.[67] Considering the resistance to the forty-five centimes tax in the depressed wine-growing areas of the west and south,[68] the reaction to the fifty-five centimes (really the one franc) tax was mild. Le Courrier de Lyon and La Gazette de Lyon noted public consternation over improper procedures and double taxation, but did not expand upon this first open criticism of Arago. Radicals and republicans, including a new conservative republican newspaper, Le Salut Public, defended the tax as necessary to open workshops, and at the end of March, few Lyonnais contested the need for workshops to occupy the unemployed.[69]

Unfortunately, the fifty-five centimes tax did not solve the immediate fiscal problem. It was a difficult tax to collect in time to open workshops.[70] By the end of March, people knew that the administration had no funds for food vouchers or workshops. Learning that the central government was sending 500,000 francs to Lyon, but not knowing its purpose, Arago publicly denied rumours that the government could not provide bread and work. Because the money was intended for the local branch of the government's discount bank, reactionaries would later raise a cry of deliberate misuse of funds. However, an official audit of his accounts exonerated Arago, who had deposited the 500,000 francs in the discount bank[71] and used a 600,000 francs loan from the Provisional Government to rescue the bankrupt program.[72]

Other major commercial and industrial cities also opened workshops in March 1848; most of these workshops did conventional public works (roadwork). The Lyonnais program differed from the rest only in so far as it ultimately employed 17,000, or more than any city except Paris, which employed 100,000; paid above the average daily rate of one franc fifty centimes, and added a bonus, a food voucher. As a consequence, Lyon had more difficulty financing their workshops than Paris, where the central government covered the enormous expenditure (14,500,000 francs), or than cities like Toulouse, where private donations covered modest expenses. Yet Lyon did not limit enrolment, reduce rates, or close workshops, as many cities did in April. In Amiens, Nancy, and Reims, attempts to curtail public work programs provoked demonstrations and even fights with the National Guard.[73] Because Arago had a healthy respect for the Lyonnais workers' capacity for revolt, he put less emphasis on fiscal restraint than on preventing confrontations. His calculated fiscal irresponsibility contributed to the essentially peaceful character of the Lyonnais revolution.

Arago's recognition that weavers preferred relevant skilled work to useless physical labour prompted a more important gesture in the interest of employment and peace. From the beginning, he urged the Provisional Government to buy the new republican flags from the *fabrique*. On the last day of March, he announced a large government order of flags to be allocated by a subcommittee of the Committee to Organize Work.[74] While the announcement helped subdue the unrest convulsing the city, it also inspired a quiet demonstration. The following day a large contingent of women "visited" the Prefecture to request that women be allowed in the new National Workshops. Arago, who had made no mention of National Workshops, consented.[75] Despite its dismay at not being consulted, the Committee to Organize Work formed a subcommittee, which obligingly recommended a National Workshop to employ women and fill the government order. After a long debate in which many members of the full committee contended that setting up a workshop would retard the beginning of work, President Morellet convinced the majority to adopt the recommendation. The committee also asked the Central Committee for a substantial sum of money to set up the workshop. A huge crowd, including 500 workers from the functioning workshops, celebrated the news.[76]

They celebrated too soon. Ignoring the Committee to Organize Work, Arago chose to have the order made up in private workshops. It was probably a wise decision, since it undoubtdly accelerated the beginning of work and likely reduced disorder by limiting, in a positive manner, the number of workers in the unruly National Workshops. Arago did try to ensure that the neediest weavers got the commissions. He named eight silk merchants and sixteen *chefs d'atelier* to a new Committee to Allocate the Government Order. Less than half his nominees belonged to the Committee to Organize Work, although the merchant Edant, the masters Benoit and Greppo, and three other *chefs* were neobabouvists. In addition, two masters were dissident Icarians and many others are identified as democratic-socialists. The communist and democratic-socialist bloc assured the election of Edant as president and Bernard-Barret, a radical republican typographer, as vice-president. In the early, policy-making meetings, Edant, Benoit, and Greppo were influential. When the committee actually assigned work, Bernard-Barret and other, less busy radicals took over.[77]

Initially, the Committee to Allocate the Government Order accepted the piece-rates set by the Provisional Government and had merchants submit lists of unemployed masters (though they did reserve the right to substitute needier *chefs*). Once masters complained about piece-rates, the committee obtained a raise. They also devised a system of assigning commissions so that they would provide work for 4,500 to 9,500 weavers (and 4,300 assistants) over a four-month period. Next they began registering masters and, by May, had approved 5,539 and rejected 477 "comfortable" *chefs*. Now they assigned masters to merchants and gave preference to registered masters. To guarantee that as many *chefs* as possible shared the work, they stipulated that a *chef* could receive only one commission.[78]

The Committee to Allocate the Government Order assumed that women, who did much of the simple silk weaving, would participate in the simple silk portion of the order. Arago did start a subscription for unemployed women; two Fourierists, Elisa Morellet and Aline Juif, chaired a Women's Work Committee to collect and disburse the monies. In view of the harsh economic conditions, people gave generously: workers in a National Workshop actually scraped together 295 francs for the fund. In the autumn, the Women's Work Committee would found a cooperative workshop to sew the double-faced flags.[79] Other cooperatives would then mount and package the order.

Although the flag order created more acceptable work and thereby promoted social peace, it failed to address the basic cause of unemployment. If the Committee to Allocate the Government Order placed enough commissions to stimulate the silk market, there was still "no real amelioration," no independent growth.[80] Despite a reform of the food relief program which reduced fraud, the Provisions Commission was still swamped with requests for relief because the number of indigents rose as the economic crisis lingered. In less than four months, the commission spent 651,452 francs on vouchers, over six times as much as the Welfare Bureau had spent in the food crisis of 1845–6. (In the same four months, the Welfare Bureau disbursed 110,000 francs in private charity.)[81] Surviving commission records enable us to profile the recipients and deduce the effect of the economic collapse on certain neighbourhoods.

The typical recipient was an immigrant aged thirty-eight to sixty, who was married and supporting three people. Over half were silk workers; almost a third were labourers. Most lived in communities where every second or third building contained thirteen or fourteen families – six or seven silk workers' families – on welfare.[82] The Provisional Government commissioner had not solved the workers' fundamental problem, unemployment.

THE CENTRAL
DEMOCRATIC CLUB

One part of Commissioner Arago's political assignment proved unexpectedly easy, for the moderate Executive Commission, the moderate rump of the Central Committee, and the *Censeur* republicans on the Prefectural Committee all accepted his leadership. Moreover, Arago was so confident of his rapport with radicals that he reinstated most of the radicals incorporated in February when he reconstituted the suburban councils. Bernard-Barret, Greppo, Grinand, and six others whom he appointed to the Croix-Rousse Council had belonged to neobabouvist or dissident Icarian societies; thirteen of the twenty-eight councillors were workers. The proportion of radicals and workers was only slightly lower in Guillotière. Nevertheless, relations with the government commissioner were amicable, largely because the suburban councils, like the city council, needed financial assistance from the central government to pay for relief.[83] Interestingly, Arago made few changes in the conservative local administrations of the arrondissement of Villefranche. Presumably, he wanted to reassure the powerful conservative local elites of the area.[84]

The second and more significant part of his political mission was to arrange the election of moderate republicans to the National Assembly. Although he quickly called electoral assemblies and ultimately endorsed a moderate republican slate, he was consistently outmanoeuvred by the conservative elite in the countryside and the Central Democratic Club in the city. The Democratic Society expanded into a club network second in size only to the Parisian network, yet managed to control more of its demonstrations and focus more on electing radicals than its Parisian counterpart. The ideologically sophisticated and politically experienced leadership of the monarchy arranged for a viable slate and elected more democratic-socialist workers than any other department.

After Arago had shorn the Police Commission of its power, the National Guard continued to be a source of discord in municipal politics. Neither the Police Commission nor the army captain who succeeded it adequately armed the militia. At Arago's insistence, the commission temporarily had halted delivery of rifles to the National Guard in order to arm the Mobile Guard. Captain Cholat waited three weeks before resuming deliveries and by then the militia had fewer than 10,000 rifles for nearly 24,000 men. When a review revealed how few Guards from workers' quarters had arms, workers renewed their seizures of arms.[85]

During the month that Captain Cholat directed the National Guard, he held a new census and elections. The second round of elections, like the first, produced a largely conservative crop of officers.[86] The Central Committee, convinced that some officers were plotting with General Le Pays de Bourjolly to overthrow it, arrested the officers without a shred of substantive evidence. Although the committee quickly released the officers, the rash move had discredited it. National Guard officers petitioned Arago to call elections for the city council; they circulated rumours that members of the Provisions Commission had profited from the sale of food vouchers. When the committee submitted a collective resignation in protest, Arago refused to accept it on the grounds that laws governing municipal elections, and the national elections, must come first.[87]

While the National Guard criticized the Central Committee, its new commander, the republican General Neumayer, continued holding elections and arming the militia. By the end of April, all officers had been elected and most men had rifles. Except in Croix-Rousse, where many officers were silk workers and twenty were radicals, the officers were mostly bourgeois of moderate to conservative opinion.[88] If Lyonnais moderates had no established elite units to keep the Guard a conservative institution, as happened in Paris,[89] they did manage the elections to the same end. The Committee of the Quai de Retz seems to have organized the Guard elections, then officers spearheaded an attack on the Central Committee.

As the Central Committee lost popularity and authority, the Democratic Society gained. A week before Arago called electoral assemblies, the Democratic Society applied to the Central and Croix-Rousse committees for a public room. Both committees refused because the moderate majorities argued that then they would have to find space for other clubs. Not until 9 March, when an armed detachment of Voraces led by an obscure neobabouvist installed the Democratic Society in a seminary in one of the forts, did the committees relent. By then, one meeting-place was insufficient, so the Democratic Society asked permission to use schools. The Central Committee opened nine schools and colleges, encouraged the church to make other seminaries available, and subsequently paid the rent for dozens of cafés.[90] Although clubs needed cheap meeting-places to attract workers, public facilities and financing meant that the government could shut the premises or cut off funds in the waning days of the revolution.

The Democratic Society was expansionist. Once settled in the seminary, it began contacting other, mainly suburban societies and dispatching "citizens" (mainly neobabouvists) to every quarter to establish clubs.By mid-March, it ordered the "neighbourhood clubs" to send it delegates and financial accounts. While twenty-two clubs and a few workers' *corporations* complied, their delegates soon challenged the Democratic Society's authority and demanded a coordinating body composed of delegates from each club, including the Democratic Society. The society deferred, yet its members, acting as delegates from other clubs, dominated the Central Democratic Club that emerged on the 18th. One result was the secession of moderate republican societies.[91]

Moderate republicans objected to the Democratic Society/Central Democratic Club because of its personnel and politics. Benoit, Grangy, Grinand, and at least six other leaders of the Democratic Society came from neobabouvist circles. Fully forty per cent of the activists in the Central Democratic Club can be identified as members of prerevolutionary radical groups.[92] Their experience in secret societies explains the society's stringent entrance requirements (two members had to vouch for a candidate's "morality and civic virtue"), which seemed to contradict its new public status and provisions for open voting. The secret society background also suggested the useful system of local clubs linked by delegates to a central committee. The ideological orientation was evident as early as 15 March, when the club's newspaper reproduced the text of a speech by the neobabouvist, Grinand, which lauded equality as "the supreme principle." Thee days later, the club killed a proposal to "fuse the three socialist parties" by denouncing the Fourierists for accepting inequality and the Saint-Simonians for selling out to the monarchy. Yet the pragmatic neobabouvists knew they needed allies on the left. A Proudhonian, Pierre Gros, and a Union member, Guillermin, collaborated with Benoit and Charavey to write the society's platform, adopted on 16 March. The platform, which included the usual democratic demands for manhood suffrage, election to all offices, and free, equal education, also urged mutual credit, a progressive income tax, and nationalization of transport, mining, and insurance companies (in short, the program Benoit presented to the Committee to Organize Work).[93] Moderates could not accept the socialist portions of the program.

After republicans seceded, workers' *corporations* adhered to the Central Democratic Club. As in Paris,[94] mechanics had called a meeting of representatives from all *corporations* to choose working-class candidates for the National Assembly elections. When they invited the Democratic Society to send representatives to explain its position, the society countered by inviting the *corporations* to send delegates to its electoral committee. The Workers' Electoral Committee disbanded because thirty-seven of the forty member *corporations*, including nine circles in the *fabrique*, the three shoemakers' *compagnonnages*, and the tailors' society, all of which had been active before 1848, affiliated with the Central Democratic Club.[95] Unlike *corporations* in the capital, they did not retain an independent political organization nor extract a promise that half the Central Club candidates would be workers. One explanation of their accommodating posture toward the clubs may be the lack of an official unifying agency such as the Luxemburg Commission.[96] A more likely explanation is the proletarian nature of the Central Club, which must have made it more attractive to the *corporations*. As table 10 illustrates, over seventy per cent of the club activists were workers, a far higher proportion than in the Parisian leadership. Moreover, the working-class membership of the clubs reflected the organized trades. Since the Democratic Society and the Central Club met in Croix-Rousse and, as table 11 reveals, three-quarters of the allied clubs met in the suburbs or working-class quarters, most members must have been workers. The *corporations'* merger with the clubs clearly enhanced the working-class quality of the clubs and strengthened them.[97]

As the elections approached, clubs proliferated. On the eve of the elections, when the metropolis supported 138 clubs, over three-quarters of them belonged to the Central Democratic Club and United Corporations.[98] These figures compare favourably with the 203 clubs in the capital, 149 of which were democratic-socialist. In all essentials, the Central Democratic Club and its affiliates resembled the Parisian club movement. In both cities, radical secret societies founded the original clubs, then transformed them into coordinating committees for other clubs. Both movements attracted mainly artisans and workers and aimed to indoctrinate the new, lower-class voters, to pressure the government, and to elect democratic-socialists to the National Assembly.[99]

Resembling Parisian societies did not, however, imply copying or obeying them. On 8 March, the Democratic Society initiated a correspondence with the prominent Parisian radical, Raspail. At that point, the Democratic Society was drafting its constitution, while Raspail had not even started his club. The few letters that followed hardly shaped Central Club policy.[100] A month later, envoys from the Club of Clubs in Paris arrived to find fifty (actually more) clubs and 500 delegates in the Central Club. Satisfied that the clubs were "perfectly organized," the envoys kept a low profile. When two became concerned about the slow pace of candidate selection and the rejection of a radical republican candidate approved by the Club of Clubs, they addressed the clubs. Although their reports mentioned an enthusiastic reception,[101] the tempo did not pick up and the candidate in question was not seriously

TABLE 10
Social Composition of Club Activists, March–
April 1848

Social Group	Number	Percentage
Silk workers	37	47
Garment workers	6	7.5
Construction workers	6	7.5
Other workers	0	0
Artisans	7	9
All workers	56	71
Petty bourgeois	12	15
Bourgeois	11	14

Source: Le Tribun du People, March–April 1848; checked against file of all militants.

TABLE 11
Location of Clubs in Central Democratic Club,
26 March 1848

Location	Number	Percentage
City		
Old Quarters	3	8
Peninsula	9	24
Slope of Mount Saint Sebastien	3	8
Total	15	40.5
Suburbs		
Croix-Rousse	14	38
Guillotière	6	16
Others	2	5
Total	22	59.5

Source: L'Organisateur Lyonnaise, 26 March 1848; eight of the forty-five listed clubs could not be located.

considered. As in most provincial cities, Parisian envoys had little influence on the club movement.[102]

Furthermore, the Central Democratic Club differed from the Parisian networks in five important ways. As we have seen, the Central Democratic Club was more proletarian and more closely aligned to the *corporations*. Second, its official membership of 8,699[103] cannot compare with the Parisian clubs' estimated membership of 100,000. Third, because of its working-class membership and small size, it was more practical than Parisian networks. Instead of debating principles like freedom of the press,[104] the Democratic Society had adopted a newspaper, named an executive board (Charavey, president, Benoit, vice-president), and set up clubs in the metropolis and major towns in surrounding cantons.[105] When they had to debate principles, they sent controversial proposals to subcommittees to hammer out compromises. While few affiliates accepted all planks of the platform (for instance, the Equality Club dominated by democratic Fourierists like Marius Chastaing of *La Tribune Lyonnaise* rejected nationalization), it did serve as a point of departure for their discussions.[106] Meanwhile, the clubs kept in touch with their constituency by taking popular stands on current issues like the organization of work and the fortifications.[107]

A fourth difference was in the type of demonstrations. Briefly, Central Club demonstrations were smaller and, after March, more independent and disciplined than Parisian *journées*. Let us contrast the 16 April *journée* in Paris with the three contemporaneous demonstrations in Lyon. When Parisian *corporations* in the Luxemburg Commission decided to bolster Louis Blanc's position in, and perhaps purge, the Provisional Government, they did not consult the clubs until the last moment, then alarmed club leaders with their peremptory tone. For the first time in the revolution, the government deployed the National Guard against the crowd. Barbes and other, mainly bourgeois club leaders joined their units of the militia rather than the crowd. Nevertheless, Parisians blamed the clubs in the hysterical reaction to the *journée*.[108]

In Lyon, the clubs were not drawn into militant actions instigated by others, nor were they severely criticized. On 15 April, the Central Club and affiliated *corporations* voted to protest a list of candidates sent to the army by the Prefectural Committee and on the 17th, they paraded to the Prefecture. The timing, one day after the *journée*, was coincidental, for the Lyonnais clubs simply opposed the moderate republican candidates on the list and the *Censeur* republicans on the Prefectural Committee who had tried to use government "influence." On the 22nd, in a driving rain, they mustered eight to ten thousand people for a march to publicize their candidates. On the 30th, they expressed displeasure with the election returns by assembling in Croux-Rousse and asking National Guards there to boycott à review in the city. The crowd stopped the few Guards who did try to attend the review.[109] None of these demonstrations induced repression or renunciation of the clubs. Neither Arago nor General Neumayer resisted their interference in a militia review, while many praised the clubs for preserving order after the elections because club leaders dissuaded small bands of workers from menacing conservative winners' homes.[110] The final demonstration released frustrations in a more constructive manner. Partly as a consequence, Lyon escaped the violence that followed the elections in two other radical cities, Limoges and Rouen.[111]

The most significant difference between the Central Democratic Club and the Parisian movement, and the main reason for Lyon's tranquillity after the elections, was the Central Club's good showing at the polls. The club, in its single-minded dedication to the campaign, avoided errors that undermined the Parisian and other provincial societies' campaigns. According to Peter Amann, the Parisians made the mistake of not nominating a plausible slate in time to publicize it. To cement their alliance with the *corporations*, they agreed to support twenty workers chosen by the *corporations*, but did not learn the names of these workers until just before election day. Many of these working-class candidates were obscure men, who needed but could not get publicity. Only six of their thirty-four candidates won, four of them as members of the Provisional Government.[112]

Conversely, the Central Democratic Club had an acceptable slate in advance of election eve. As early as 8 March, the Democratic Society started proposing candidates and struck a committee to consider their suitability. The first names proposed included Joseph Benoit, Felix and Louis Blanc, Charavey, Cabet, Dézamy, Greppo, Guillermin, Proudhon, and Raspail. The electoral committee included Grangy and Maurin-Béraud, the neobabouvist who had installed the society in the seminary. When the Central Democratic Club amalgamated with the politicized *corporations*, its effort to keep the selection process in the electoral committee (in line with its policy of sending controversial matters to carefully chosen subcommittees) caused a revolt. The club had to make the committee more broadly representative of the clubs and *corporations*, reduce its own role to providing information about candidates whose names were submitted by the clubs and *corporations*, and let the entire membership vote on the slate.[113] Despite the procedural delays and the laments of Club of Club envoys, the membership voted in a well-rounded slate on 18 April. In addition to the predictable Parisian radicals (Cabet, Proudhon, and Raspail), local communists (Benoit, Blanc, Edant, and Greppo), and a more obscure Reformed Carbonari, Vindry, they chose two democrats with ties to the *corporations* (the typesetters Doutre and Pelletier) and three prominent moderates (Arago, Lortet, and Laforest). Four of the five workers – Benoit, Doutre, Greppo, and Pelletier – were in effect public figures. The typesetter Pelletier had operated a cafe that served as a meeting-place for radicals. The third weaver, Vindry, and the token peasant, Faure, were less familiar to the Lyonnais.[114]

The selection process was not easy. In the enthusiastic response to the first test of manhood suffrage, 215 men offered themselves as possible candidates.[115] Increasing the confusion, virtually every one claimed to be a supporter of manhood suffrage and amelioration of the workers' lot. Many candidates presented their cases to one or more clubs, where, if the sparse records are representative, they were rarely questioned in detail. When they were questioned, it was about their commitment to equality and their solutions to the economic malaise. Presumably the biographical and political information about candidates provided by the electoral committee helped club members distinguish one candidate from another. The reason for the exclusion of conservatives like the marquis de Mortemart, who emphasized "order and respect for family, property, and religion," is obvious. The exclusion of the *Censeur* republicans, despite their stress on educational equality and "association," is equally explicable, given the prerevolutionary rift over the banquet and the recent protest over the list sent to the army. For the most part, the clubs and *corporations* preferred democrats and communists (most of whom called themselves democratic-socialists) who promised a "guaranteed right to work" and "the organization of work" in cooperative work-shops.[116] The inclusion of prominent Parisians may reflect a lack of local bourgeois radicals; it certainly reflected the workers' respect for Cabet and Raspail.[117] The public positions and personal popularity of Arago, Laforest, and Lortet, and a desire to appeal to many different con-stituencies, account for their names on the slate. Moderates and conserva-tives also tried to appeal to a wide variety of voters, for Doutre, Faure, Laforest, and Lortet were on two other lists, while Benoit and Greppo were on one other list.[118]

Although the *Censeur* republicans constituted their own electoral committee, they seemed increasingly ineffectual after they blundered in sending their list to the army.[119] The conservatives were the democratic-socialists' formidable opponents. As elsewhere,[120] Lyonnais notables laid low until mid-March. Archbishop de Bonald had ordered the clergy to obey the republic as early as 27 February, but *Le Courrier de Lyon* had not accepted manhood suffrage until 10 March. Within days, Arago's dissolution of the Jesuit order provoked the legitimist/Catholic party. On the day that the Central Club materialized, the archbishop's circular reminded the clergy of their rights as citizens and urged them to exercise their rights in the interests of the "peace and public order." About the same time, Ledru-Rollin's instructions to the Provisional Government commissioners moved *Le Courrier* and the new conservative republican *Salut Public* to describe the commissioners' extraordinary powers as "dictatorial." Conservatives united after Ledru-Rollin advised commis-sioners to use their office to promote republicans of long standing in the national elections and the Prefectural Committee sent a list of *Censeur* republicans to the army.[121]

By 27 March, Orleanists had organized conservatives into a General Committee of Clubs consisting of delegates from fourteen clubs. In the next three weeks, seventeen more clubs adhered. Some clubs had broken with the "coterie controlling" the Central Democratic Club; the Eighth Battalion and other National Guard clubs had never joined the Central Club. By 1 April, the General Committee and the General Committee of the Rural Cantons had agreed to a common slate. At first the General Committee eliminated *Censeur* republicans and democratic-socialists, but, in an effort to attract proletarian voters, it eventually included Laforest, two other liberals, the radicals Benoit and Doutre (and, of course, two conservatives). The General Committee of the Rural Cantons chose Mortemart, three other local notables, and two liberals to satisfy their more conservative constituency. Under pressure from the urban conservatives, they finally agreed to a token moderate republican.[122]

While the two club movements considered candidates, they waged propaganda campaigns. In addition to the Central Club organ, *Le Tribun du Peuple*, the Equality Club's *Bulletin*, and Chastaing's *Tribune Lyonnaise*, sixteen other democratic-socialist newspapers sprang up during the campaign. These newspapers published club minutes and notes on candidates and editorialized about the need to elect socialist workers. Furthermore, the Central Club reached out to two hostile constituencies, the soldiers and the peasantry. In March, they had assured the soldiers' right to attend clubs; in April, delegates set up clubs in rural communes. Free copies of *Le Tribun du Peuple* and another neobabouvist organ, *La République*, went to soldiers and peasants.[123] But the Central Club could not compete with the large landowners in the General Committee of the Rural Cantons who, like "natural leaders" of the countryside in other departments, ably exploited fears of the *loi agraire* (equal division of property) and anger about the forty-five centimes tax. In the metropolis, the General Committee's *Bulletin* and the established conservative press took a less extreme line.[124]

Voter turnout was high; the two-day vote quiet; the four-day count slow due to unfounded allegations of irregularities.[125] While the metropolis voted solidly for the Central Democratic Club slate, the countryside sustained the General Committee. The initial reports of a democratic-socialist victory, based on the urban returns, were reversed by the late rural returns. In the end, six Central Club candidates and ten General Committee candidates won. Three of the top four vote-getters (Laforest with 126,943, Doutre with 104,841, and Lortet with 83,644) were on all lists. Two other Central Club candidates (Benoit, ninth with 63,981, and

Greppo, last with 45,194) were on one other list. Only Pelletier, second from the bottom with 45,471 votes, represented the Central Club alone. Laforest, Lortet, and Doutre (who had been sent to a silk-weaving commune as an emissary) had some rural support; Benoit, Greppo, and Pelletier won on the strength of the urban vote. Conversely, six candidates won on the strength of the General Committee's endorsement and rural support. Only three of the representatives can be considered moderate republicans; four were democratic-socialists; seven proved to be conservatives.[126]

Politically, the Rhône deputation diverged from the National Assembly as a whole in having a lower proportion of moderate republicans (two versus three-tenths of the entire Assembly) and a higher proportion of democratic-socialists (three versus one-tenth in the overall Assembly). Socially, it had far more workers than any other department; indeed it sent five of the total of twenty-three workers in the Assembly. Unlike all but one other working-class deputy (Perdiguier, the *compagnonnage* reformer), Benoit, Doutre, Greppo, and Pelletier voted consistently with the radical group known as the Mountain. Benoit, Doutre, and Pelletier were also unusually forceful spokesmen for their working-class constituents (and Greppo was active in radical circles behind the scenes).[127] In short, the outstanding feature of the Rhône results was the radical, working-class minority. Benoit summed up and accounted for the anomaly: "But in Lyon the elections had a socialist character which they had nowhere else, not even in Paris. The population voted for ideas which had been upheld by the clubs, newspapers, and speeches, but which were also the result of working conditions."[128] He might have given credit to the band of democrats, socialists, and communists who, like himself, had proselytized for years before the republic.

Explaining the moderate republicans' defeat is more difficult. Clearly, they bungled in sending a list to the army. Republicans on the Prefectural Committee took full responsibility, even counselling the Provisional Government commissioner to deny any knowledge of the list, because they worried that partisans of the old regime would use the opportunity to decry central government interference and revive federalist sentiments. The recent history of Lyon and protests against commissioners in Bordeaux and Besançon suggest that their concern was realistic.[129] For his part, Arago had been unusually reticent about sending "patriots" to the countryside "to form public opinion." When a member of the Central Committee proposed the use of emissaries to educate the peasantry, Arago countered that government-sponsored emissaries might alienate the peasantry (although he did send a few, like Doutre, to silk-weaving towns).[130] Probably his concentration on the metropolis and inaction in the countryside – both stemming from his laudable desire to limit conflict – hurt moderate republicans in the elections.

If Arago's cautious approach to both the radicals of Lyon and the conservatives of the rural cantons did hurt the moderate republicans, it also eased the general acceptance of the new regime in a turbulent and divided department. All Arago's so-called failures – to elect moderates, to restrain spending, and to retrieve the cannon – derived less from his diplomatic conduct in a difficult assignment than from the presence of an assertive club movement, a devastated major industry, and an independent paramilitary unit. Alternatively, his main accomplishment, a peaceful change of regimes, must also be attributed to the proletarian club leaders who steered the populace into practical, peaceful, electoral pursuits. Although this leadership was ideologically radical, they had long ago understood the need to educate and organize the working class for democracy.

CHAPTER FOUR

Reaction, May–July 1848

Arago's replacement, Martin-Bernard, had been commissioner-general of the Rhône and three adjoining departments since mid-March. From 14 April, when Arago asked to be relieved, until his departure after the elections, Martin-Bernard had coadministered the Rhône, so that the new commissioner was not as complete a stranger to the local elite as his predecessor had been. Yet Martin-Bernard was one of the radical republican conspirators defended by Arago in 1839 and, like his predecessor, was willing to propitiate demonstrators. His appointment did not relieve conservatives, especially since it was followed by a resurgence of luddism and Vorace "policing." Because Martin-Bernard had to cope with militant workers in the context of a more confident, coherent conservatism and a deflated, disorganized club movement, he had to dissolve the Voraces and dismiss the Central Committee. However, with the aid of the clubs which were revived for the municipal elections, he was able to preserve the peace though the period of transition which provoked an insurrection in the capital. Despite this amazing accomplishment, he was retired and the clubs suffered reprisals from his successor. The first republican prefect in the Rhône, Ambert, a moderate republican,[1] dismantled two official republican institutions, the National Workshops and the National Guard.

The late revolutionary period saw the pendulum swing toward reaction and repression without violent resistance, but not because the revolutionaries had capitulated. If the extraordinary feature of Martin-Bernard's term of office was the quiescence in June, the remarkable aspect of Ambert's first month in office was the persistence of the clubs. When the National Workshops were modified in June, the clubs which had eschewed demonstrations for two months restrained the workshops. Martin-Bernard also contributed to the peaceful resolution of this menacing situation by making overtures to the crowd until the danger of fighting passed, then deferring to the forces of order. The clubs' sensible assessment of the efficacy of street fighting in a city surrounded by an army and the commissioner's delicate juggling of the crowd and the forces of order explain why the city famous for working-class insurrections avoided class warfare in June 1848. The calm acceptance of the changes in the workshop meant, in turn, a more benign repression and a rapid recovery for the clubs.

THE MAY DAYS

After the elections of April 1848, the Lyonnais developed a new pattern of revolutionary outbursts and counterrevolutionary repression. In May, a new round of luddism and Vorace intervention in police and judicial affairs evoked the first serious conservative counterattack and the first real repression since the containment of the luddites in February. Without an electoral focus, the clubs lost direction, and, without club guidance, the Voraces and Workshops reverted to their earlier, less calculated kind of behaviour. For the first time, outsiders played a significant role in the agitation. The resulting altercations rallied the conservatives into campaigns against the Voraces, the one radical unit of the National Guard, and the Central Committee. Although Martin-Bernard was able to spare the Voraces a bloody battle and almost certain defeat, he had to concede the dissolution of the Voraces and the Central Committee. By their aggressive defence of their comrades in the workshops, the Voraces hastened the dissolution of the revolutionary committee.

Two weeks after Martin-Bernard assumed sole responsibility for the Rhône, another wave of unrest washed over Lyon. On 8 May, the Central Committee responded to local clubs' complaints about the statue of Louis XIV in Bellecour square by ordering it removed. Conservatives, worried that the committee would destroy the symbolic masterpiece, screamed vandalism. Conservatives and radicals congregated in the square and inevitably some came to blows. While Voraces arrested critics of the removal order, the National Guard stood watch over the statue – and the Voraces. Since the factions reflected class divisions and each commanded a paramilitary unit, the dispute could have escalated into a major confrontation. Fortunately, Martin-Bernard imposed a cooling-off period by referring the matter to the central government and placing the statue "under the safeguard of the Lyonnais population." Although groups gathered in the square for days, no significant collision occurred.[2] The statue was ultimately lodged in a museum, as the Central Committee had originally proposed, and replaced by a statue of the "Man of the People." Neither side in the dispute felt completely satisfied.[3] With the opposing sides acting like armies girding for battle, a *casus belli* soon presented itself.

On 14 May, a semirural National Workshop outside Croix-Rousse halted wagons hauling mechanical looms to a factory in a nearby commune and burned the looms. The luddites believed that the owner was breaking a promise made in the early days of the revolution not to reopen the factory. (The owner claimed, not very convincingly, that he only intended to store the looms to save warehouse rent.) The next day police arrested seven of the ringleaders, a move which angered clubs and Voraces in Croix-Rousse, where many of the ringleaders lived.[4] The Democratic Club, now called the Jandard Club, entertained a motion to march on the prison and liberate the accused workers, while another club organized a patrol of the commune to stop any further arrests. Into the breach barged Police Commissioner Galerne and eighteen policemen, only to be surrounded and shot at by one hundred armed Voraces. Galerne and sixteen policemen withdrew to Lyon after the Voraces seized and held two agents captive in the communal jail. About four hundred people gathered and sent delegates to the Prefecture with an offer to exchange the agents for the machine-breakers. When Martin-Bernard refused, the National Workshops built barricades at the two main entrances from Lyon and other strategic spots in Croix-Rousse. News of the first barricades in revolutionary Lyon, conveyed to the commissioner, did not change his mind.[5]

The same day (17 May), a new Provisional Committee of Voraces invited all members and workers' *corporations* "to liberate the Voraces and patriot prisoners" that night.[6] Three hundred men did encircle the prison that night, then asked two *procureurs de la République* to release the prisoners. When both demurred, the Voraces kidnapped the second *procureur*, Tabouret, and took him to their café in Croix-Rousse. In the morning, they let Tabouret go on condition that he would return if the luddites were not freed. When he returned with information that the Appellate Court was reviewing the case, he was permitted to leave. However, he was recaptured as he tried to discourage a crowd which was not under the control of the Provisional Committee from besieging the courthouse. The court's decision to drop charges against the machine-breakers did not sway his captors,[7] because the crowd now wanted twenty-two other workers detained for similar offences liberated. Martin-Bernard had his secretary and a popular wine merchant talk the crowd into freeing Tabouret and the two sequestered policemen.[8] At this conciliatory juncture, a band of Voraces moving toward the Prefecture to pressure Martin-Bernard into releasing the twenty-two workers met a company of the National Guard. After someone discharged a rifle, apparently inadvertently, the Voraces fled in a panic. Rumours about fighting sped through Croix-Rousse; drummers beat the call to arms; a second column descended to Lyon. There they encountered another detachment of Guards and both sides ostentatiously, almost ritualistically, loaded their rifles before the Voraces retreated. Back in Croix-Rousse, barricades rose again, but came down a day later, since the militia did not approach the suburb.[9]

Up to this point, Martin-Bernard had urged the judiciary to review the case leniently and generally had acted as a mediator. Now, he yielded to Acting Attorney-General Loyson, who advocated punitive measures. On 23 May, Martin-Bernard dissolved the Voraces, the Carbonari (who had declined to protect the Prefecture against "the People"), and all irregular corps.[10] Loyson, a conservative republican appointee, initiated judicial proceedings against Tabouret's kidnappers. The victim himself was not vindictive: his deposition noted that the Provisional Committee did not want to hold him the second time and that the demonstrators were "deeply convinced of the justice of their position" – in other words, that the old moral economy prevailed. He further testified that all but one had treated him respectfully and identified only the exception, whom he exonerated for being drunk, and a guard, whom he praised for his "protection." The Appeal Court acquitted the drunk but sentenced the guard to two years in prison.[11]

The May Days coincided with the third revolutionary *journée* in the capital. While Lyonnais tempers flared over the statue, Polish refugees inflamed Parisian clubs over the oppression of their homeland and the clubs persuaded a new Centralizing Committee to pressure the government into supporting the liberation of Poland. The Centralizing Committee, cautious and not fully in charge, struggled in vain to avert an armed march on the Chamber. One day after Lyon's luddite incident, a Parisian crowd invaded the Chamber Hall, dissolved the National Assembly, and proclaimed a radical provisional government. The security forces quickly suppressed the rising and arrested the leaders; the City Council began expelling clubs from public buildings.[12]

Three facts suggest that this *journée* did effect the Lyonnais agitation. Parisian club envoys visited local clubs in the first half of May; someone, presumably an envoy, posted a list of the members of the new provisional government one day after the Parisian rising – and one day before the Lyonnais rising; and most definitively, the Voraces, who had met with Club of Club envoys a month earlier, had "news from the capital" just before they overthrew their old leadership and elected new leaders who precipitated the courthouse incidents.[13] If, however, knowledge of the *journée* revived the Voraces, it did not awaken the lethargic clubs. After initial interest in the arrests, the clubs, which had always opposed luddism and had, since March, avoided other people's demonstrations, stayed out of the fray. The new Vorace leaders were obscure journeymen, not club leaders in another guise. Nor did knowledge of the *journée* change or politicize the issue for the Voraces, who expressed little interest in the Polish cause. The most salient parallel may be the contemporaneous outbursts by National Workshops and Voraces in surrounding communes. Like the Croix-Rousseans, they were motivated by local economic conditions and/or the newly assertive judiciary. At least one workshop copied the Croix-Rousse model of taking a *procureur* prisoner. [14]

Despite the dissolution order, the Voraces did not disband immediately. Few members acted upon the authorities' suggestion that they enlist in the army or militia; some entered clubs or National Workshops, where, according to the police, they fomented trouble. Almost half the Voraces continued to meet, surreptitiously, through the autumn. Attendance fell in the winter, but the forty or fifty who came to the Jandard café faithfully compensated by organizing along the lines of a traditional secret society. Although members would be prosecuted for their part in the insurrection of June 1849, the secretive new society would survive until the end of that year. [15]

The agitation in May finally activated Lyonnais conservatives. Already, the surprisingly favourable election returns had invigorated some to the extent that the local director of an insurance company, Edouard Reveil, and twenty-nine other Lyonnais businessmen had led the opposition to the proposal to nationalize insurance. [16] The local "outrages" fully mobilized legitimists, Orleanists, and conservative republicans, who campaigned on two fronts. After the statue affair, officers in the National Guard attacked the one radical corps in the militia; following the courthouse incidents, the National Guard and the reactionary press turned on Commander Neumayer and the Central Committee.

On 1 April, the Central Committee had ordered the formation of four batteries of artillery to be organized by the commander of the Civil Guard, Felix Blanc. In less than a week, 1,200 men responded to posters soliciting volunteers for this special and usually elite corps. Over 700 volunteers, including 220 former artillery officers, were rejected before the unit elected Felix Blanc lieutenant-colonel. Soon complaints about exclusions and communist control reached the commander of the National Guard. General Neumayer replied that the corps "appeared to be properly organized" and the elections had been conducted according to regulations. He persisted in his efforts to get an artillery instructor, armaments, and a fort for the unit. [17]

Shortly after the army provided armaments and a fort, a dozen artillerymen joined civilians who entered the fort and demanded ammunition. Although the artillerymen desisted when the commander refused, they were wrongly accused of stealing cartridges. The charges encouraged the 220 ex-artillery officers to petition for a reorganization of the corps on the grounds that it was illegal and admitted men who did not meet the physical standards. They publicized the petition and the conservative press took up the issue.[18]

On 18 May, in the course of the courthouse incidents, a lieutenant in the artillery left his post and fraternized with the crowd in Croix-Rousse. His desertion doubled criticism of the corps. Seventy petty officers and artillerymen resigned and asked the central government to reconstitute the unit and eliminate men who did not meet the height standard. The petitioners also wanted the corps confined to city-dwellers – a slap at the more radical and proletarian suburban Guards. Finally, they wanted the lieutenant court-martialled and the men who followed him on the 18th discharged. Neumayer recommended that the central government authorize the corps and replace one-quarter of the men (forty for abandoning their post, eighty-nine for not meeting height requirements). The government had not acted on his recommendations when they dismissed the entire Lyonnais National Guard a month later.[19]

After the 18th, conservatives also censured General Neumayer. Journalists asked pointed questions about the failure to mobilize until the prisoners were released; they chided the two officers who refused requests to protect the courthouse and rescue Tabouret because they had "no orders." Individual Guards were blunter. Neumayer had to issue a bulletin justifying his conduct and denouncing his detractors for undermining discipline. He weathered this storm, and even quashed conservatives' attempts to form another elite corps.

The reactionaries reserved their heaviest fire for the Central Committee, which had intervened on behalf of the prisoners. Right-wing newspapers decried the authorities' "weakness" and blamed the Central Committee for all the disorder since February. They insinuated that the committee had considered proclaiming a provisional government and that members of the Provisions Committee had sold food vouchers. More constructively, they helped officers of the National Guard gather signatures on another petition for municipal elections. The officers sent delegations to Martin-Bernard, who forwarded their request to the central government.[20]

In the interval, many members of the committee submitted their resignations in protest against the slander. Since Martin-Bernard did not accept them, many members simply ceased attending committee meetings.[21] A much depleted and largely radical committee voted to oust the Brothers of the Christian Doctrine from the communal schools. As always, a threat to the church's role in primary education brought a prompt rejoinder from archbishop de Bonald, though now, in deference to the republic, he spoke of defending "democratic principles." His rather restrained circular was complemented by personal vilification in *La Gazette de Lyon* and *L'Union Nationale* (a new conservative Catholic newspaper).[22] Two days later, Martin-Bernard announced municipal elections for 6 June. The reactionaries who had been slow to assert themselves were among the first to force the removal of a revolutionary council. They also pressured the government into calling suburban elections after committees there tried to secularize education and rename streets in honour of revolutionary heroes.[23]

In May 1848, renewed luddism, challenges to the constituted authorities, and a radical gesture by the revolutionary committee hastened the demise of the unofficial paramilitary unit and the semiofficial Central Committee. Disruptive workshops, an assertive popular militia, and intervention in church affairs forged a new conservative coalition, something the conservatives had not been able to accomplish on their own. Aggrieved by the attack on property, the police, the court, and the church's hegemony in education, reactionaries formed a secret society known, according to the police, as the Friends of Order.[24]

REACTION, JUNE 1848

After a turbulent May, Lyon remained tranquil through the transition from the revolutionary to the reactionary phase of the republic. Due to a streamlined, aggressive electoral campaign, the conservatives won the second democratic election. The Central Democratic Club, which resurfaced for the election, suffered, by comparison, from its democratic and decentralized structure. Weak leadership, constant internal negotiations, compromises, and ambivalence about its candidates ensured a hesitant democratic-socialist campaign. Although demoralized by the defeat, the essentially parliamentary character of the movement precluded any irrational, violent response to the provocative changes in the National Workshops. The explicit rejection of street fighting checked other, more excitable groups. Still, such self-control might have been insufficient without Martin-Bernard's concession on changes in the workshops, compensation in new flag commissions, and, after these appeased most workers, intimidation of any possible malcontents by means of a massive armed mobilization. Together, the radicals in the clubs and the radical republican in the Prefecture stemmed the ebb and flow of insurrection and repression.

One day after learning of the Lyonnais election, the conservative General Committee resumed its meetings, suspended since the national elections. Now, committee members represented companies of the National Guard rather than clubs and operated in a more hierarchical and expeditious manner than in April. By 6 June, the committee had compiled a slate of forty-two candidates. Their National Guard list excluded all members of the Central Committee except Laforest, two other liberals, and three conservative republicans. Compared to the liberals, republicans, and democratic-socialists on the General Committee's national slate, the exceptions were token concessions to moderates. Conversely, the list included Edouard Reveil and two dozen other postmonarchical conservative politicians.[25]

While the General Committee considered candidates, their allies took the offensive. The counterrevolutionary press branded the Central Committee a "foyer of communism" and "agent of anarchy." Although reactionaries had precipitated the election before a new electoral law took effect, they objected to using updated voters' lists from the national elections. The National Guard sent representatives to every street to register new voters on the assumption that conservatives had not registered for the previous election. The newspapers complained about the Central Committee supervising the distribution of voters' cards and the polling, then complained about the last-minute postponement of the vote. Disputing Martin-Bernard's explanation that there had been too little advance preparation, they charged that the "revolutionaries" feared the outcome.[26]

The radicals responded to the conservatives' aggressive campaign very defensively. Like its opponent, the Central Democratic Club reassembled for the election campaign. Unlike its opponent, the Central Club was smaller, had less dynamic leaders, and a less efficient process of selecting candidates than in April. Partly as a consequence, they ran a less lively campaign.

Following the national elections, the Central Club disbanded and the number of local clubs dropped drastically. This was hardly surprising, given the club movement's focus on elections (a similar plunge occurred in Paris).[27] Even when the new campaign generated new interest, however, only fifty delegates came to the Central Club meetings. Because the delegates had insisted on frequent changes of executive and because the Executive Commission met frequently, few of the original, committed leaders could or would enter the commission. Early in June, the Central Club had to persuade Vindry, the unsuccessful candidate in the national elections, to accept the presidency.[28] Although the club decided to repudiate lies about the Central Committee by choosing its candidates from the committee, it vetoed the Jandard Club's proposal for a parade to express their appreciation of the committee and publicize their candidates.[29] The hostility toward the committee after the vote against the Christian Brothers' subsidy may account for club members' lukewarm support; the antipathy toward crowds after the courthouse episode explains why they renounced a tactic they had used effectively in the previous election. In general, the low level of enthusiasm in most clubs counselled a quiet campaign.

The Central Democratic Club asked clubs, *corporations*, National Workshops, and neighbourhoods to vote on their proposed candidates in one designated club for each electoral section. This grass roots approach proved to be more cumbersome and less cohesive than the General Committee's delegate vote on candidates. In some bourgeois sections, the Central Club had to open clubs. One such club substituted Laforest and two like-minded bourgeois for three working-class radicals. The Central Club accepted these substitutions. When another club replaced all the proposed candidates, in one case with a worker suspected of being a police informant in the 1844 crackdown on communists, the club rejected the replacements, occasioning a secession. But the club often compromised, for the final slate included only twenty-three incumbents (many dispirited members of the Central Committee refused to run) and twenty democratic-socialists.[30]

The democratic-socialists did try to rally their supporters by alerting them to the consequences of a conservative victory. Their one remaining newspaper, *Le Peuple Souverain*, appealed to readers to preserve the republic: "The Revolution is in power ... the reaction raises its head ... it is up to the revolutionaries ... to consolidate their work." The editors warned that a victory for the "privileged" would mean lower wages, therefore strikes, "brutal suppression," disarming of the populace, closing of clubs, and "the end of liberty." As things transpired, their prediction was accurate.

The Committee of the Quai de Retz and *Le Censeur* compiled their own lists, dominated, respectively, by liberals and *républicains d'hier*. Only nine workers appeared on the combined slates. This time, the prominent democratic club known as the Equality Club broke with athe Central Club because it would not merge its list with *Le Censeur*'s. Acutely aware that republicans had to present a united front against the unified reaction, the Equality Club culled names from all slates and publicized their eclectic list in Chastaing's *Tribune Lyonnaise*.[32] The right-wing press ignored the moderates, save for sniping about the republicans' inability to govern, and aimed their barbs at the "smocks" (a reference to workers' shirts) and "communists" in the Central Democratic Club.[33]

Despite efforts to combat apathy, turnout was low, which helped the National Guard list triumph.[34] Over three-quarters of its candidates won, two-thirds of them (twenty-three) with the General Committee's endorsement alone. Although eight Central Club candidates were elected, five of them were also on another slate. No liberal or republican was returned on the strength of Committee of the Quai de Retz or *Censeur* support. The moderates consoled themselves with the fact that a majority of the new council were republicans, albeit conservative republicans.[35]

Compared to the Lyonnais clubs' relative success in the national elections or to the Parisian clubs' "modest success" in the June by-elections for the National Assembly, the results were disappointing.[36] The difference was due to more complex voting procedures, the reactionaries' streamlined organization and hard-hitting campaign, and the radicals' disorganized, lifeless campaign. Forced to defend an unpopular administration, the clubs could not summon the enthusiasm needed to counter the Central Committee's bad image. The Central Committees' reputation for arbitrary measures, culminating in the sudden suspension of subsidies to religious schools, had been cultivated by selective reporting in the conservative press; it also contributed to the conservative victory.

Although it was public knowledge that the forthcoming law on municipal elections would necessitate another election,[37] the new City Council and Mayor Reveil did not hesitate to act on their mandates. Their agenda consisted of returning to the formal procedures of the monarchy, restoring the city to solvency, and reviving commerce – an amalgam of the conservative and moderate republican programs.[38] Fiscally, they focused on reclaiming 787,000 francs "advanced" to the central government for the National Workshops, plus 696,987 francs spent on food relief. They contended that the city should be reimbursed because the Provisional Government had proclaimed the organization of work, and therefore was financially responsible for the workshops and relief, because relief went to the unemployed who could not be accommodated in the Workshops. Everyone but Edant, one of a handful of holdovers from the Central Committee, welcomed the cost-saving change from daily to piece-work pay in the public works program. The council's response to the destitution attendant on the shutdown of the public works was the old standby, a public subscription.[39]

Concern about financing relief was not solely ideological. In Croix-Rousse and Guillotière, where the elections had been delayed until the new electoral law came into effect, the revolutionary committees also worried about mounting debts. However, the committees confined themselves to asking the national government for more funds to distribute food. Since they did not contribute to the National Workshops, though their working-class communities benefited from them, they protested cutbacks in the workshops.[40]

Aversion to the National Workshops had spread among the bourgeoisie; even *Le Censeur* joined the critics. Under Martin-Bernard, the problem of improvised projects and unsupervised personnel continued to plague the program. At the beginning of May, he had promised a restive crowd of 3,000 workers enrolled but not employed in the workshops that he would find them work. He then prodded engineers into building a rail line to Geneva, a worthy project, but, because of the urgency, begun before adequate surveys or expropriation procedures had been completed. In a matter of days, hundreds of workers were knocking down walls and moving though fields on farmland worth six to seven thousand francs a hectare. Five hundred silk and construction workers strung out for miles could not be properly supervised, with the predictable result that some workgangs destroyed valuable crops and woodlands. As details of the senseless destruction became known, an outcry arose.[41]

The clamour had not died down when the semirural workshop burned the mechanical looms and sparked the May Days. This time the Voraces and Central Committee bore the consequences; the next time workshop employees felt the full weight of repression. On 31 May, the underemployed Perrache workshop seized 475 rifles destined for the Army of the Alps, whereupon soldiers from the nearby barracks surrounded and searched the area, recovering 300 rifles and arresting eighty suspects. A month later, thirty-six men were tried.[42] Even *Le Peuple Souverain* deplored this "pillage," though the editors attributed it to *agents-provocateurs* because of the troops' prompt arrival.[43]

In the last half of May, National Workshops all over France caused disturbances and, partly in response, the central government decreed a change from daily to piece-work pay. News of the decree, coming on the heels of the Perrache episode, pleased reactionaries and republicans alike.[44] Instead of imposing the change immediately, Martin-Bernard commissioned a report on its impact and implementation. By 20 June, the director of the National Workshops reported that piece-work would eliminate over a third of the employees and recommended reorganizing the remaining men into squads of twenty to be paid by the square metre. Martin-Bernard (and the City Council) ordered him to institute the new system on the 22nd.[45] Martin-Bernard probably temporized because the situation remained tense. In the first week of June, soldiers were subject to reprisals for their role in the Perrache affair. The following week, men enrolled in the workshops demonstrated for an increase in their food allowance and men employed in the workshops petitioned for a holiday with pay. Their attitude did not presage passive acceptance of the new system.[46]

When the new regulations were announced on 20 June, many workshops did stop work and send delegates to the government commissioner. Martin-Bernard pacified them by postponing the new regulations for a few more days.[47] Here matters stood when rumours of the insurrections in Paris and Marseilles began circulating. While workers in private as well as public workshops left their jobs, most of them merely stood talking in "calm," "serious" groups in the streets. In Croix-Rousse, a poster invited the National Workshops to gather in the Grand Square, where speakers were exhorting the crowd to fight, but no one heeded this advice. By 27 June, the metropolis was tranquil.[48]

Contemporaries and historians have asked why the workers who revolted twice in the 1830s did not revolt in June 1848? Attorney-General Loyson answered by pointing to his call-up of all the regiments of the Third Division of the Army of the Alps. The foremost historian of the Lyonnais revolution, François Dutacq, gave greater weight to Martin-Bernard's action in appeasing the crowd until he could announce the Parisian insurgents' defeat. Only then did he allow Loyson to summon the troops and only then did the resort to force have a deterrent effect.[49] A brief survey of insurgents' response to force confirms Dutacq's argument that Martin-Bernard's restraint was the more decisive factor. Troops and National Guards converging on the capital did not deter insurgents there.[50] Nor had a considerable military presence stopped the Voraces in February. Given the National Workshops' hostility toward the army after the Perrache affair, an influx of soldiers before the Lyonnais learned of the bloody suppression of the Paris rising might well have incited violence.

There are good reasons, however, for considering another agent of peace. Lyonnais reactionaries argued that 30,000 soldiers prevented an uprising because they, and other reactionaries, believed in a conspiracy by clubs in the capital. They based their conspiracy theory on the fact that word of the Parisian insurrection spread prior to the official news release and on the allegation that Parisian club members were agitating in Lyon.[51] But Peter Amann has proved that Parisian clubs neither planned nor precipitated the June Days; instead clubs were drawn into the fray by the National Workshops after the government's policy on the workshops triggered the battle. In the weeks preceding the rebellion, the clubs had exercised a moderating influence, although the closure of clubs made them more sympathetic to the insurgents.[52] In Lyon, by contrast, the authorities had not closed clubs (though many clubs set up for the civic election shut down voluntarily after the polling). Furthermore, although suburban clubs held emergency sessions during the June Days and a few entertained motions to turn to the streets, every one of these clubs decisively rejected any notion of fighting.[53] The clubs not only diverted "firebrands" into parliamentary debates, they convinced them of the futility of street fighting against a much larger and better-equipped army or at least used peer pressure to stop them from taking up arms. They likely used their long-standing links with the workshops to calm angry workshop employees.

The contrast to Marseilles is also instructive. Fear that the ten-hours decree would be retracted and anger over the commissioners' treatment of Parisian refugees kindled the revolt in Marseilles before the populace knew of the simultaneous insurrection in the capital.[54] No local issue ignited the usually volatile Lyonnais populace. With the exception of construction workers,[55] Lyonnais workers had shown little interest in the ten-hours day because it held little attraction for family workshops and could not be enforced in thousands of silk workshops. Martin-Bernard had smoothed the friction over piece-work by postponing its introduction. More significantly, he realized that the silk workers who filled the workshops were less committed to unproductive work in National Workshops than to meaningful work in the *fabrique* Accordingly, he pressed the government to follow up its flag order with a five million francs payment. He did not release dispatches about the Parisian insurrection until he could also inform the public of the five million francs.[56]

Since April, the *fabrique* had experienced a modest recovery due to the stimulus from the flag order. By the end of May, some silk weavers were leaving the National Workshops to return to their *ateliers*.[57] However, the Provisional Government had appropriated only enough money for advances to *chefs d'atelier* for two months and by 24 June, the money was running out. Thus the decree of 24 June 1848, raising the original credit to five million francs, meant that *chefs* who had completed their orders would be paid in full, while other masters could mount their looms for two months' work.[58] Employing nearly half of the master weavers, the group which had fomented and led previous rebellions, clearly reduced the likelihood of rebellion.

In short, Lyonnais workers' refusal to engage in battle did not reflect either a weak radical impulse or lack of interest in the organization of work. On the contrary, the Lyonnais workers did not combat changes in the public works program because their clubs were strong and highly disciplined and local workers had a very different conception of the organization of work. From their insurrectionary heritage (see table 6), Lyonnais radicals and workers knew the price of armed resistance against artillery. Their previous electoral success pointed to another route to attain their goals. Certainly, their radical reputation ensured the appointment of a radical republican commissioner who eased the transition from revolution to reaction and therefore encouraged the workers' passive acceptance of the transition.

REPRESSION, JULY 1848

With the Cavaignac "dictatorship" and the installation of a moderate republican prefect, the country and the department of the Rhône tilted from revolutionary to repressive policies. Because the city of Lyon had not put up a futile resistance, the immediate repression was not as devastating for the remaining popular revolutionary institutions as, for instance, in Paris. Although the new prefect disestablished the two official revolutionary institutions (the National Guard and the National Workshops) to the applause of the exultant conservatives and the symbolic protests of the democratic-socialists, efforts to eliminate unofficial radical organizations failed. In fact, while the complacent conservatives let their electoral machine deteriorate, the chastened clubs applied the lessons of the disastrous municipal campaign and won in the suburban elections.

For a few days, Martin-Bernard tried to moderate the repression. On 24 June, he and General Gemeau received orders from their respective ministries to recover the fortifications and artillery in Croix-Rousse and the rifles taken from army arsenals. Judging the moment inopportune, Martin-Bernard did not inform Attorney-General Loyson until the 26th. When Loyson prompted him to act, Martin-Bernard refused to authorize a search and seizure operation. The resourceful Loyson took a letter from the new adjoint mayor of Lyon warning of a "bloody collision" to General Gemeau and forced his hand. Loyson, who had already written the minister of justice that he would have to disarm Croix-Rousse without the help of (en dehors de) Martin-Bernard, recovered the forts and cannon without the commissioner's approval. Martin-Bernard did manage to delay the search for small arms.[59]

By July, the familiar fears about the approach of Parisian insurgents, exaggerated by fantastic rumours about plots to blow up the gasworks, had spread panic. Conservative newspapers criticized Martin-Bernard for his "intimacy with socialists in the Parisian clubs" and "excessive indulgence to the agents of disorder." Aware that the commissioner was being retired, Loyson, in his report to the minister of justice, accused Martin-Bernard of being "a demagogue" who had encouraged the clubs to incite the National Workshops.[60] Weeks after commissioners in less troubled departments, Martin-Bernard was replaced by the first republican prefect of the Rhône. Like half the new prefects, Ambert was a moderate republican associated with Le National.[61] He initiated a systematic repression of revolutionary institutions.

Until Ambert arrived on 8 July, Loyson and General Gemeau continued their erratic and heavy-handed sanctions. Loyson had squadron leaders in the National Workshops arrested for yelling "*Vive la République!*" and attempted to close workshops alleged to be "in full revolt" because they met to discuss piece-work. On the 3rd, 500 soldiers and 500 National Guards repossessed the fourteen cannon loaned to the controversial artillery unit of the National Guard. (Their former protector, General Neumayer, had been transferred to Paris at the end of June.) Two nights later, so many regiments of infantry, cavalry, and artillery were bivouacked in major squares that "the city resembled an army camp." Absurd predictions that 1,500 Parisian insurgents would enter the city occasioned the military occupation. When no one came, police took advantage of the propitious circumstances to arrest "known socialists" addressing a crowd.[62]

If these measures hardly approximated the disbanding of National Workshops and thousands of arrests in Paris,[63] the new prefect's first moves were more commensurate. Acting on instructions from the minister of the interior, Ambert dissolved the National Guard in Lyon and the suburbs and ordered all arms returned. A poster released the same day (13 July) justified dissolution and disarmament as preludes to reorganization. Two days later, he dismantled the National Workshops and directed the destitute to apply to the city for relief.[64]

Disarmament proceeded rapidly: the Guards returned over 33,000 of the 37,000 rifles and muskets within a week. Some of these arms went to militias recently formed in rural communes to stop "armed bands of workers ravaging the harvest." Afraid that radicals would retreat to the countryside, the authorities saw the rural militias as a means to contain "the revolution."[65] For the most part, disarmament was accomplished peacefully. After the announcement about the National Workshops, however, troops occupied Croix-Rousse so that police could search for arms.[66]

How did the Lyonnais respond to the legal repression? Reactionaries welcomed Cavaignac's assumption of power and Ambert's appointment, which they construed as the end of "the exceptional and revolutionary regime." Despite their association with the National Guard, they disliked its democratic constitution and therefore liked its "regularization" and disarmament. They were, of course, pleased by the cancellation of the public works program. The conservative press followed the nation-wide tendency to blame socialists and communists for the class warfare in the capital. A new popular organ, *La Verité*, lashed out at "utopians" who "broke the links of the social chain"[67] – a line of attack the Right would perfect in the months to come.

Republicans, democrats, and democratic-socialists were less unanimous, an ominous portent. A subdued *Censeur* rallied to Cavaignac and

Ambert and defended the disestablishment of revolutionary institutions. *La Tribune Lyonnaise* showed its democratic as opposed to socialist colours by congratulating Cavaignac for preserving the social fabric and approving Ambert's "corrective" ordinances. A very alienated Chastaing reacted to the June Days by breaking with his former allies to the left. Not until the end of July did he express reservations about Cavaignac's dictatorial powers or the indefinite "reorganization" of the militia. *Le Peuple Souverain*, like other left-leaning newspapers, warned that the dictatorship would be a transitional stage on the way to monarchy or, more presciently, to another Napoleonic Empire.[68]

The city councils acquiesced in the changes. Predictably, the Lyonnais council thanked Cavaignac for saving France from the "abyss" – defined as the destruction of property and family. They raised no objections to the abolition of the militia created by their detested predecessor. In Guillotière, the revolutionary committee debated as usual, save for an outburst by a neobabouvist, Perret, over the National Guard's loss of artillery. In Croix-Rousse, the committee did convoke National Guards, Voraces, and clubs to discuss whether to cede the cannon entrusted to them since March. After a lively discussion, the committee and militia voted to release them. Voraces and clubs, meeting separately, agreed. Nonetheless, Generals Gemeau and Neumayer led five units of light infantry, twenty squadrons of cavalry, four batteries of artillery, and one and a half battalions of the National Guard up to Croix-Rousse for the recovery. Only scattered shouts of "*Vive la République!*" and nine arrests for "exciting hatred" disturbed the operation.[69]

During the disarming, there were only isolated, symbolic protests such as handing in rifles festooned with black and tricolour ribbons. Others withheld their rifles, which resulted in widespread house searches in the suburbs. The searches provoked Croix-Rousseans, who hurled rocks at police until the police refused to come to this "foyer of revolution." Even searches by soldiers failed to unearth many arms in the suburbs. With suburbanites clearly hiding arms in the countryside, the prefect suppressed the new militias in the communes near the metropolis.[70] Radical officers in the Guard, moderate republicans, and club leaders petitioned for a "democratic reorganization" of the Guard until February 1849, when the minister of the interior, Faucher, responding to a question by Representative Pelletier, stated that it would be "imprudent" to distribute arms to a "revolutionary population."[71]

Closing the National Workshops threw over 17,000 people out of work and deprived 12,000 enrolled but not yet employed of food vouchers. Not surprisingly, a sizeable crowd assembled outside the Prefecture and complained noisily. The infantry dispersed the crowd after arresting a few of its more obstreperous members. Although people talked of another demonstration and a more meaningful organization of work, most discharged workers simply went on relief without further ado. The public works program, always an ill-conceived compromise, had few supporters due to its wastefulness – one conservative critic estimated it did work worth 50,000 francs at a cost of over one and a half million francs.[72] Silk workers, who filled the workshops, gradually found "real work" as the *fabrique* picked up orders.[73] Even they showed little interest in reopening the workshops, as opposed to more rational ways of organizing work.

According to François Dutacq, the decree abolishing the National Workshops marked "the end of the revolutionary era in Lyon." In so far as he, like many early historians of 1848, focused on official bodies such as the Central Committee, National Guard, and National Workshops, he was correct. His final assessment of the Lyonnais revolution as uniquely radical yet strangely nonviolent still stands after many regional studies have added to our knowledge of 1848.[74] However, subsequent histories of other cities suggest that Dutacq paid too little attention to the unofficial voluntary associations spawned by the revolution. Although cooperatives remained in the planning stage, they would flourish in the reactionary phase of the Second Republic. More important, the Central Democratic Club, that forerunner of modern mass political organization, would operate for another year.

To be sure, the Central Democratic Club was no longer the agent of mass demonstrations. At two critical junctures during the crisis of late June, the Central Club intervened to preserve peace. On the 26th, its former (and better-known) executive commission calmed an angry crowd in Croix-Rousse. Two days later, the club ratified the decision to give up the controversial cannon and thereby repudiated any resistance to the unpopular move. Nevertheless, Loyson issued warrants for the current leaders' arrest and locked a public building where many neighbourhood clubs met. He later explained that the moves were preventive, since clubs "could influence" workers. The Central Club and a few affiliates continued to meet and voice opposition to disarmament. These "incendiary" sentiments, combined with rumours about a demonstration over the workshops, resulted in an official closure on 18 July.[75]

The Central Club, which had already opened its meetings to the public in anticipation of the club law (see chapter 5), took advantage of another loophole in that measure to reopen for the municipal elections at the end of July. Learning from its mistakes in the previous election, the Central Club first prepared a slate and *then* sent it to the neighbourhood clubs for ratification. Although they still chose up to half of their candidates from the revolutionary committees, this was a wise decision in the suburbs, where committees had not alienated their constituencies. To unite the Left against the unified Right, they tried to enlist the support of liberals and moderate republicans. However, the Committee of the Quai de Retz and *Le Censeur* found their democratic-socialist slate unacceptable and mounted their own slates.[76]

The returns showed that the Central Democratic Club had regained its clout. In Croix-Rousse, eleven members of the revolutionary committee were "reelected" to the twenty-eight member council. Four new councillors had been active in the Central Club and three others were "fellow-travellers." *Le Peuple Souverain* proclaimed a victory. In Guillotière, eleven incumbents were "reelected" and twenty-one other club candidates won seats. The four opposition candidates were returned by the two bourgeois electoral districts. In Lyon, a more complex pattern can be discerned: three workers' districts chose ten of their eleven councillors from the club list; three socially mixed districts elected seven club candidates, and three bourgeois districts shunned their candidates. Seventeen of the councillors had been endorsed by the club, eight by *Le Censeur*, and seventeen by the conservatives. *Le Peuple Souverain*, drawing solace from the twenty-five republican councillors, pronounced the results "generally satisfactory."[77]

Conservatives, who had run the same slate as in June, consoled themselves with the observation that a slight majority of the Lyonnais councillors had sat on the preceding, conservative council. But their newspapers recognized their defeat in the suburbs and blamed the apathy of bourgeois voters.[78] They overlooked the small number of bourgeois voters in the suburbs and the conservatives' complacent, elitist campaign. Far from discouraging the radicals, the repression had lulled the reactionaries. However, the returns alerted the Right to concentrate on the city and, in national elections, on the countryside.

To the extent that the revolution of 1848 is seen as the first test of manhood suffrage and early socialist programs, with its central innovations being a precocious form of mass political mobilization and an early element of the welfare state, the Lyonnais revolution may be said to have expired with the closure of the Central Democratic Club and the National Workshops. By the same token, the resurrection of the club network after the introduction of the restrictive club law proves that the revolutionary era left a legacy of popular political consciousness and organization. Similarly, the survival of an admittedly attenuated Committee to Organize Work permitted further experimentation with another popular voluntary association, producers' cooperatives. If the first blast of the reaction crippled the most distinctive popular association of the revolution, the Voraces did recuperate as a secret society. They and club leaders would use the old devices of cover organizations, in particular consumer cooperatives, and secret society networks to maintain the personal contacts and organizational web developed before and during the revolution. Some members of these consumer cooperatives and societies would resist the gathering repression to the point, one year later, of insurrection.

CHAPTER FIVE

Resistance,
August 1848–May 1849

While the authoritarian Cavaignac administration limited the recently acquired rights of association and freedom of speech, the president's moderate republican colleagues in the National Assembly tried to direct the popular penchant for voluntary association into carefully charted channels. Accordingly, the National Assembly passed laws regulating the clubs and political press and subsidizing narrowly defined producers' cooperatives. This two-pronged policy of managing voluntary associations, which would be perfected under the liberal empire, was first implemented in Lyon by a moderate republican prefect. After the presidential election in December 1848, the new conservative prefect was seconded by a brutal and reactionary general, whose arrival signalled a shift from legal regulation to open confrontation with democratic-socialist clubs and newspapers.

The radicals resisted both regularization and confrontation until June 1849. Although having themselves developed cooperative theory and practice in the 1830s, workers in metropolitan Lyon submitted fewer requests for government loans than other urban, industrial workers[1] because they objected to the government's preference for producers' associations of workers *and* capitalists. They did found twenty independent producers' cooperatives without government funding or private investment capital. These enterprises reflected local cooperative, corporative, and mutualist traditions.

Meanwhile, the Central Democratic Club and its important affiliates survived and flourished by exploiting exemptions in the club laws. After floundering in their fall and winter campaigns, the democratic-socialists regrouped under the impulsion of the New Mountain, a democratic-socialist campaign network, and ran a completely successful campaign in the spring 1849 elections. In Lyon as in most of southeastern France, the "drift to the right"[2] culminated in large majorities for Louis Napoleon in

December 1848. His victory, followed by the appearance of General Bugeaud, relaxed the Right but reinvigorated the Left. In the Legislative Assembly elections, radical candidates won all the seats in the Rhône and, of greater import, took most of the seats in neighbouring departments to the southeast.

PRODUCERS' COOPERATIVES

The National Assembly's subsidy to appropriately capitalistic producers' cooperatives, at best a token gesture, had very little effect on Lyon. Most workers were indifferent because they preferred the more egalitarian (conservatives would say communist) version of producers' cooperatives elaborated by the workers' press of the monarchy. In particular, they disliked the Assembly's guidelines about private financing and dividends for investors. Five of the seven Lyonnais applications for loans were rejected, largely because they did not have any private financing and did not provide for dividends. Although the two successful applications included investors, and one had fairly prosperous worker-shareholders, both enterprises succumbed to the maladies common to government-funded cooperatives, to wit, poor investment policy and rapid repayment schedules, as well as the poor credit ratings, inexperienced administrations, and disputes between directors and shareholders that debilitated all producers' cooperatives. More workers, notably those organized before the revolution, realized that the Committee to Organize Work could no longer arbitrate strikes and returned to the successful strike tactics of the monarchy. Many brought their own cooperative schemes to the Committee to Organize Work, which helped them establish twenty independent producers' cooperatives. These cooperatives better represented the workers' desires for *corporative* and mutualist elements.

On 3 July, the National Assembly voted a credit of 3 million francs for industrial "associations." Instructions accompanying the act specified that workers should purchase the means of production "above all, by their own efforts." Accordingly the state offered loans, not grants, to cooperatives with "serious guarantees of success." An Encouragement Council would decide which associations qualified, prescribe a repayment schedule, and dispense the monies. The former director of *L'Atelier*, the Christian Socialist organ, reassured the Assembly that the decree would only create "islands of collective property" in a sea of capitalist enterprise; it would not restructure the economy.[3] The allocation reflected the "moderate interventionist" views of many republicans, notably the Christian Socialists. Lyon's moderate republicans approved because they considered the allocation an acceptable way of providing incentives and employment for workers. Local conservatives, even the laissez-faire Orleanists who deplored "general association" as "mitigated communism," tolerated small-scale, single-industry cooperatives.[4] Radical workers, who had never shown much interest in Christian Socialism, expressed less enthusiasm than their peers in Paris. The radicalized workers disliked the government's insistence on including private investors. One asked: "Why do ten thousand workers not offer the government as many guarantees, through retainers on their wages, as one applicant who does not work?"[5]

Both Lyonnais associations awarded government loans included investors. A silk broker, Felix Martin, had conceived of a cooperative before the revolution and applied for half a million francs before the law came into effect. By September 1848, he was advertising for simple silk weavers to buy shares on the assumption that he would get the money. Five months later, the Encouragement Council accorded him a loan of 200,000 francs when 300 shares had been sold and half of each 100-franc share had been paid. In May 1849, ninety-two shareholders incorporated as the Simple Silk Fabrique and two months later the council deposited 100,000 francs in the Fabrique's account.[6]

Like many cooperatives,[7] the Fabrique was soon embroiled in disputes about management and the distribution of work. Within six months, half the shareholders petitioned the prefect to remove the director, Martin, because they considered him "authoritarian" and "arbitrary." In his defence, Martin revealed that shareholders had paid only 750 francs – three friends had loaned him the rest of the 15,000 francs required by the council – so he had refused work to shareholders until they paid for their shares. Gauthier, a habitué of the radical clubs and former member of the revolutionary municipal committee in Guillotière, organized forty impoverished members living in that suburb to take over the Adminstration Council. When a general meeting sustained Martin, the dissidents withdrew but the company had to buy their shares in the middle of the slow season. To hold the remaining members, Martin had to pay the high piece-rates set by the Administrative Council and employ forty-eight looms when he had only enough orders to occupy thirty looms. Concerned about inadequate financing and mismanagement, the Supervisory Committee of three merchants advised revoking the loan. Early in 1850, Martin had to liquidate company assets and begin reimbursing shareholders. Creditors eventually took him to Commercial Court, which ordered him to pay the government 38,251 francs and other creditors 3,783 francs.[8]

A velours merchant, Covillard, originally proposed the Velours Weavers' Union to the Lyonnais Committee to Organize Work. When the committee rejected his proposal on July 2nd, 1848, Covillard, Ennemond Brosse, another velours merchant, and a bookkeeper on the committee, plus six velours masters not on the committee, revised the plan to present to the national government. None of the founders had been prominent in radical circles before or during the revolution. Their statutes called for a limited liability corporation of 2,000 shareholders. Masters would contribute their looms and 500 francs a loom, payable in instalments, in return for piece-rates and dividends. Thirty per cent of net profits would go into a pension fund, benefits for sick members, widows, and orphans, and a "solidarity bank" to help other trades plagued by unemployment.[9] The master weavers' mutualist backgrounds explain the protective and provident provisions.

The chairman of the Committee to Organize Work, the acting mayor of Lyon, and the workers representing the Rhône in the National Assembly supported Covillard's request for a 500,000 francs loan. Early in 1849 the Encouragement Council accepted a modified version of the statutes and authorized a 200,000 francs loan on conditions similar to the Fabrique's. In the spring, 284 shareholders incorporated as Brosse and Company and in the summer, the company received half the loan.[10] The Velours Weavers' Union was a better risk than the Simple Silk Fabrique in so far as it had more substantial shares and more "dependable" shareholders.[11] Although the union overspent in its first five months, the Encouragement Council bailed it out by releasing shareholders' payments and the second instalment of the loan. One half of the shareholders (those who obtained work from the union) made their second payment on schedule and forty-nine shareholders lent the company 9,183 francs. In 1850, the company earned nearly 266,000 francs, realizing a net profit of 20,464 francs, and paid the 6,864 francs interest on its loan.[12]

Unfortunately, velours went out of fashion the following year, when the company was to begin repaying the principal. The company had to ask for a two-year, and subsequently a third year, delay in the repayment schedule. By 1854, it owed 25,500 francs toward the principal, plus 9,400 francs interest, and it fell further behind on the annual payments toward the principal. In 1856, the Supervisory Committee reported a deficit of 9,403 francs due to the incompetence of the company's agent in the capital but did not recommend "rigorous action" because Brosse assumed the directorship after the deficit was discovered. However, suspicious shareholders forced an audit which revealed that the company had lost 216,430 francs since 1852, including 131,138 francs in payments on shares. The previous director had drawn on the capital budget to meet operating expenses and converted the resulting "profits" into dividends. Bankruptcy proceedings dragged on for eleven years.[13]

The failure of both cooperatives financed by the government does not imply that Lyonnais cooperators were especially inept. Only five of the twenty-six provincial cooperatives and nine of the thirty Parisian cooperatives funded by the government survived to 1856, suggesting that the law or the way it was implemented can be faulted. Since the law set relatively high interest rates and the Encouragement Council insisted on rapid repayment, heavy burdens were imposed on struggling new enterprises. Moreover, the Assembly's preference for associations of workers and capitalists assured conflicts of interest. Trouble also arose because the council often invested in declining industries, like velours. These problems, more than inexperienced managers, undermined many cooperatives "encouraged" by the government.[14]

The five Lyonnais projects denied government assistance ranged from a grandiose Workers' Union, which was to build sections of the Paris-Marseilles railway lines, to a tiny Fraternal Association of Silk Printers. The Ministry of Public Works sidetracked the union, perhaps because the ambitious organizers claimed to represent 6,000 workers and wanted to provide health care, among other benefits! The council rejected the silk printers and another silk project because "there are enough cooperative experiments" in the *fabrique*. They turned down a construction workers' cooperative for tending "toward corporativism and against free contracts." However, they only rebuffed one association on grounds of "insufficient guarantees for success." No doubt the council was influenced by all five associations' failure to provide for private financing or dividends.[15]

Lyonnais interested in cooperatives also approached the Committee to Organize Work. In the summer and autumn of 1848, the committee intervened in only one strike and then its conciliation board could not get the support from the Prefecture needed to gain concessions from the master dyers. The dyers' workers, who had won some of their demands three years earlier, had to return to work on the masters' terms.[16] Like workers in other textile towns,[17] workers in Lyon held job actions through the autumn of 1848. No less than eight trades walked out to impose settlements signed in the spring on recalcitrant employers. After staying out four months, painters, tanners, curriers, and stone masons drifted back to the blacklisted shops and accepted less favourable contracts. The police only arrested the leaders of the simple silk weavers' strike against merchants paying below the revolutionary *tarif*, for this action jeopardized the *fabrique* just as the silk market began to recover. The arrests, and the difficulty of maintaining a blacklist when weavers were desperate for work, destroyed the strike. Learning from the débâcle, the velours weavers' circle reverted to the tactics of 1844: they postponed a strike vote until February, when spring buyers arrived and velours weavers were in demand. Then they had only to threaten to get the revolutionary rates restored.[18]

Instead of settling strikes or organizing public works, the Committee to Organize Work, like the Luxemburg Commission,[19] now debated Proudhonian and Fourierist schemes. First, it endorsed a scheme combining Proudhonian credit ideas with Fourierist cooperative concepts. An industrialist, J.F. Coignet, advocated "communal agencies" to be capitalized by central government bonds and local mortgages. The agencies would convert these securities into negotiable bills to loan to producers, who would consign their products to a communal warehouse which would sell the merchandise. To get government backing, Chairman Morellet, Coignet, and a third member of the committee spent fruitless weeks in the capital. Generally, the committee favoured cooperatives along Fourierist lines, save for the insistence on government supervision. Next, it adopted another Coignet proposal for associations of everyone in an industry, with profits to be divided between workers and capitalists "according to the importance of their shares in the association." The state would determine the precise division of profits and guarantee wages "sufficient to afford a comfortable existence."[20]

At the committee's invitation, forty-three workers' *corporations* sent delegates to its meetings. Although most delegates only brought grievances they wanted the committee to rectify, a few like the shoemakers' delegate, Camus, came regularly to urge workers' cooperatives. When the committee recommended Coignet's plan, Camus denounced it for the usual reason: it gave the profits to the capitalist. When delegates submitted the plan to their *corporations*, most of them rejected it because of the division of profits between workers and capitalists. By this time, more delegates were attending committee meetings than were appointed members. In this period, especially when Morellet and Coignet were absent, the committee approved most of the projects submitted to it by *corporations*. None of the projects made provision for investment capital or dividends.[21]

Clearly, the twenty independent producers' cooperatives in Lyon shared the aversion to investment capital evinced by their counterparts in the capital. They also had the corporative and mutualist bias of producers' cooperatives all over France.[22] All but two of these cooperatives were unique in their *corporation* and most were in trades like construction or clothing, which had been organized under the monarchy. Workers in twelve of these trades had struck during or after the revolution; the stone masons had founded their cooperative as part of a strike settlement. Perhaps because of their previous success in unionizing and striking, workers in Lyon did not use cooperatives as resistance societies, as, for instance, workers in Lille did.[23] However, their cooperatives did have typically syndicalist features. All five extant constitutions mention pension plans plus accident, sickness, and death benefits. Three include unemployment insurance, while the other two had funds for schooling children.[24] In addition to their syndicalist/mutualist tenor, they incorporated some Fourierist features. Passages in the constitutions decrying competition and lauding union might have been lifted from the Fourierist propaganda circulating in prerevolutionary Lyon. More substantively, the constitutions set minimum wages but allowed pay differentiation according to skill. (The joiners, who prescribed equal wages, nevertheless had a fund to encourage "the talented.")[25]

The construction cooperatives had eventful histories. In September 1848, the joiners' association mentioned in chapter 4 opened a workshop employing thirty of the forty members. Government patronage and other cooperatives' purchased helped the workshop prosper. The Committee to Allocate the Government Order bought boxes for flags; the municipal councils commissioned furniture for schools; a consumer cooperative ordered shelves and counters. By the end of the year the association opened two more shops and employed sixty to eighty workers. As the shops became centres for all master and journeymen joiners to discuss occupational concerns and the "social question," hundreds applied for membership and 260 were admitted. The two *compagnonnages* overcame their rivalry and offered to merge into one *corporation*. After the *compagnonnages* adhered, nearly all masters and journeymen belonged to the association.[26]

Unfortunately, if not unexpectedly, expansion brought dissension. As early as October, members employed in the shop walked out for two and a half weeks over piece-rates. Next, new members voted in a new executive board which got into a dispute with the director. He retaliated by calling a general meeting which revoked the executive board. Rebuffed, the executive board and thirty-two supporters resigned and tried to initiate bankruptcy proceedings. Up to this point, the narrative parallels the brief history of Felix Martin and Company, but the Commercial Court refused to hear the case so the denouement was postponed.[27]

The dispute may have been due to the decision to unite with the masons' and carpenters' cooperatives to build an apartment/workshop complex. The masons and carpenters had also incorporated and expanded in the autumn. By winter, when the associations could not provide work for their combined membership of 614, they pooled their resources, purchased some land, and made tentative arrangements to finance a project. When the private investor reneged, the cooperatives applied for a government loan. Although any housing project in the rapidly growing suburbs was viable, they did not get a loan because of the joint venture's "corporative tendencies." This ambitious but abortive venture killed the carpenters' cooperative and injured the other two. The joiners, who had invested the most, lost over 10,000 francs and half their shareholders. Nevertheless, they survived until the coup d'état of December 1851, despite another split, seizure of their tools, and a court case. The masons also held out until the dissolution of most cooperatives after the coup.[28]

The other producers' cooperatives founded in the year following the revolution had fewer shareholders, modest goals, and no open quarrels. For instance, the 100 shareholders of the Fraternal Association of United Shoemakers had 5,000 francs capital and operated one and later two shops quietly until the coup.[29]

The first chronicler of cooperation in Lyon, Flotard, found that the joiners did over 80,000 francs' worth of business in the year of the housing project fiasco and over 60,000 francs in the year of the second secession. Even after that blow, the joiners had nearly 3,000 francs in savings as well as enough orders and supplies to employ thirty to forty members for six months. The stone masons' cooperative did 120,000 francs' worth of business in its twenty-seven months of existence. Flotard (and subsequent researchers) could find no financial information about the other cooperatives.[30] Since the lack of court records for most cooperatives suggests they functioned smoothly, we can conclude that the producers' cooperatives of the Second Republic were moderately successful. Although they suffered from inexperienced administration, inadequate credit, and internal dissension, it took the coup d'état to administer the coup de grâce.

CLUBS AND COMMITTEES, AUGUST–DECEMBER 1848

Even as the cooperative movement expanded in a favourable political climate, the radical political movement contracted in response to intense repression. Yet the small band of radicals who persisted made their presence felt in Lyon, the Rhône, and surrounding departments. The most sophisticated political organizations, the clubs, survived due to the devotion of several hundred democratic-socialists and a series of election campaigns, now their only official *raison d'être*. As police surveillance and harassment mounted, many clubs were buried, but the major one arose from the ashes as an electoral committee. After successful campaigns for practical slates in a third round of local elections, this committee supported a candidate with limited appeal in the fall by-election for an Assembly seat and a rump committee endorsed him again in the winter presidential election. A weak candidate and, in the second case, disunity, combined with their opponents' forceful, unified campaigns, account for the radicals' disastrous showing in the first national elections fought under the new restrictive laws.

While encouraging a safe kind of economic association, the National Assembly limited the rights of association and free speech. A 29 July law (passed by 629 votes) subjected all meetings to government authorization. Meetings had to be open to the public and to police agents who could halt any discussion "contrary to public order." The act also prohibited correspondence between clubs. The only exemptions were for political banquets and electoral committees, though police could still observe them and arrest speakers. In August, the Assembly revived the bond required of newspapers dealing with politics. Although the republican press law set lower bonds than its predecessor, provincial newpapers suddenly had to raise 6,000 francs. A slightly reworded seditious libel act instituted severe penalties for "attacks" on the republic, private property, or the family. In the fall, a departmental ordinance improved enforcement of the club law by extending the jurisdiction of Lyon's Central Police commissioner to the suburbs, where most clubs met.[31]

Even before the ordinance, Police Commissioner Galerne moved against the suburban clubs. On the night the civic election results were announced, crowds stoned the suburban properties of newly elected conservative councillors. Since the victims (including the *canut*, Auberthier) were not the most unacceptable conservatives elected, the vandals must have selected targets where they thought police would not intervene, in the suburbs. Commissioner Galerne dispelled any illusions of immunity in the suburbs by arresting suburban club leaders without any evidence that they had incited or joined the riot. Galerne probably hoped that the arrests would serve as a warning; at any rate, he recorded that they subdued the clubs.[32]

Within ten days, the prefect annulled the suburban elections and called new elections for suburban councils, as well as partial elections for one-third of the seats on the General Council. During the overlapping campaigns, the Central Democratic Club had to disband and the neighbourhood clubs had to report the names of their officers, their meeting-places, and meeting-times. Police raided the one club that met without fulfilling these requirements and arrested its four executive officers (three silk weavers and a typesetter). Since the new club law prohibited ideological names, most of the clubs dropped their revolutionary names for locational ones. The Equality Club, which retained its name, was shut until renamed the Rue du Boeuf Club. After the National Assembly reintroduced the bond for political newspapers, the owner of *Le Peuple Souverain*, the one truly radical newspaper remaining in Lyon, informed his readers that the 6,000 francs bond was beyond his means.[33]

In spite of the onslaught, the democratic-socialists conducted effective campaigns for the municipal and departmental councils. The Central

Club became the legal Democratic Electoral Committee of the Rhône and collected a campaign chest; Le Peuple Souverain went public to pay its bond. The Democratic Committee, which could not correspond with local clubs, communicated indirectly by publishing slates in Le Peuple Souverain. While the slates for the suburban councils retained Bernard-Barret, Gauthier, Guillermin, Perret, and all the radical working-class incumbents, the list for the more elitist General Council included Laforest, two bourgeois republicans, and two respectable radicals, Morellet and Edant. Only Vallier, a socialist weaver and Croix-Rousse councillor, seemed out of place on this politically expedient list.[34] Reactionaries, who had complained about irregularities until they forced the annulment of the previous suburban elections, gave up on the suburbs. Although they put more effort into the campaign for the General Council, the legitimists and Orleanists could not agree on candidates and, absorbed in infighting, did not get out their voters. Democratic Committee candidates won all the seats,[35] making Vallier "perhaps the only worker to sit on a General Council in 1848." Influenced by the Lyonnais example, surrounding departments elected democrats, if not socialists, to the councils so long dominated by notables.[36]

Radicals on the two suburban councils interpreted their large majorities as mandates to secularize the elementary schools. The Guillotière council, which had been feuding with a local cleric over the schools, commissioned a report on the teaching orders. The report condemned the orders for their "retrograde tendencies" and "monarchical spirit"; the council voted to dismiss the Brothers of the Christian Doctrine and Sisters of St Joseph with the political and moral justification that the orders could not provide a "sincerely republican education" to prepare "men worthy of liberty." The Christian Brothers protested the "attack on freedom of education" and gathered 2,000 signatures on a petition to prevent it. Both orders appealed to the prefect and the minister of the interior; Ambert and subsequently Tourangin asked for a postponement until Organic Laws had been enacted (on the grounds that one of these would set educational policy). Meanwhile radicals on the council prepared their own petition in favour of lay education and obtained 5,000 signatures. In February 1849, the council replaced the clerics with twenty lay teachers.[37]

Conservatives responded to their electoral defeats and the attack on religious instruction in a variety of ways. The conservative majority in the General Council compromised on the minority's motion to end state support of the church, with the surprising result that the council halved its allocation to the clergy. They likewise agreed to continue the subsidy to the Committee to Organize Work. More predictably, the reactionary press fought secularization and criticized Orleanists and legitimists for failing to put differences aside during the elections. In truth, the two factions were sufficiently shocked by their defeat and by secularization to unite behind one moderate candidate in the September by-election for an Assembly seat. The candidate was Rivet, former prefect of the Rhône.[38]

On the other side, the Democratic Electoral Committee nominated Raspail, who was popular in the city but not outside (and was unable to campaign because he was in prison over his alleged role in the May and June Days). When Le Censeur called a meeting to decide between two of their candidates, the Democratic Committee printed their own invitations and ballots, flooded the meeting with their supporters, took over the podium, and conducted the vote. Of 766 ballots cast, 758 were marked Raspail. Something similar happened at a liberal electoral assembly. Accordingly, republicans and liberals held small, private assemblies, where each chose a (different) moderate candidate.[39] Although their newspapers publicized their candidates, the campaign was really two-sided. Ambert, who worried about dividing the moderate vote, persuaded the liberal, Petetin, to renounce his candidacy. The campaign was rough, in accordance with the reactionaries' new emphasis on "a battle between civilization and barbarism." In the suburbs and old quarters, radicals terrorized Rivet's agents and tore down or trashed his posters. In the countryside, conservatives made radicals equally uncomfortable.[40]

Although Rivet's victory conformed to the overall results of the September by-elections (fifteen of the seventeen seats went to conservatives), analysis of Lyon's returns shows that all the cantons in the metropolis favoured Raspail. Guillotière gave the biggest margin: 71 per cent of the ballots versus 21 per cent for Rivet. Croix-Rousse came second with 5,409 or 59 per cent of the voters casting their ballots for Raspail. In the metropolis as a whole, he received 26,388 votes, nearly 12,000 more than his nearest competitor, Rivet. The front-runners were followed by Louis Napoleon with 2,370 and the Censeur candidate with a paltry 955. This stunning success for the Democratic Electoral Committee was completely reversed by the rural vote: 7,977 for Raspail, 27,422 for Rivet. Nothing reversed the pitifully low vote for the Censeur candidate.[41]

Just before the polling, crowds from Croix-Rousse and Guillotière marched to the city singing the "Marseillaise" and promoting the radical candidate. During the five-day count, hundreds of workers milled around the Hôtel de ville and once forty of them invaded the counting room. When the mayor finally mounted the balcony to announce that Rivet had won, the crowd in the square simply booed. To forestall any post-election disturbances, Ambert sent in the troops, who arrested fifty. This ended the noisy expression of discontent with the results.[42]

The fighting that broke out a few days later had little to do with the election. Since Martin-Bernard's departure, authorities had given few assignments to the Mobile Guard, who had become demoralized. Members of the militia had been apprehended for assault and battery, theft, and drunkenness. Although people had seen the unit's dissolution early in September as a sign of the reaction, no one had protested owing to the unit's bad reputation. Most Guards simply returned their rifles, though some participated in the demonstrations at the Hôtel de ville. By October, five or six hundred Guards, tired of waiting for severance pay, went to the Prefecture to demand it. When Ambert explained that he did not have the money yet, the crowd howled and scuffled with the police until three hundred dragoons cleared the square. Half the Guards followed a red flag to Croix-Rousse, where they met and menaced a local police commissioner. The inhabitants actually defended the commissioner, who was a revolutionary appointee, When the Guards tried to rally the populace of this insurrectionary commune by beating the *rappel*, only a few workers joined them in a futile effort to build a barricade. The arrival of troops, notification that the National Assembly had approved their severance pay, and a heavy rain halted the disturbance.[43]

After the September elections, radical republicans all over France held banquets to commemorate the anniversary of the founding of the first French Republic. In Lyon, the Democratic Electoral Committee also celebrated Raspail's election in Paris. By charging a low admission price (one franc twenty-five centimes), the committee drew 1,800 people and turned away 2,000! Yet Lyon remained calm compared to Toulouse, where diners roared "*Vive la guillotine!*" Instead, club leaders made the usual toasts, such as Charavey's to equality, or the dissident Icarian, Razuret's, to socialism. The only new note came from Grinand, chairman of the Democratic Committee, whose toast to "prosperity, the family, and religion" prompted the omnipresent police agent to report a "conversion." Neither the committee nor *Le Peuple Souverain* interpreted it as a conversion.[44] More likely the committee was trying to allay fears that they were communists, fears so ably exploited by conservatives in the last campaign.

Following the banquet, the Democratic Electoral Committee ceased public functions for over a month. In the interval, ten neighbourhood clubs met in Croix-Rousse, Guillotière, and the old quarters. Half met daily, half thrice weekly; at most 1,000 attended regularly. The police reports mention fifty-six speakers, most of whom gave radical speeches (the agents probably omitted moderate speeches). Grinand, Charavey, and other democratic-socialist luminaries spoke, as did nine members of the fraternal association then forming. Although aware of the police agent's presence, they were not intimidated because the agents gave them some leeway. The authorities prosecuted Dr Borne for repeatedly denouncing "God, religions, and their ministers" but ignored Grinand's diatribe against the clergy. They tried only eight club members, half of whom were accused of convoking a general assembly of clubs when they were really calling a cooperative meeting. As the presidential campaign began, they closed one club because of speeches critical of the constitution and the president. The closure brought the first formal suggestion that the clubs should be cautious.[45]

In the relative freedom up to this point, a prominent Fourierist, Juif, went from club to club advocating phalanges and the Proudhonian, Pierre Gros, promoted exchange banks. The same clubs applauded both speakers. Generally, though, the clubs touted the revolutionary "organization of work" and the postrevolutionary cooperatives. Politics was a constant preoccupation. At first the speakers censured Cavaignac's treatment of workers; then the speeches dwelt on the promulgation of the constitution. Having seen the results of manhood suffrage, the clubs abandoned their earlier support for ratification of the constitution and opposed direct election of the president.[46]

By mid-November, the clubs focused on selecting a presidential candidate. No one proposed the once-popular Lamartine, now accused of "organizing the reaction." The Mountain's candidate, Ledru-Rollin, had detractors and defenders: some claimed he and Lamartine had used the republic "in their own interests" while others called him and Raspail "our most intimate friends ... because they alone want the workers' welfare and our social republic." Raspail remained the favourite and when the clubs learned that the Parisian socialists were sponsoring him, they endorsed him. They did not consider the two favourites, Cavaignac and Louis Napoleon, though the latter had some adherents.[47]

While the clubs discussed candidates, the Democratic Electoral Committee reemerged to announce an electoral banquet. Now it was known as the Socialist Democrats' Committee to distinguish it from the more moderate Progressive Democrats' Committee. Though the Socialist Committee was more petty bourgeois than it had been in previous incarnations, Grinand (who had become a teacher and herbalist since the early 1840s), Pierre Gros, and Charavey had kept in touch with suburban clubs. So, too, had ex-corporal Beauvoir, the shoemaker Guillermin, and the weaver Razuret. Although most Socialist Democrats preferred Raspail, they did not announce their support until the eve of the election, owing to the departure of the clerk, Lentillon, and the typesetter, Cautel-Baudet, who, as Republican Democrats, worked with the Progressive Democrats to swing the clubs over to Ledru-Rollin. The Republican Democrats were not reconciled until the day before the polling. Torn by dissension, the democratic-socialists did not campaign

vigorously, Aside from an early, inconclusive banquet, which nevertheless attracted thousands, they held only one other large meeting to
announce their candidate.[48]

The presidential election forced moderate republicans to endorse
Cavaignac, albeit with less enthusiasm than elsewhere and with the
excuse that he had the best chance of defeating Louis Napoleon. Notables
in Lyon, Paris, and the Nord wavered between Cavaignac as a necessary
bulwark against socialism and Louis Napoleon, but gravitated to
Napoleon because they felt he had the best chance of winning. On 7
December, *Le Courrier de Lyon* endorsed Napoleon on the assumption
that the conservative Committee of the rue de Poitiers, in Paris, had
endorsed him. (They misinterpreted individual support.) On the 9th and
10th, the legitimist newspapers followed suit, citing Louis Napoleon's
commitment to "religious and educational freedom." Only the Bonapartists were decisive. They put out a local organ (*Le Président*),
distributed pamphlets, and persuaded electoral meetings in bourgeois
districts to opt for their candidate.[49]

The results – Louis Napoleon 41,986; Cavaignac, 12,432; Raspail,
8,561; and Ledru-Rollin, 1,624 – are not surprising considering the
solidarity on the Right and division on the Left. The fact that Bonaparte's
share of the vote (62 per cent) exceeded that of all other major cities except
Rouen, another radical city, is less startling if we remember that the
working-class sections of Paris, as well as Lyon and Rouen, gave sizeable
majorities to Bonaparte (though peasants provided the largest majorities). In a complete turnabout from the previous election, every Lyonnais
canton favoured Louis Napoleon and repudiated Raspail. The electors of
Guillotière, who had cast 480 ballots for Louis Napoleon in the
by-election, cast 10,063 ballots for him in the presidential election. At 73
per cent of the vote, this was his biggest majority in the metropolis.
Raspail's share of the vote plummeted from 71 to 11 per cent. In the
canton containing Croix-Rousse, Raspail dropped from 59 per cent to 19
per cent of the vote.[50]

What accounts for this dramatic shift from Raspail to Bonaparte in less
than two months? Referring to Paris, though his remarks also apply to
Lyon, A.J. Tudesq answers that voters distinguished between electing a
representative and electing a president. They realized that voting for
Raspail, who was still in prison and was not known nationally, would
waste votes in a presidential election. More positively, Tudesq argues that
the Bonapartist campaign revived a *popular* Napoleonic legend.[51]
Something similar must explain the Lyonnais clubs' hesitation about
Raspail and receptivity to spokesmen for Bonaparte. On the other hand,
the radicals' divisions distracted them from campaigning among and
gaining support from the uncommitted. In Lyon they ignored one

important constituency, the army, despite the soldiers' predominance in electoral sections in Guillotière. These sections voted heavily for Bonaparte.[52]

Immediately after the results were announced, the army held a review. Since civilians had recently clashed with the troops over the rebuilding of the Croix-Rousse fortifications, the military command assigned a regiment to watch the spectators. The decision to use a regiment infamous for its repression of the second Lyonnais insurrection invited violence. Fifteen hundred spectators stoned and then chased the regiment back to the barracks. This outburst of hostility was the only post-election disturbance and it was denounced by the radical leaders. In Lyon, as elsewhere, the radical infrastructure emerged from the electoral defeat in disarray. After Christmas, a Socialist Democrats' banquet attracted only 600 stalwarts.[53] This was far removed from the 1,800 attending, and 2,000 turned away from, the banquet following the by-election.

THE LEGISLATIVE ASSEMBLY CAMPAIGN, JANUARY–MAY 1849

By the time the democratic-socialists had sufficiently revived to plan their celebration of the proclamation of the republic, the situation had deteriorated. In the interval the new prefect, Tourangin, had begun his administration by promising to implement "the principles of order" and preserve "the fundamental principles of all regular society." More specifically, he ordered the removal of all symbols of the red republic. Unlike other prefects who instituted this assault on freedom of expression,[54] Tourangin was seconded by Marshal Bugeaud. On his arrival in Lyon, the marshal, notorious – and detested – for his brutal suppression of the June Days, ominously announced that the new Army of the Alps could not engage in external warfare, its ostensible purpose, as long as it left behind "a formidable civil war." Lest this was ambiguous, he told officers that he would lead those who wanted "to defend society" if the red republicans captured the country. Conservatives, who were relieved by the appointment of Tourangin, were delighted by Bugeaud. They interpreted his statements to mean he would "strike the Lyonnais demagogues with a lightning bolt."[55]

Sending a general who had perfected the strategy of deploying artillery against urban revolts to remove the symbols of the red republic both threatened and taunted the red republicans. To their credit, the democratic-socialists neither resigned themselves nor yielded to the temptation of challenging Bugeaud. They redoubled their propaganda, analysed their mistakes in the preceding election, and, prodded by Parisian radicals, patched up their differences. Systematically correcting their previous errors, they mounted a triumphant campaign in the Legislative Assembly elections. Moreover, their victory was complemented by the unexpected success of their political allies to the south and east.

Bugeaud started by asking the mayor to remove the statue of the "Man of the People" from the main square. When the mayor demurred because the move might provoke the populace, Bugeaud withdrew the sentry stationed beside the statue, which drew hundreds of workers (probably Voraces) to the square to guard the statue. After five noisy nights, the City Council sent in troops to clear the square. When small groups reassembled in the surrounding streets and one group beat an officer, his men charged with their sabres and left one civilian wounded, one dead. The next evening, as soldiers and workers grappled again, fifty-four workers were arrested. Finally, the City Council reaffirmed its commitment to the statue and convinced the demonstrators that it would be safe without a guard. In less than a fortnight, a young royalist mutilated the "Man of the People." Workers resumed their round-the-clock patrols until the council voted to restore the statue and place it on a pedestal for safekeeping.[56]

During these confrontations, Tourangin initiated more familiar parts of the repressive policy and began with a purge of republicans on the judicial staff. The prosecutors, under pressure, harassed the press. Between January and 15 June, *Le Peuple Souverain* appeared before the courts eight times. Although juries usually acquitted the director, Faures, he ultimately spent two months in jail and paid over 1,000 francs in fines. A new radical newspaper, *Le Républicain*, was prosecuted for six articles. In the spring campaign for the Legislative Assembly, the central authorities ordered police surveillance of electoral meetings and Lyonnais police closed six clubs and sent six speakers to trial for remarks in the clubs.[57]

Mounting repression did not stifle the reinvigorated radicals, nor did it drive them, as it did radicals in Lille and smaller places, to express their political opinions in symbolic ways at Carnival. Like the Parisians, they talked politics in clubs and organized their campaign though a secret society, the Rights of Man or Republican Solidarity.[58] In February, two suburban clubs had over 600 people in attendance, while a new city club had 250 people at its first meeting. When police shut clubs, they reopened immediately. As the campaign began, many clubs were converted to electoral committees in the vain hope that this would lighten police pressure. In time, the threat of arrest reduced attendance figures from, in one case, 800 to 150. Since the number of electoral committees rose considerably, it is probable that as many people participated in this campaign as in the last one. Before the election, clubs debated current political affairs, notably the new, harsher club law; after the campaign began, they put their effort into propaganda.[59]

The left-wing press was equally undaunted by the repression. In February alone, six issues of Le Peuple Souverain were impounded for articles criticizing Tourangin and Bugeaud for their mishandling of the statue affair. (The authorities did not otherwise object to the newspapers' commentary on the affair, because the editorials responsibly argued for calm.) Although a new ordinance against street peddlers cut sales by 1,000, this left a respectable circulation of 7,500.[60]

A new radical organ appeared just as the repression intensified.[61] During the presidential campaign, Charavey, Drivon, Grinand, seven other Socialist Democrats, and nine like-minded club members published a prospectus for a newspaper. Because of the divisions in the democratic-socialist camp and demoralization after their electoral defeat, it took a month to form the joint stock company. By then, the stockholders and editorial board included partisans of Ledru-Rollin. Representative Greppo and other members of the Paris-based Republican Solidarity had encouraged the reconciliation in their nation-wide campaign to unify the Left for the upcoming elections. The introductory issue demanded "the democratic and social republic"; the first regular issue promoted "work associations" with pay according to need. Le Républicain also published Grinand's toast at the banquet commemorating the founding of the Second Republic: "To the revolutionary spirit, the tyrant's terror, the consolation of the oppressed, and the people's vengeance." Although the censors tolerated this, they rejected articles calling Bugeaud "a man who coolly meditates massacre." Neither censorship nor insolvency intimidated Le Républicain. When the policy of sending free copies to soldiers brought the newspaper to the brink of bankruptcy, Greppo and the other worker representatives, as well as representatives Chaley and Laforest, municipal councillors Edant and Juif, and other bourgeois shareholders rescued it by issuing and buying new (five francs) shares. Circulation peaked at 9,400, then levelled off at 6,400 copies daily.[62]

The negotiations to establish Le Républicain were only part of broader negotiations to unify the Socialist and Republican Democrats in a sixty-member Central Democratic Committee. United and determined, the committee planned the largest of the dozens of banquets celebrating the anniversary of the February revolution. Once again, six thousand celebrants sat down to dinner! Early in March, the committee asked workers' corporations and cooperatives to send them delegates. Recognizing a Central Democratic Club tactic, the police commissioner dispatched up to 300 agents and soldiers to the committee's public meetings. Despite constant harassment, the committee compiled a list of candidates for the Legislative Assembly. Early in May, the Progressive Democrats and *Le Censeur* adopted their list.[63]

The presidential election and Bugeaud's belligerence taught the Left the virtues of compromise. However, the Progressive Democrats and *Censeur* republicans made most of the compromises. The slate included the four worker representatives to the National Assembly who had voted with the Mountain on major issues. Benoit, Doutre, Greppo, and Pelletier had even joined the tiny minority voting against the constitution because it did not provide for the "social republic." These humble men had spoken forcefully for the right to work and to strike. Greppo, the only representative to support Proudhon's credit proposals, stood almost alone at the end, as he presented petitions to indict the cabinet and retain the Assembly. The Socialist Democrats added a prominent member of the Mountain, Mathieu de la Drôme, a former weaver and dissident Icarian, Sebastien Commissaire, and two peasants. They did substitute Benjamin Raspail for his incarcerated brother, François, but their only real concessions to the Progressive Democrats and *Censeur* republicans were the bourgeois socialist, Morellet, and the moderate republican representative, Chanay.[64]

The defeat in December and the fighting in February convinced the radicals that they had to appeal to soldiers. They not only wanted the military vote; they wanted to cultivate sympathy in case of disorder or, given Bugeaud's attitude, a coup. The radical newspapers delivered free of charge advised the troops that: "The soldier owes only the duty of passive obedience before the enemy ... Inside the country, when ordered to march against fellow citizens, he has the right to examine what is right and wrong." When Bugeaud prohibited these papers in the barracks, bands of up to 150 soldiers went to the newspaper offices to pick up copies. When the commander placed the offices off limits, thirty to fifty men from one regiment walked by the offices to catch bundles of papers thrown down to them by the staff. As a thousand civilians gathered in the streets to applaud, soldiers from another regiment were dispatched to clear the streets. At this point the municipal authorities blockaded the streets, so the editors distributed copies unobtrusively to defuse the explosive situation.[65]

Despite Bugeaud's interference, despite the transfer of soldiers implicated in the press incidents, the garrison voted "entirely red." The only other garrison to return "reds" in May 1849 was in Paris, where the Mountain had also made a special appeal to the troops.[66]

The radicals' campaign in the countryside contributed more to their victory, for the peasants provided the margin of victory in the Rhône as in the rest of the southeast. Since December, the radical leadership had tried to reassure the peasantry that they did not stand for the *loi agraire*, nor were they opposed to the family and religion. Articles in the urban press had made little impression, so their newspapers ran series and printed supplements addressed to peasants from March through May 1849. The authors of these pieces included the famous peasant propagandist, Pierre Joigneaux; they criticized the forty-five centimes tax, asked probing questions about legitimists' promises to peasants, advocated cheap rural credit, and generally offered solutions to rural grievances. The committee subsidized these newspapers and sent emissaries to the countryside to dispense free copies. The emissaries were so active the police commissioner estimated, with some exaggeration, that they dispensed 300,000 "red" pamphlets. The committee also held banquets in St-Genis (setting of a luddite attack in February 1848) and twelve more distant villages. By keeping the cost of admission low, they attracted hundreds to each rural banquet. [67]

While the Mountain employed these techniques throughout the provinces, nowhere were they as effective as in the Rhône. In the Legislative Assembly elections, only six of the department's twenty-six cantons, all of them in backward, mountainous regions, voted for the "white" slate. [68]

The local reactionaries were divided and undecided until the last minute and their campaign suffered. Although Orleanists, legitimists, liberals, and Bonapartists agreed with the Committee of the rue de Poitiers on the need to unite before "the menace to society itself," the legitimists in the rural cantons balked at the inclusion of a few conservative republicans on their joint slate. After weeks of hard negotiations between the Orleanist and legitimist committees, the latter accepted two conservative republicans along with Representative Rivet, Mayor Reveil, and two other Orleanists. They buttressed these "moderates" with Representative Mortemarte and two other legitimist notables, plus General Lebon-Desmottes (a replacement for their first choice, Bugeaud, who preferred to stand elsewhere) and Auberthier, the token worker representative "who had voted correctly in the National Assembly." The Napoleonic Committee, never a serious contender in this election, folded days before the polls opened. Until the reactionaries had a slate, they waged an offensive against the socialists. Despite vows to combat the socialists' "indefatigable propaganda" with the "same tactics," they only occasionally distributed free newspapers to the peasantry. Nor did they hold banquets. [69]

The bitter contest between two extremes induced four-fifths of the electorate to exercise their franchise. The united and disciplined party, in this instance the democratic-socialists, delivered their voters. Their candidates won with 72,659 to 69,302 ballots, while the conservative candidates lost with 50,345 to 46,038 ballots. The *Censeur* republican, Chanay, headed the list, with three of the radical incumbents, Doutre, Pelletier, and Benoit, close behind. The most radical and proletarian incumbent, Greppo, came seventh with 70,233 votes. All the radical, proletarian incumbents save the front-runner increased their mandates by over 10,000 votes. Benjamin Raspail, who ran last among the winners, got 60,000 more ballots than his better-known brother had received in December and doubled his brother's vote in the more comparable September election. The metropolitan area contributed more than half of the red list's total count, with the canton containing Croix-Rousse giving the biggest mandate: 75,121 votes. Guillotière followed with 69,399 votes.[70]

As before, the unique feature of the Rhône results was the election of so many radical, working-class spokesmen. Benoit, Doutre, Greppo, Pelletier, and the new member, Commissaire, represented nearly half the democratic-socialist workers in the Legislative Assembly.[71] Long years of service to the radical cause in the secret societies of the monarchy and the clubs of the revolution, as well as the incumbents' records in the National Assembly, faithfully reported in the local democratic-socialist press, help to explain their success. The truly popular character of the Lyonnais club movement, the Central Democratic Committee's skilful campaign, especially in the countryside, and their opponents' disunity also account for "red" victories. Two other factors complete the explanation: the textile city's frequent contacts with its hinterland through putting out and migration and the dissatisfaction of peasants in the vineyard and absentee landlord areas of the Rhône.

The combination of a unified, disciplined, and determined group of urban radicals, reaching out to a peasantry disaffected from large landowners, also accounts for the more startling success of democratic-socialist lists through much of central and southeastern France. In the first democratic election showing a precise division of political opinion, the Rhône was only one of fourteen departments returning all the candidates of the Mountain. In fact, the Rhône ranked only tenth in terms of the proportion of the vote accorded to radicals. But five of the departments with larger majorities – the Saône-et-Loire, Isère, Drôme, Jura, and Ain – lay in the Lyonnais sphere of influence along the valleys of the Saône and the Rhône. These five, and one other department according an absolute majority to the democratic-socialists, sent migrants to Lyon, migrants who joined the secret societies and clubs of the radical movement. The Central Democratic Committee certainly corresponded with the surrounding departments and probably used contacts of club members from these departments. Since they could muster hundreds to go to banquets in the rural areas, it is likely that they sent at least some members to Vienne and other nearby towns in these departments. Historians such as Vigier and Loubère, who study the early acceptance of the Left in rural areas of the south and southeast, stress the importance of urban propagandists from textile towns bringing in new concepts. Both historians mention Lyonnais missionaries.[72]

Clearly the creeping repression of the first postrevolutionary year had, if anything, strengthened Lyonnais radicalism. Unhappily, the dynamic of repression and resistance had also goaded some radicals underground, into secret societies which would instigate a third Lyonnais insurrection.

CHAPTER SIX

Insurrection, June 1849

Secret societies were also targets of the club law, especially as interpreted by the minister of justice and local officials. Even before the law of 29 July 1848, Police Commissioner Galerne was reporting on the activities of "secret" societies. Initially, this zealous official submitted accounts of a wide variety of meetings, including an Icarian gathering to plan the emigration to America. Throughout his year-long surveillance, he watched consumer cooperatives as carefully as political committees. Not always aware of differences between economic and political associations, he usually lumped them together and inflated his estimates of membership in clandestine groups. On 8 January 1849, he claimed that 25,000 men or three-fifths of the adult male population belonged to clandestine groups. Five months earlier, Acting Attorney-General Loyson spoke more generally of "a vast secret society in Lyon and the surrounding communes" which recruited among "the numerous communist sects in Lyon."[1]

Police and judicial reports exaggerating the extent of the democratic-socialist threat have led historians to dismiss the authorities' fears as unreasonable.[2] More recent analyses of police, attorney-generals', and prefects' reports suggest that the threat was real up to, and in many cases after, the insurrections of June 1849.[3] It is argued here that Lyonnais authorities who were overly concerned about consumer cooperatives nevertheless had cause for alarm until the state of siege was imposed after the insurrection. With the closure of the Central Democratic Club and many of its affiliates in July 1848, the committed democratic-socialists did not abandon their political debates or their socioeconomic theories. Most joined the three legal consumer cooperatives which they, like workers and authorities elsewhere, considered practical applications of democratic-socialism. In addition to symbolizing a radical ideology, the consumer cooperatives seemed threatening because their central administrations and local shops resembled the secret society networks of the monarchy. However, only two of the cooperatives were disguised political associations and only one, or rather some members of one, played a role in the insurrection. A smaller group of radicals retreated to small, private assemblies to sustain political discussion. As Agulhon discovered and Merriman substantiated for seventeen departments: "The era of clubs was followed by the age of *chambrées*."[4] Because Lyonnais and Parisian radicals had experience with secret societies under the monarchy, their *chambrées* were coordinated by an elaborate secret society known as the Rights of Man in Lyon and as the Republican Solidarity elsewhere.

As we shall see, the secret societies were largely responsible for the chief insurrection of June 1849. If members of the New Mountain did instigate an abortive rising in the capital, the modest, legal demonstration that ensued hardly bears comparison with the full-scale insurrection in Croix-Rousse, where insurgents formed a revolutionary municipal council, built barricades, and defended them at the cost of twenty-five civilian lives. Surprisingly, the Voraces were the principal instigators, indicating a more political, and national, orientation on the part of these journeymen.

CONSUMER COOPERATIVES, DECEMBER 1848 – JUNE 1849

Lyon's consumer cooperatives actually flourished in the face of police surveillance and harassment. While workers who had relied on corporative action during the revolution turned to producers' cooperatives, club activists who felt the need to supplement the circumscribed clubs formed consumer cooperatives, much as Mutualists had flowed into the first consumer cooperative in 1835. A few of the founders conceived of the cooperative cafés as fronts for political meetings, but most of the members sincerely worked at making the cooperatives economically viable enterprises. The minority attracted the authorities' attention, but the majority were responsible for one of the three outstanding experiments in consumer cooperatives under the Second Republic.[5]

Within days of the introduction of the club law and the drop in club attendance after the civic elections of July 1848, groups of workers met in the old quarters, Croix-Rousse, and Vaise to set up an association to apply for a government loan. Though the groups referred to themselves publicly as *corporations*, many of the leaders had been presidents of now-defunct clubs, so that some of the groups must have been the rumps of clubs. At the first meeting, proponents of a producers' cooperative clashed with the more political advocates of a consumer cooperative.

Soon the apolitical spokesmen left to organize the Workers' Union, which was later denied a government loan. Still, meetings at the end of August attracted up to 800 people, who spent as much time criticizing the government as they did ratifying the constitution of the Fraternal Association of French Industries.[6]

On 1 September, the Executive Committee of the French Industries published their constitution on a red poster. The eighteen members of the Executive Committee had belonged to clubs affiliated with the Central Democratic Club. One, a former weaver Blaise Murat, had fought in the 1831 insurrection, joined the Commerce Veridique, contributed to *L'Atelier* in the 1840s, and sat on the Central Committee and edited *Le Censeur* in 1848. Not surprisingly, the preamble to the constitution contained what was a very political appeal for a general association: "Instead of coming powerfully to the aid of the suffering classes, as it should and could, the Government has handed them over, as in the past, to monopolists, speculators, usurers ... The workers have had to find in themselves a remedy for their ills ... They have found it in association ... Association by *corporation* or by industry carries a stamp of exclusivism ... General association ... is the only one which offers ... the advantages a worker lacks ... We have tried to put this program into practice."[7]

After a digression in support of Raspail in the by-election, the Executive Committee asked all *corporations* to unite with them and held meetings in the suburbs to collect subscriptions. By December, the cooperative was selling coal to members at a discount and had opened two grocery shops, one in Croix-Rousse, one in Guillotière. By February, it had sold 1,225 shares and realized a profit of 2,152 francs.[8]

At this time, the French Industries incorporated as Chaboud and Company. Chaboud was a silk merchant who had been a master, one of the earliest Mutualists, and a supporter of the Commerce Veridique. Since September, the Executive Committee had lost Murat and seven club activists, most of them petty bourgeois, and added fourteen members, thirteen of them workers. Three of the workers had also contributed to the first French consumer cooperative. The charter of Chaboud and Company omitted the political preamble and prescribed a structure similar to the Commerce Veridique's: it called for a limited liability company "to purchase, sell or exchange any product." Half the capital was to be raised by the sale of 200,000 one-franc shares. (The other half was supposed to come from a government loan, but the company directors never approached the government, perhaps because they realized that the Encouragement Council, with its preference for producers' cooperatives and dividends, would not approve.) Like the other Lyonnais cooperatives, the company did not offer dividends or permit sale of shares until dissolution, in ninety-nine years.[9]

Events proved that Chaboud and Company had shed its parapolitical character and decided to operate as a purely economic venture. Between February and June of 1849, the company added a butcher shop, sold 455 more shares, and realized a profit of nearly 2,000 francs. Although the authorities shut the shops after the insurrection of 1849, they found no evidence implicating either the company as a corporate entity or any of its known members. The shops reopened but the paranoid police remained suspicious that the company's cheap shares and appeal to all workers signalled a bid to take over the whole economy or that the central committee with local shops hid a secret society network. Despite constant surveillance, the police never caught members of Chaboud and Company in a compromising political position, so the cooperative functioned until the coup d'état. Three members of the Executive Committee were arrested at that time, not because of open opposition to the coup but because of their political affiliations prior to joining Chaboud and Company.[10]

Two other consumer cooperatives sprang up in that fertile year following the revolution. Since they were more political, they will be considered in detail below. The point, here, is that apolitical *and* political consumer cooperatives had broad objectives and expansive organizational arrangements. Like the French Industries and the producers' cooperatives, they expressed an interest in the education and ethical development of all workers. Their concern for the workers' intellectual and moral welfare parallelled that of the Owenites in England[11] and the Mutualists at home. From their experience in the Mutualist Society, the Commerce Veridique, and the club movement, they borrowed the useful structure of a central bureau with an unlimited number of local branches. Their antecedents, pretensions, and large but coordinated format made all consumer cooperatives menacing to the authorities, whether or not they had specifically political goals.

Lyon's early experimentation with mutualism and cooperation also influenced consumer cooperatives in two distant cities during the Second Republic. Two doctors who participated in the first flourish of mutualist and cooperative ideas (in 1830s Lyon) established fraternal associations in Nantes and Reims. In the former city, Dr Guépin combined a producers' and a consumer cooperative; in the latter city, the association included mutual aid and engaged in electoral campaigns. Both associations prospered until they, too, fell victim of official fears and dissolution, in their cases before the coup d'état.[12]

The second flowering of consumer cooperatives in Lyon had a more immediate impact. A few months after the French Industries incorporated in the city, a United Workers' Commercial Enterprise incorporated in nearby Vienne (in the Isère). Like other radicals in that community, the

United Workers imitated Lyonnais models. Thus their constitution reproduced the French Industries' preamble and borrowed many provisions, not to mention the name, from another Lyonnais prototype. The copy was less democratic in structure owing to the prominence of Fourierists in the Vienne cooperative. Once in operation, the United Workers followed the Chaboud and Company pattern of abandoning political goals to build a successful economic undertaking and, despite this, disappearing after the coup.[13]

Both the consumer cooperatives founded in Lyon after the Fraternal Association of French Industries combined political and economic concerns. Some of their members used the cafés, shops, and meetings to talk politics and read newspapers; some of these members followed their political convictions, and allies, into insurrection; the majority pursued the associations' economic goals.

The French Industries had been depoliticized by the defection of many political associates. While it collected subscriptions in November 1848, Murat, the editor of Le Censeur, left to establish the Democratic Association of United Industries and took with him an editor of Le Républicain, F. Drivon, the neobabouvist city councillor, Edant, and a prominent dissident Icarian, Poncet. They and a few other political activists paid twenty francs apiece to set up a Democratic Café and a Fraternal Butcher Shop. By the spring, they had recruited forty members and incorporated. Their statutes resembled those of the French Industries except that the Democratic Association was capitalized at only 100,000 francs and all the capital was to be raised by the sale of two-francs shares. In short, the radical association omitted the hopeless clause about a government loan.[14]

The insurrection revealed that few members treated the Democratic Association as a "front" for subversive activities. The Democratic Café manager (who was a Reformed Carbonari) helped to build barricades and took up arms to defend them. After the insurrection, he disappeared with the association's funds, was tried in absentia, and sentenced to deportation. However, only one other member, Poncet, was convicted of taking up arms and his conviction was invalidated on appeal. The military authorities shut the shops because they felt that a company without dividends or inheritable shares was not a commercial venture but "the realization of socialism." Although the prosecution charged that the Democratic Association was a club network, the military court disagreed and permitted the shops to reopen. Now the weaver Drivon, who had not been incriminated in the insurrection, changed the association into a strictly economic enterprise.[15] It functioned quietly until the coup d'état, when cooperatives were dissolved.[16]

During the winter of 1848, some workers in the original Croix-Rousse club, the Jandard Club, pooled their fuel money to purchase coal in quantity. Once the coal was dispensed and the presidential election was over, they decided to expand into the grocery business. Owing to seasonal unemployment, they were unable to get credit and had to pool their limited resources to buy some produce. They made one home a distribution centre, laid planks over boxes for counters, borrowed a scale, and weighed and packaged their produce. This makeshift arrangement worked so well that they were besieged with customers.[17] By 23 December, their new Fraternal Association of United Workers had seven to nine hundred subscribing customers. In February 1849, it registered at the Commercial Court as Naudé and Company. It was less ambitious than the Democratic Association, for its 100,000 francs capital was to be raised by selling one-franc shares on the instalment plan. Naudé and Company was also more capitalistic – or expedient – than the other cooperatives in providing for dividends; it was also more realistic about dissolving in five years' time.[18]

The twenty-four men who signed the constitution of Naudé and Company had considerable club, secret society, and cooperative experience. A herbalist, Naudé, a loom merchant, Démard, and a silk folder had presided over the parent club. Naudé, Démard, and a silk weaver also belonged to the radical lodge of the Free Masons located in Croix-Rousse. A clerk, an ex-soldier, a shoemaker, and two other weavers had been prominent in the Jandard and other Croix-Rousse clubs. The clerk was a long-time Fourierist, J. Rémond; the ex-soldier was Corporal Beauvoir, who had alerted the clubs about Sergeant Gigou's disappearance in March 1848; and the shoemaker was Vincent Guillermin of the politicized Union of 1847. Another shoemaker can be traced back to the Reformed Carbonari of 1842. A silk weaver, Pierre Millet, had hosted dissident Icarian meetings in 1844, fought in both insurrections in the 1830s, and helped found the Mutualist Society in 1828! At least four co-signors had contributed to the Commerce Veridique of 1835. Only six of the co-signors (all silk weavers) cannot be connected to some political or economic association.

In the spring of 1849, the fifteen directors and the employees of Naudé and Company continued to be politically active. The directors met in the Jandard and other cafés that had been club centres and, according to the ever-present police agent, discussed political more than commercial affairs.[19] During the insurrection, the Jandard café, which doubled as Voraces' headquarters, figured as a rendez-vous for insurgents. Naudé and Company's bookkeeper, Deschaud, wrote the telegram that ignited the conflagration. Two other employees, Corporal Beauvoir and a dissident Icarian, Bacot, felt sufficiently compromised to flee France after the fighting. Arguing that the shops were disguised clubs and company money had been expended on "political ends tied to the insurrection," the authorities closed the cooperative. They tried Deschaud in absentia and convicted him of conspiracy to overthrow the government and participation in rebellion. The manager, Guillermin, spent three months in prison for "seditious remarks." Bacot returned to face trial voluntarily and was acquitted.[20]

In spite of political distractions, the directors were good administrators. On the day the battle began, Naudé and Company had a central headquarters, six grocery stores, a bakery, pastry shop, delicatessen, wine warehouse, and coal depot. From Croix-Rousse the outlets had spread to other suburbs and the old quarters of the city in response to demand in these working-class districts. In six months, the number of shareholders had nearly doubled to 1,500. The company employed forty to fifty shareholders who would otherwise have been unemployed and paid them a respectable two francs fifty centimes to three francs a day (one-third of it in merchandise). Daily turnover fluctuated between twelve and thirteen hundred francs; the semiannual profits reached 6,000 francs, and total assets were evaluated at 60,000 francs.[21]

Obviously the shareholders did not want to liquidate their successful venture. When the imprisoned manager resigned, they replaced him with Naudé, who had not been implicated in the insurrection and had just been reelected to the Croix-Rousse City Council. After months of petitioning, Naudé got the ban on the cooperative lifted. By then, the repressive atmosphere of the state of siege had persuaded Naudé to keep the company out of politics. The police searched the shops and the directors' homes in February 1850, but found nothing incriminating (except of Naudé and two other directors, who were subsequently convicted of belonging to a secret society, the radical masonic lodge). In 1851, the company ran fifteen or sixteen shops, which did 900,000 francs business and earned a gross profit of 30,000 francs. In Mutualist fashion, the shareholders voted to open two primary schools, one for their sons, one for their daughters. Since they were already supporting eight pensioners, they considered establishing a retirement home. After the coup d'état, the authorities recognized the company's commercial character by allowing it to be liquidated by an auditor appointed by the Civil Court.[22]

THE SECRET NETWORK,
JULY 1848–JUNE 1849

If consumer cooperatives were only peripherally political, *chambrées* were quintessentially political. Unlike the *chambrées* of Provence or eastern France, the *chambrées* of Lyon (and Paris) were direct descendants of the secret societies of the monarchy.[23] Consequently, they benefited from the organizational experimentation of the monarchy and began as formal, relatively integrated entities. Following the national elections and especially the inception of the club law, political activists withdrew from the dwindling, closely watched clubs to resuscitate secret societies. In the summer of 1848 Commissioner Galerne's reports mention the Family, the Rights of Man, the Reformed Carbonari (which had functioned as a security force and a club in the revolution), and the radical masonic lodge (now known as the Friends of Man). Although he misinterpreted an informal gathering of old Family members as a reorganizational meeting, he soon realized his mistake. Similarly, he came to see the Reformed Carbonari and the Friends of Man as small and secondary. However, in the case of the Rights of Man, he correctly perceived the resurrection of an important political infrastructure.

The individuals named by Commissioner Galerne are familiar from the secret societies of the monarchy and the clubs and committees of the revolution. Bernard-Barret, Castel, Murat, and Vincent had been in the Rights of Man in 1840 (and Castel came from the tailors' society of 1837). Benoit, Edant, Greppo, Grinand, and Juif had belonged to the Equals in 1840, while Benoit and Grangy can be traced back to the Flowers of 1837. Curtet and Razuret had been dissident Icarians since 1844; Vindry was a Reformed Carbonari. Furthermore, Cautel-Baudet, Charavey, and Vindry had presided over the Central Democratic Club and nearly half of the thirty-four named individuals had been active in the Central Democratic Club. Nearly two-thirds had sat on the Central Committee. Table 12 provides a more detailed breakdown of their political and economic antecedents. Since Galerne watched for known leaders, he named mainly bourgeois and petty bourgeois leaders, but he insisted that the rank and file were workers, especially silk workers.[24]

Repressing clubs had the paradoxical but predictable effect of driving militants from overt to covert political endeavours – the very development the authorities feared. The history of Lyon's *chambrées* over the next six months confirms the reciprocal relationship between *chambrées* and clubs/electoral committees. Attendance at the private assemblies rose when the public clubs/committees retrenched and fell when the clubs/committees were full. Although the neobabouvist, Charavey, the Fourierist, Juif, and a few other habitués of *chambrées* propagandized at the clubs on a regular basis, most only frequented the clubs during the election campaigns, when leaders of the secret societies stepped forward to form the democratic-socialist committees. In the presidential campaign, half the members of the Socialist Democrats' Committee and just under half the members of the Progressive Democrats' Committee had previously been identified by Galerne as participants in private political meetings. As electoral committees folded after each campaign, members

TABLE 12
Economic and Political Antecedents of Secret Society
Members

Period	Activity	Number
Monarchy	Insurrections	4
	Mutual aid societies	5
	Occupational circles	2
	Commerce Verdique	2
	Fourierists	6
	Secret societies, 1830s	7
	Rights of Man, 1840	4
	Equals	5
	Dissident Icarians	2
	Workers' and radical press	6
Revolution	Central Committee	21
	Work Committee	10
	Suburban committees	8
	Central Democratic Club	16
	National Guard	5
	Voraces	3

Source: ADR, M, Police générale, Rapports journaliers, 18 July–28 December 1848

flowed back to their clandestine groups, where they maintained the democratic-socialist alliance between elections.[25]

During the state of siege, the military seized the papers of the most important secret society. Their dossier on the Society for the Rights of Man offers a rare opportunity to verify Commissioner Galerne's reports. As might be expected, the reports exaggerate but do not seriously distort the society's general purpose and specific efforts.

Shortly after the National Assembly elections of April 1848, and after the Society for the Rights of Man was reconstituted in the capital, the society reemerged in Lyon. Although it predated the club law, it foresaw the need for secrecy and retained its clandestine structure, screening procedures, and oaths to assure loyalty. It subdivided into sections of fifteen to thirty members who were not, in theory, to know who belonged to other sections. Sections elected a Central Committee to coordinate their joint activities. To join a candidate had to be sponsored by two members who would vouch for his "morality," be examined by two other members, and be approved by all but one member. An approved candidate had to swear "to do everything I can to make non-member citizens understand and adopt the principles enunciated in the Declaration of the Rights of Man." Dues were five centimes weekly plus five francs monthly (they had trouble collecting the latter). The sections met weekly for "moral and political edification."[26]

In three months, the number of sections increased from twenty-one to fifty, although many sections did not have fifteen members. By the end of October, when Galerne reported thirty sections meeting in one evening, over 360 members voted in a new Central Committee. The editor of *Le Censeur*, Murat, received 266 votes; two typographers, Cautel-Baudet and Bernard-Barret, got 307 and 224 votes, and two others had 195 and 189 votes. Incomplete membership lists support the commissioner's contention that the rank and file were workers but indicate that the Central Committees were more artisanal and petty bourgeois than he believed. In seven months the society raised 835 francs and spent most of it on publication of 2,050 copies of the constitution, 2,000 copies of the Declaration of the Rights of Man, unspecified pamphlets, election campaigns, and banquets (the remainder went for sick relief and funeral expenses for members).[27] Presumably one of the pamphlets was Gabriel Charavey's evaluation of the constitution, since Charavey was a member, the constitution was one of the society's concerns, and his pamphlet was definitely subsidized. In a classic democratic-socialist statement, Charavey denounced the "purely political" constitution for failing to organize work and for ignoring workers' needs.[28]

Following the disastrous presidential campaign, the society became more aggressive. First, it sponsored a pamphlet condemning the president politically and personally. Next, some prominent members contributed to a promising new propaganda device, an *Almanach démocratique et sociale des clubs lyonnais de 1849*. While their written contributions were temperate – they include Vincent's speech assuring peasants that democratic-socialists did not want to destroy property and the family – other articles were provocative. The editor was Maurin-Béraud, the neobabouvist who had seized the seminary for the Democratic Society in March 1848. True to his principles, Maurin-Béraud reprinted an old Buonarroti piece praising the Hébertists (radical revolutionaries of 1794, who supported the terror, economic controls, etc.) and documents on Babeuf's conspiracy. The society also published the tract that initiated the campaign to win the military vote in the Legislative Assembly elections. Although the tract discouraged confrontation, it was threatening to Marshal Bugeaud, who dreaded attempts to indoctrinate the troops.[29]

Behind the new aggressive stance lay a new solidarity. As the clubs shut down after 10 December, *chambrées* and *cercles* sprang up so suddenly that the confused police theorized about two almost mythic secret societies, the Vauteurs and the Ventre-creux, perhaps because a pamphlet linked these societies to the Voraces. By mid-January 1849, the police commissioner recognized that the circles were new sections of the Rights of Man/Republican Solidarity set up by former Provisional Government Commissioner Martin-Bernard, Representative Greppo, and other members of the Mountain. Until Greppo and six other emissaries from the Mountain visited Lyon in the second half of January, the sections were divided between the bourgeois republicans of the Progressive Democrats' Committee and the more proletarian Socialist Democrats' Committee. The emissaries unified most of the sections around *Le Républicain* and a Provisional Committee. For about a month the only signs of the Provisional Committee were brochures sent to soldiers and advice to radicals to stay away from the statue of the "Man of the People" during that dispute.[30]

Lyon, however, was one of the first and most significant outposts in the Republican Solidarity's crusade to unite the Left and convert the countryside for the Legislative Assembly elections.[31] Behind the scenes the Provisional Committee completed the work of unification and corresponded with Montagnards in surrounding departments, urging them to organize sections and promising them free publications for "peaceful propaganda." They also planned the banquet commemorating the February revolution and designated the Central Democratic Committee that directed the Legislative Assembly campaign.[32] From mid-March to mid-May, the sections collaborated with the clubs in distributing electoral posters and publications in the countryside. When the police harassed clubs, many sections converted into electoral committees to campaign openly. At this time, the Rights of Man/Solidarity was centred in Croix-Rousse and composed principally of silk workers and secondarily of tailors and shoemakers. It maintained such good relations with the Voraces and Mutualists that the latter broke their tradition of avoiding politics by donating forty francs to the radical campaign.[33]

The wide contacts and general militance of the Rights of Man worried the authorities. Early in March the police raided the homes of Bernard-Barret, Castel, Cautel-Baudet, Murat, and other members of the Central Committee, but confiscated only one pistol, one National Guard sword, one Declaration of the Rights of Man, and some brochures. The searches were repeated five weeks later with equally disappointing results. By the beginning of May, the panicky police commissioner claimed that there were 30,000 socialists in the metropolis (an underestimation if we count all those who would vote democratic-socialist). Although he realized that the "demagogic party" was relying on an electoral victory, he cautioned that some sections, especially in Croix-Rousse, were prepared to take up hidden arms. On the eve of the vote, he added that the Voraces had sworn to kill Marshal Bugeaud.[34] The "victor of June" moved in regiments from neighbouring departments and prepared to attack the city if the "reds" won a nation-wide victory. Only the news that most of France had voted "white" induced him to set these plans aside.[35] Meanwhile, the Central Committee of the Rights of Man publicized this warning: "Citizens, everything suggests victory ... The enemies of the Republic, defeated at the polls, seem to want to foment disorders ... Let all democrats be calm and dignified."[36]

A warning was necessary, because some democratic-socialists were excited, even arrogant, about their electoral victory. For two days after the announcement of the metropolitan vote, the suburbs celebrated and the Voraces held emergency sessions. Even after the returns from conservative regions came in, weavers in Croix-Rousse remained so insolent to merchants' clerks that many clerks refused to check on orders in that suburb.[37] The urban returns caused a "veritable panic" in the business community, with the stock exchange registering a steep decline, gold disappearing into private safes, and the silk market "completely paralysed." Some bourgeois families moved out of the city. To heighten reactionaries' anxiety, Marshal Bugeaud was elected from another department and left after learning the national results. Reactionaries had little faith in Bugeaud's successor, General Gemeau, whom they remembered as a republican general during the revolution, when the military command did little to stop the Voraces and luddites.[38]

As the generally conservative results became known, silk merchants resumed their purchases and silk weavers returned to their abundant spring orders. When the situation stabilized, the Republican Solidarity resolved to step up its propaganda, staying within the law until the "great day."[39] They started, as always, with a victory banquet. Although advertised only one day in advance, the banquet attracted 3,000 people, including representatives from Rive-de-Gier and other radical towns in the area. The Solidarity was determined to maintain the network generated by the election. They increased the circulation of *Le Républicain* to 10,000 copies and appealed to workers' *corporations* to buy shares in the newspaper as well as to subscribe. They still sent free copies to soldiers and received requests from delegates in villages like Crémieux, in the Isère, for free subscriptions to help them proselytize.[40]

After the election, radicals all over France censured France's armed intervention in the Roman Republic. Communications from the Parisian to the Lyonnais Solidarity switched from sporadic efforts to cool passions to regular directives to hold emergency sessions. The Lyonnais hardly needed encouragement. The clubs which had faltered after the election revived as they, and the democratic-socialist press, aimed a constant barrage of criticism at the government. Speeches in the clubs and editorials in *Le Républicain* and *Le Peuple Souverain* urged the Mountain to impeach the president and assured them that, if impeachment failed, they had the backing of "twelve million ardent and devoted citizens, always ready to die to defend you." Twice the Voraces, and probably other secret societies, held emergency sessions. Late in May, the police broke up six sessions; on 11 June, they only observed, because by then

Commissioner Galerne was exceedingly worried about the next few days.[41]

After the months of simply sustaining the democratic-socialist alliance had culminated in the disastrous presidential campaign, the Rights of Man, prodded by the Republican Solidarity, organized a triumphant campaign for the Legislative Assembly. From January through May of 1849, the system of small, anonymous sections synchronized by a secret committee that had evolved under the monarchy, complemented by the republican innovation of public clubs coordinated by the same committee operating openly, functioned as an efficient political machine. Furthermore, the two-tiered arrangement kept the peace, for the democratic-socialists refused to be distracted from their primary objective by Bugeaud's taunts. Only after they attained their electoral goal, and after their Parisian and Vorace allies began to agitate, did they adopt a menacing tone.

INSURRECTION, 15 JUNE 1849

On 12 June, the Legislative Assembly rejected the bill to impeach the president, whereupon Ledru-Rollin and other leaders of the Mountain hesitantly threatened to resort to force. The next day, they issued a manifesto and call to arms, yet at the same time organized a peaceful demonstration. The Parisian populace remained indifferent, partly because many were debilitated by the cholera raging in the working-class districts and perhaps also because many were deterred by memories of the harsh repression a year before. On the 13th, no more than eight thousand demonstrators assembled, only to be dispersed, with more than necessary bloodshed, by the army. Although minor disturbances occurred in many towns in the southeast, the only other major outbreak happened in Lyon,[42] or more precisely, in Croix-Rousse. The Croix-Rousseans were not suffering from cholera, nor had they experienced a brutal military reprisal in the preceding year. If the leaders who had so recently threatened popular revolt preferred to wait for a definite signal from the capital, the Voraces and less sophisticated members of the rank and file rushed forward to defend the red republic. They encountered the army they had humiliated in February 1848, now prepared, indeed dedicated, to humbling their old opponents.

Even as the Parisian demonstration disintegrated, the Lyonnais agitation accelerated. Late in the afternoon of 13 June, *Le Censeur* published a special edition with a report of the French army's defeat and retreat from Rome. Murat did not fabricate the report, just took it from Turin's republican newspaper without checking for accuracy. The prefect's behaviour was more irresponsible. Tourangin had in his possession letters which disproved the defeat, yet did not release them until the following day, when he appended them to the inflammatory communiqué about the Assembly's rejection of the bill to impeach the president. Until then, the false information spread and evoked a great deal of interest. That evening, one Croix-Rousse club admitted 600 people to its meeting about the events in Italy.[43]

On the morning of 14 June, *Le Républicain* and *Le Peuple Souverain* reprinted the Turin article and added their own articles exhorting soldiers to help them defend the constitution. That afternoon, as the public learned the truth about Rome and the impeachment vote, rumours about a revolt in the capital began circulating. Hundreds of people converged on the Hôtel de ville and the Prefecture demanding news of Paris and yelling "*Vive la Montagne!*" Tourangin, who had no more news, dispatched 600 soldiers to the courtyard of the Hôtel de ville and 500 more to the square in front of the Prefecture to disperse them. The outnumbered crowd did not resist so no one was hurt in this first engagement.[44]

Finally, the leaders of the Republican Solidarity stepped into the spotlight. Unhappily, their performance was almost as ambiguous as the Mountain's one day earlier. At about six P.M., Castel, Grinand, Juif, the directors of *Le Républicain* and *Le Peuple Souverain*, and a few other members of the Solidarity went to the Prefecture to ask Tourangin if he had received a telegram telling of a coup. Tourangin said no, but some delegates may have doubted him, given his delay in releasing the letters from Italy and his predecessor's stalling tactics in February 1848. Castel, Juif, and Faures returned to the *Peuple Souverain* office to await further news; Grinand accompanied the director of *Le Républicain* to dinner, then to the *Républicain* office at 9 P.M. In that three-hour interval, Director Burel later claimed, one of his editors (the United Industries bookkeeper) had composed a telegram proclaiming a convention and signed "the Democratic-Socialist Electoral Committee of Paris," and had printed and distributed copies. The editor-bookkeeper, Deschaud, confirmed this story from his exile – and immunity – in Lausanne. However, other members of the deputation and the military court reasoned that Burel must have collaborated in the preparation, if not the execution, of this provocation. Burel certainly sympathized with its intent, for the next day he (and the director of *Le Peuple Souverain*) published a message from the Mountain calling for an armed uprising and announcing fighting in the capital. They took the message from a Parisian correspondent's letter, dated 13 June.[45]

Once the radicals had a cue from the capital, they acted promptly yet peacefully. On reading Deschaud's telegram, the Voraces and the clubs sitting in emergency sessions spilled out into the streets and made the familiar, by now almost automatic trek down to the Hôtel de ville in Lyon. Along the way, they gathered spectators, until fifteen to eighteen thousand people had crammed into the square in front of the Hôtel de ville and the narrow streets feeding into the square. So far the crowd merely shouted slogans like "*Vive la République démocratique et sociale!*" and departed when troops came to clear the area. As they left, many promised to return better prepared, though few did, and only to display their dead.[46] Henceforth all the action was in the old quarters and the suburbs.

That same evening, 14 June, smaller bands assembled in the main square of Croix-Rousse. Some followed red flags; others boasted a few armed escorts, but all remained orderly. One of the larger bands left the commune for the Veterinary School in the old quarters, where they insisted that the students, many of whom were sympathetic to the radicals, join their demonstration. The school had no protection, so the principal acquiesced after a few minutes. Many students fell in, marched to Croix-Rousse, consulted with radicals, and returned to their college. At 6 A.M., in an obviously prearranged manoeuvre, someone in Croix-Rousse beat the *rappel* and hundreds mustered at the Mountain Club and Jandard Club/Voraces café. Counting the supporters they picked up en route to the Veterinary School, they numbered 1,000 to 1,200. Since the principal had called in 150 soldiers and refused to open the compound, the crowd scaled the walls around the school and disarmed the soldiers with very little opposition. Some students and even soldiers accompanied the partly armed crowd back to Croix-Rousse, where they disarmed two small military posts at the jail and Town Hall. By 10 A.M. on the 15th, ten of the participants, all political neophytes, had constituted a provisional municipal committee at Town Hall.[47]

The absence of opposition up to this point, the hope that the soldiers would uphold the constitution, and likely memories of the army's passivity in February 1848 deceived the insurgents. General Gemeau did not deserve the reactionaries' distrust: he had dispatched all units to their riot stations. When insurgents approached a station in the Croix-Rousse fortifications, yelling "*Vive la ligne, l'armée est à nous!*", the officer in charge refused them admittance; when they became angry, he ordered a volley which felled many of them and scattered the rest. Over the next few hours there were desultory exchanges, while the infantry awaited the artillery and the rebels erected barricades across the Grande rue and fifteen other arteries leading into the commune. The bombardment began at 1 P.M. and took two hours to level the barricade over the Grande rue and six hours to blast through all the barriers. After each barrier collapsed, soldiers "mopped up" along the streets and alleys behind it. Most rebels who tried to escape into the countryside encountered a girdle of patrols around the suburb. Many were taken prisoner.[48]

General Gemeau had applied Bugeaud's strategy for suppressing rebellions as developed for the June Days and adapted for Lyon. His objective was to confine and stop the fighting before it escalated into a full-scale rebellion; his means were a massive display of force in most of the metropolis and artillery fire in the rebel suburb. Two divisions of the Army of the Alps were quick-marched toward Lyon; a battalion of infantry, two batteries of artillery, and a company of dragoons occupied Bellecour square; another battalion guarded the Prefecture; a third battalion and three other companies protected the Hôtel de ville. Four and a half battalions and eight cannon were deployed against Croix-Rousse; half attacked from the city, the other half approached from the rear. The two-front operation inflicted a terrible beating on this "foyer of revolt." The Jandard Club/Voraces café was completely demolished; several buildings on the Grande rue were seriously damaged; cannon balls pierced over one hundred buildings and nearly all the shop windows on the main streets were shattered. The human cost was equally high. Twenty-five civilians and twenty-one soldiers lost their lives; at least seventy-one were wounded and seven to eight hundred "suspects" were arrested.[49]

There were half-hearted and belated efforts to help the embattled insurgents. In the city, a group led by a veterinary student tried to raid a gun shop and two gangs invaded churches to ring the tocsin. Police and infantry restrained them. In Guillotière and Vaise, radicals beat the *rappel*, formed columns, and searched for arms; one contingent actually left Vaise for Croix-Rousse. The huge, obedient Guillotière garrison discouraged Guillotière columns; artillery units on the boundaries of Croix-Rousse kept the Vaise contingent from entering the besieged commune. Something similar happened to the reinforcements from their allies in Rive-de-Gier in the Loire. After hearing of the fighting, radicals there formed a column, sacked an armory, and marched toward the metropolis on the night of 15 June. Sighting an artillery unit on the periphery, they sent scouts ahead and turned back on learning that the revolt had been crushed. Montagnards in other towns influenced by the Lyonnais solidarity – Macon and Tournus in the Saône-et-Loire, Vienne and smaller silk-weaving villages in the Isère – tried blocking the departure of troops. Troops from Vienne had to dismantle three barricades on the road to Lyon.[50]

If General Gemeau had successfully contained the rebellion, he had not kept it from being the largest rebellion in 1849. Whereas the nationally known deputies of the Mountain had inspired only six to eight thousand demonstrators, the locally known leaders of the Lyonnais Solidarity had induced fifteen to eighteen thousand to demonstrate and several thousand to defend their commune. From one perspective, the response was a tribute to the success of the radical leaders who had proselytized in their communities and disciplined their working-class followers. Workers who had heeded the cautious advice of the clubs one year earlier now accepted the aggressive posture of secret societies. From another perspective, the response raised questions about the culpability of leaders who incited violence in a city surrounded by an army – even if they had some reason to expect certain regiments to defect. The military tribunals found fourteen members of the Solidarity guilty of inciting violence, but only three guilty of fighting, which suggests that they were irresponsible.[51]

A glance at who did not instigate or fight in the rebellion helps to answer the perplexing question of why radicals who had so long forsworn violence and so often prevented conflict would encourage or engage in such a hopeless battle. First, it is noteworthy that the leaders of Lyonnais communism and socialism were not among the instigators or combatants. Benoit, Doutre, Greppo, and Pelletier were in Paris, where they were not incriminated in the *journée* of 13 June. Only Deputy Commissaire, who had been politicized by the Rights of Man demonstrations in 1840, *not* by reading communist propaganda, went into exile.[52] Similarly, most prominent prerevolutionary neobabouvists were absent, like Felix Blanc, or abstained from the agitation, like Edant. The notable exceptions, the exiles Grinand and the Fourierist, Juif, had merely inquired about events at the Prefecture and been innocent victims of the telegram plot. As the most visible democratic-socialist leaders, they certainly had reason to go into exile, for police arrested many club and committee leaders on speculation that they must have been involved. Bernard-Barret, Castel, and others who had been radicalized by the Rights of Man demonstrations of 1840, then had joined the *Censeur* campaigns for reform, seem to have been playing the *Censeur* role in February 1848. Their wait-and-see attitude suggests that they had no intention of initiating anything until the local authorities capitulated, as in February 1848. It was the revolutionary recruits to radicalism, Burel and Deschaud, who fabricated and printed the false telegram. Few of these men were visible after the demonstration at City Hall, the last obvious parallel to February 1848.[53] Some radical leaders were following a familiar revolutionary script, almost ritualistically, *until* other actors deviated from the script.

As for Rights of Man combatants, only Bert(h)ault was a neobabouvist. Since Bert(h)ault had joined the peaceful, propagandistic Communist Workers of Lyon after his trial as a Reformed Carbonari in 1844, he may have used the more acceptable, public group as a temporary refuge in a period of police pressure. Just as old members of the Rights of Man had some background in street agitation, the Reformed Carbonari had a tradition of conspiracy and experience in a paramilitary organization as a security force in 1848. The two other members of the Rights of Man who "mounted the barricades" were (so far as can be determined) neophytes among the radical leadership. One joined in the disarming of a military post in his neighborhood and then defended his neighborhood; a fifty-one year-old café operator followed most of his customers into battle. Most of these were Voraces.[54] Three other café operators, who had no connection with the Rights of Man, also catered to Voraces or Carbonari.[55] If we look beyond the Rights of Man and café operators (always represented among alleged insurgents in Croix-Rousse), we find dozens of revolutionary recruits to radicalism. The only identifiable group was the Voraces. Eight Voraces, including Perret *dit Sans Rancune* (leader in March 1848), were convicted as insurgents because of their association with the march to the Veterinary School, the attacks on military posts, and the provisional communal committee.[56] They also copied revolutionary models, but their models were the revolutionary crowds of February 1848. The constitution of a provisional committee was also reminiscent of the Rhône Volunteers' alternative government in 1831.

The solution to the puzzle presented by the apparent spectacle of mature, experienced democratic-socialists inciting a poorly armed population to fight an army is that few of the men who had eschewed revolutionary for evolutionary change did precipitate or participate in the revolt. The more recently politicized, less sophisticated Voraces, seconded by the Carbonari and a few old Rights of Man members, instigated and fought in the insurrection. As a result of their experience as a paramilitary unit, and especially their seizure of the forts without serious resistance or reprisals in February 1848, the Voraces had unrealistic expectations in regard to their own prowess and their opponents' will.

If the radicals of 1848 deserve reproach for fanning false hopes about the possibility of revolution, the government deserves most of the blame for creating a climate of opinion in which revolution seemed the only way to achieve political change. Restricting the rights of association and free speech and repressing all open forums for the expression of political dissent caused discontent yet deprived dissenters of legal outlets to express their discontent. More specifically, Tourangin's slow and provocative response to the false report of the army's defeat at Rome let the crisis escalate into rebellion.

The people prosecuted for fighting the rebellion bear a striking resemblance to the insurgents of 1834. Once again, over one-third were silk weavers; nearly one-third were other workers, and one-sixth were petty bourgeois, particularly café owners. (Ten soldiers were prosecuted for their part in the rebellion; the rest of the deserters were shot on sight.)[57] As in 1834, about 70 per cent were under thirty-five years of age and nearly 60 per cent had immigrated to the metropolis (see table 3).

However, the insurrection of 1849 differed in three respects. First, it engaged fewer people. One acute observer believed that many sympathetic *canuts* avoided the battle because they remembered the repression of the previous insurrection.[58] One suspects that many radicals remained aloof for the same reason. Second, the Voraces played a more prominent role than the Ferrandiniers in 1834 or the Rhône Volunteers in 1831. Third, the insurrection of 1849 was more political. Whereas the insurgents of 1834 had reacted to a specific act threatening the existence of their associations, the insurgents of 1849 mobilized in anticipation of an attack on the constitution to protect the red republic. By taking the initiative against an impending constitutional threat, the Voraces proved that journeymen had been politicized by the revolution and the post-revolutionary resistance to repression.

CHAPTER SEVEN

State of Siege,
June 1849–
December 1851

After the insurrection the government declared a state of siege in Paris, Lyon, and adjacent departments in the Sixth Military Division, thereby placing these areas under the jurisdiction of the military courts and investing all administrative powers in the local military commander.[1] In Lyon, the military tribunals (called War Councils) spent seven months trying accused insurgents and devoted five more months to cases arising from the insurrection. Because Lyonnais authorities believed that the population remained "in the grip of revolutionaries" and did not trust civilian courts, the government did not lift martial law at the same time as it did in Paris, so that military tribunals judged civilians charged with political crimes through 1851.[2] General Gemeau made extensive use of his authorization "to take any measure to assure order": he closed cooperatives, clubs, and all the cafés, cabarets, and brothels in Croix-Rousse; suspended *Le Censeur*, the only republican newspaper not silenced by the flight or imprisonment of its staff, and prohibited the peddling of newspapers, pamphlets, or books. He insisted that the police report directly to him, rather than through the normal channel, the prefect. Tourangin, who resigned after the insurrection, was replaced by a more tractable Orleanist, Darcy.[3]

Repression intensified after Louis Napoleon broke with republican forms by appointing an extraparliamentary ministry on 31 October 1849. The new ministry imposed restrictions on the municipal franchise and implemented a more systematic suppression of democratic-socialist propaganda. New Lyonnais officials launched a sweeping offensive against the remnants of the radical movement.[4] First, an extraordinary commissioner to the Sixth Military Division was empowered to ensure "public safety" in the Rhône and adjoining departments. The appointee was the dean of the prefectural corps, a long-time Orleanist prefect, De la Coste. His arrival coincided with a cluster of press trials that finally eliminated all but one of the reopened radical organs, including the venerable *Censeur*. In his first month alone, De la Coste banned twenty-eight radical brochures, almanachs, and periodicals. Allegations that General Gemeau was not vigilant enough against moderate republicans compelled his transfer in May 1850. His successor, General Castellane, not only supervised the police but regularly intervened in their affairs.[5]

Because the military and judicial authorities concentrated on Lyon, the state of siege was more effective there than in the rural areas of the Sixth Military Division. Its prompt and forceful application restored business confidence so quickly and completely that the "momentary interruption" in silk orders was succeeded by brisk sales. For a year and a half after the insurrection, the *fabrique* flourished as rarely before and silk weavers enjoyed almost full employment. The business boom and employment rate reassured conservatives that the "age of disorders" was over.[6] Even when the silk market collapsed and half the looms shut down in the spring of 1851, Attorney-General Gilardin confidently, and correctly, reported that "our insurrections have always occurred in times of prosperity." This extremely cautious Bonapartist official informed his superiors that the repressive machinery was slowly but surely demobilizing the democratic-socialist movement.[7] Although tenacious radicals mounted a defence of their leaders at the trial of insurgents and retained their hold on the suburban councils, conspiratorial societies declined, as the falsely labelled "Lyon Plot" and the peaceful reception of the coup d'état revealed. During the plot and the coup, the only resistance was in some surrounding departments.

DEFENCE,
JUNE 1849–AUGUST 1850

For six months, the political life of Lyon revolved around the prosecution and defence of insurgents and, secondarily, election campaigns. A more intensive repression of radical activities, with very little resistance, dominated political life in the first half of 1850.

Since the community empathized with the imprisoned insurgents, the prosecution was hindered by a paucity of witnesses. The prosecutors were able to indict only 235 people from the metropolis and convict 133 of them; few sentences exceeded five years' incarceration. The problem was not a lenient court, as the frustrated attorney-general suggested. When the military tribunal could prove guilt or assume it owing to flight, they imposed heavy sanctions: one death penalty, one life imprisonment, and thirty-four deportations. But the prosecutors' staff had trouble finding compliant witnesses and their case was undermined when some witnesses retracted sworn statements.[8] Although no one physically intimidated informers, as had happened after the insurrection of 1834, neighbours ostracized them or subjected them to other forms of moral suasion.

Of course, the radicals at liberty came to the aid of their leaders in jail or in exile. The leaders corresponded with their followers through letters to the reviving radical newspapers. One hundred and fifty exiles in Switzerland wrote to *Le Censeur* when it resumed publication in August 1849, thanking Swiss democrats for their help and implicitly asking Lyonnais democrats for help. The Lyonnais held illegal lotteries and Grandperrin *dit* Laurier, a Vorace who had fled to Vevey in Switzerland, returned to France to smuggle the proceeds.[9] After Marius Chastaing left prison, he started a subscription for the refugees, prisoners, and their families. The military command, which had imprisoned Chastaing because his *Tribune Lyonnaise* was printed at the same shop as *Le Républicain*, permitted him to resume publication on condition that he submit each issue to the attorney-general twenty-four hours before delivery to the public. In spite of this constraint, he collected 3,400 francs and clothing for the refugees and prisoners.[10]

Other republican and democratic-socialist newspapers reappeared briefly and lent their assistance. Although *Le Censeur* appointed a moderate Surveillance Committee to supervise the editor, the newspaper survived only until December 1849. The official reason for closure was "insulting" the president, the Assembly, and religion; the real offence was defending the accused insurgents and editorializing on their trials. As the most affluent newspaper to take up the defendants' cause, *Le Censeur* paid most of the defence costs – much as the paper had done for political prisoners in the 1830s. Simultaneously, their editorials exposed the flimsiness of the prosecution's cases. In the last issue to reach the public, Murat pointed out that four of the thirty-two men charged with conspiracy (including Cautel-Baudet of the Rights of Man and Cornu of the Mutualists) had been tried solely because of their political pasts. All four were acquitted.[11]

Democratic-socialist newspapers did not endure to December. After the arrest of the management of *Le Peuple Souverain*, their Parisian correspondent, Gustave Naquet, returned to put out one issue under the old title before the military command forbade the newspaper. Naquet then published a satirical review called *L'Esope*, but a "modern fable" about red birds preyed upon by "birds of many feathers" induced closure after one issue. Naquet tried a monthly, which appeared twice and raised 500 francs for the prisoners, but after September 1849 he was so encumbered with fines and prison terms that he could no longer manage a newspaper.[12] *Le Républicain*'s successors were not as polished papers, because the exile or imprisonment of its editors meant printers had to edit. (They found other workers to act as directors of their seven papers. Some directors had been Voraces; some were members of the Reformed Carbonari.) For four months, this series of newspapers supported the defendants and upheld the right to work, the organization of work, and generally social reform along Fourierist or Cabetian lines. Their ideology prompted speedy trials, convictions, and suspensions until, early in 1850, the owner of the printing shop and all the directors had been condemned to large fines and long jail terms.[13]

In the last half of 1849, the police also searched street pedlars selling inexpensive printed material and arrested dozens with material "tending to trouble tranquillity." Numerous trials ensued.[14] By 1850, the extraordinary commissioner, De La Coste, was outlawing periodicals and pamphlets tolerated under the monarchy (*La Démocratie Pacifique* and *Qu'est-ce que la Propriété?*). In the course of that year, he and the military command banned sixty-one publications on the often dubious grounds that they were inflammatory. Police combed bookstores and homes for illegal printed matter; they closed one bookstore and confiscated 8,000 copies of "communist propaganda" at the home of the innocuous Icarian correspondent.[15] Like radicals elsewhere, groups tried forming joint-stock partnerships to raise money for the bond required of, and the fines expected by, democratic-socialist newspapers; unlike radicals operating under civil law, the Lyonnais were arrested before any newspaper appeared. Cautel-Baudet and sixteen others paid twenty-five to one hundred-franc fines and went to jail for up to two months for establishing "a clandestine agency to distribute forbidden books and newspapers" or merely publicizing "a project to publish a democratic-socialist newspaper."[16]

Individuals also came to the defence of the accused. By September 1849, Rémond (the Fourierist founder of Naudé and Company) and other radicals still at liberty organized a Defence Committee to provide free legal counsel. Three of Lyon's working-class deputies, Benoit, Doutre, and Greppo, returned to Lyon to raise money for legal fees. Later, attorneys Morellet and Alphonse Gent, a prominent member of the Republican Solidarity, argued the cases of the thirty-two men charged with conspiracy, They obtained acquittals for thirteen, including one editor and the printer of *Le Peuple Souverain*, and reduced sentences for five, including the other editor and the director of *Le Peuple Souverain*. Since they could do little for the thirteen tried in absentia, men like Burel of *Le Républicain*, Bernard-Barret, Grinand, Juif, and Vincent of the Rights of Man, received verdicts of deportation. Vincent eventually turned himself in and was acquitted,[17] but he and the fugitives were henceforth *hors de combat*.

Immediately after the insurrection, radicals who avoided prosecution engaged in electoral politics. Deputy Commissaire had left the country after the insurrection and had to be replaced. While most departments postponed by-elections until March 1850, the Rhône held its by-election on 8 July 1849. Apparently the administration expected to capitalize on the democratic-socialists' disorientation, for General Gemeau even exempted electoral meetings from the ban on public assemblies. Although a few democratic-socialists met in old club settings, they spent most of the time venting their frustrations about the repression. Fortunately, the *Censeur* republicans kept their wits and chose a compromise candidate, Jules Favre, to unify the Left. Despite misgivings about the moderate republican (who would be a *ministrable* under the Third Republic), the democratic-socialists helped distribute 25,000 campaign circulars, especially in the rural hinterland.[18] The Orleanists tried a similar strategy: they endorsed Rivet as the candidate "most likely to rally the various political nuances." The Bonapartists, who had rejected Rivet a year earlier, now accepted him as the moderate candidate with the most supporters, but the recalcitrant legitimists remained faithful to Mortemart and criticized their former allies.[19]

Instead of exploiting democratic-socialist weakness, the administration helped the debilitated radicals to recuperate. The election revealed that the first blast of repression had frightened and united the Left but reassured and divided the Right. Predictably, the candidate of the united factions won: Favre received 41,334 ballots, Rivet 27,391, and Mortemart 11,739. Attorney-General Gilardin took some comfort from the fact that Favre got 30,000 fewer votes than Commissaire two months earlier. The Bonapartist organ, *Le Salut Public*, drew the fateful conclusion that the moderates should try to attract "the segments of the working class that wavers" in its support of the red republic.[20]

Within a week, the prefect called municipal elections in Croix-Rousse because he was dissatisfied with the council's sympathy for the accused insurgents, among them some councillors. Once again the democratic-socialists sponsored electoral meetings and denounced the authorities. After two weeks of arresting offending speakers, General Gemeau refused permission for any more electoral meetings. Even without a public forum, the democratic-socialists reelected a majority of the old council. The Bonapartists, seeking some consolation, noted that there were eight more moderates than on the preceding council; indeed, an Orleanist councillor returned after an absence of a year and a half from the council. The thirteen conservatives were nevertheless outnumbered by fifteen radicals, including still-imprisoned radicals like Guillermin (manager of Naudé and Company) and Rey (a café operator and *père* of the Voraces).[21]

The insurrection induced, and the Croix-Rousse election impelled, a bill to fuse the urban and suburban governments and transfer the administration of all police to the prefect. After the previous insurrection, the government had proposed incorporating the suburbs and centralizing the police, but the local governments had vetoed all except the Central Police commissioner's post. Now too, local councils protested the loss of communal liberties: the urban council objected to loss of jurisdiction over the police; the suburban councils opposed absorption and higher *octrois*. The irrepressibly radical council in Guillotière complained about the "political motivations behind the proposal," specifically, "easier domination of ... the eminently democratic spirit" in the suburbs. The Assembly did not place the political and criminal police under the prefect until June 1851; the government delayed administrative unification until after the coup d'état.[22]

Orleanists and legitimists had expressed reservations about incorporating the suburbs, for they feared that suburban voters would elect a communist council. The Bonapartists, who had faith in their popular base and their electoral machine, had fewer reservations. All conservatives applauded the restrictions on the municipal franchise introduced in the autumn of 1849, because they felt that limiting eligibility to legal residents and ratepayers would reduce the radicals' working-class constituency. To their dismay, the new regulations did not loosen the radicals' grip on the Lyonnais suburbs.[23]

During Louis Napoleon's official visit to Lyon in the summer of 1850, the Guillotière council voted by a narrow margin to boycott the welcoming ceremony. Conservative members submitted a joint resignation; the right-wing press raised a hue and cry, and the prefect called an election in the hope of replacing this difficult council. By holding banquets and importing deputies Greppo and Bernard Raspail to combat apathy about the third municipal election in three years, the radical coalition aroused their dedicated supporters. Although legitimists reinforced their campaign against lay education with attacks on individual lay teachers, other conservatives did nothing. Only one-third of the reduced electorate bothered to vote; the radical voters in working-class sections returned the left-wing majority; the bourgeois sections in Brotteaux returned the conservative minority, and the debate over subsidies to the religious schools continued. When the majority rejected a motion to resume subsidies a few months later, the prefect revoked the council again. The 1851 election strengthened the radicals' hold on the council to thirty-two of thirty-five seats and the large turnout (half the 7,632 electors) served notice that the radical voting block was not an isolated group in the new electorate.[24] The frustrated prefect called no more elections before the coup, which ended the administrative independence of the suburban communes.

The attorney-general's reports on the "political spirit" of the suburban population corroborate the democratic-socialist sway. In December 1849, Gilardin recorded that "to be a socialist here is a sort of profession of faith, in conformity with which one regulates relationships and conduct from the workshop to the secret society session to the barricades. Too little time has passed for this mania to recede." A month later, he astutely assessed the reasons for this fanaticism: "there is little professional diversity in the Lyonnais working population; a strong class and party discipline reigns here as a result of old strike habits." In the summer of 1850, he wrote of "two parties in ardent opposition" because of a population "troubled by twenty years of industrial conflict."[25] By the next summer, he assumed that abundant work and arrests of radical leaders had brought some "amelioration." He remained confident through 1851 due to the trial of a secret society network and other societies' reversion to parliamentarism.[26]

These excerpts from the attorney-general's reports summarize the geographic and economic foundations of Lyonnais radicalism. They pinpoint the independent suburban communes dominated by workers in an industry notorious for its strikes, insurrections, and, more generally, its highly developed class conflict. He did not comment upon the demographic, social, and political bases of the radical movement: the break with tradition through migration, the absence of a paternalistic elite to mediate class conflict, and the presence of workers dedicated to radical propaganda and organization. But Attorney-General Gilardin did not omit any of the measures taken to demolish the radical periodicals, societies, and networks. The mass arrests and closures of June–July 1849, the constant observation of radicals, their cafés and cooperatives, and the obsessive search for a regional secret society are all minutely recorded. As the reports register the loss of one democratic-socialist leader, organ, and organization after another, it becomes evident that the cumulative effect of arrests, trials, imprisonments, and vigilant surveillance was the dismantling of the democratic-socialist infrastructure constructed over twenty years.

DEMOBILIZATION, JUNE 1849–DECEMBER 1851

John Merriman has ably documented the relentless repression of urban economic and political dissent and the pursuit of every lead about clandestine organizations in the waning years of the Second Republic. In Lyon, the process was complicated by the variety of voluntary societies and the discovery of a secret coordinating network throughout south-eastern France. Nevertheless, Attorney-General Gilardin eliminated or intimidated every local society, arrested radical "contacts" throughout the southeast, and arranged a trial of the alleged conspirators before Lyon's military tribunal. The "Lyon Plot" trial finished any lingering resistance to the emerging police state.

In Lyon, cooperatives which strayed from narrowly industrial or commercial concerns to question the status quo were instantly closed. Before the insurrection, the Fraternal and Laborious Association of Shoe- and Boot-Makers issued a provocative prospectus: "We appeal to all Democratic-Socialists. ... Individualism is our enemy ... Far from having annual dividends, our profits will be capitalized indefinitely and will serve the general cause ... Courage! soon there will be neither exploiters nor exploited." After the insurrection, the military command delayed the opening of this political association for six months, and, when it opened, police shut it down. They terminated another cooperative after communist and Fourierist members clashed over equal versus graduated pay. The sixteen other producers' associations observed these events and prudently avoided political complications until they too were dissolved during the coup d'état.[27]

In this climate, apolitical consumer cooperatives multiplied. On the one hand, schisms in old consumer cooperatives resulted in new establishments. The autumn of 1849 saw three shareholders in the French Industries and two shareholders in the Democratic Association found a Workers' Union in Croix-Rousse. Next, Guillermin and Bacot, who had been ousted from Naudé and Company because they were implicated in the insurrection, set up the French Society, Dumas and Company in Croix-Rousse. Both establishments survived until the coup. Late in 1850, shareholders in Naudé and Company who lived in Vaise incorporated as the United Workers of the West of Lyon. Although their constitution stated that fees would be used "to the profit of the democratic and social cause," the United Workers eschewed politics and therefore endured to December 1851.[28]

On the other hand, a new type of consumer cooperative foreshadowed the cooperatives of the Second Empire. The five associations incorporated in the first half of 1850 stipulated that they would split into independent branches once they reached a certain size, usually a modest sixty to eighty members. This limitation, and clauses in their constitutions prohibiting political discussion, made them more acceptable to the authorities than earlier consumer cooperatives. The most prosperous new association, the Fraternal Society of Beavers, persisted as a collective purchasing arrangement after 1851. This society exhibited the distinguishing features of the tractable cooperatives encouraged by the empire: it was decentralized into sixteen independent branches; it dispensed with paid intermediaries by having members work for free; it mandated equal holdings (one twenty-five franc share for each member).[29]

A handful of abortive strikes taught unions that industrial militancy would no longer be tolerated. Two months before the insurrection, construction workers had held out for the ten-hour day despite the arrest of forty-eight strikers and the prosecution of fourteen strike leaders. When they struck to retain ten hours the next spring (as construction work resumed after the winter lull), their strike collapsed after ten masons were sentenced to one week in jail. That summer, steam-boat builders walked out for the ten-hour day, but they too returned when courts sent six strikers to jail for two weeks to two months. In the following year, the preemptive arrest of the entire strike committee prevented any job action.[30]

If economic militants suffered, radical journalists and political activists bore the brunt of the repression. Everywhere law enforcement bureaucrats considered periodicals one of the Left's most powerful weapons; only in Lyon, where martial law remained in force, were they able to destroy local periodicals, bar imported newspapers, and close cafés where newspapers were read aloud.[31]

The June 1850 press law imposing higher bonds on political monthlies forced the one moderately radical organ still publishing in Lyon to resort to subterfuge. Marius Chastaing converted *La Tribune Lyonnaise* into a bimonthly, with one issue dealing with economic and social matters, the other treating of politics. Judicial officials saw through the ruse and prosecuted Chastaing as well as the legally responsible director. When the civil court respected the letter of the law and acquitted Chastaing (while sentencing the director to one month in jail and fining him two hundred francs), the attorney-general appealed. When the Appellate Court reversed the lower court, Chastaing contested his conviction. The newspaper appeared as long as the court proceedings continued, but the editorials took on an uncharacteristically pessimistic tone: "*L'Echo de la Fabrique* was the first newspaper, even in Paris, to inaugurate the proletarian press; *La Tribune Lyonnaise* is the last." After winning his expensive appeal in February 1851, Chastaing stopped publishing the newspaper, which had lost 856 francs in its five years of existence.[32] This ended a twenty-year career as the most influential local democratic journalist.

With all avenues for open political activity blocked, the police focused on covert political activity. In the spring of 1850, they had arrested several Voraces and Mutualists but had not found enough evidence to press charges against the Voraces or convict the Mutualists. However, they had discovered documents that led them to the radical lodge of the Free Masons. Table 13 indicated that many members had come from the Mutualists, radical press, and secret societies of the monarchy, that almost as many had belonged to the clubs, militias, and

TABLE 13

Social Composition, Residence, and Antecedents of Radical Masons

Social composition	Silk workers	Petty bourgeois	Bourgeois
	12	3	3
Residence	Croix-Rousse	Lyon	Guillotière
	10	4	2
Antecedents in July monarchy	Mutualists	Commerce Verdique	Occupational circles
	4	2	3
	Radical press	Rights of Man, 1840	Other secret societies
	4	3	3
Revolutionary activities	Suburban councils	Clubs	Suburban guards
	5	4	3
Postrevolutionary affiliations	Suburban councils	Rights of Man	Fraternal associations
	6	3	3

Principal source: ADR, R, Insurrection du 1849, Saisie des journaux, dossier on Amis de l'Homme.

secret societies of the republic, and that the Friends of Man continued to be a force in the suburban councils and fraternal associations. The leader or "Venerable," Murat, and twelve others went to prison for six months to two years. Papers at Murat's home revealed that the Reformed Carbonari were regrouping without disclosing names. A year later, when a member of the Young Carbonari offered a suspiciously high reward for a lost insignia, a brothel keeper informed the police. They traced the hapless man and compiled evidence to send three Young Carbonari to prison for six months to two years.[33]

    While stiff sentences killed the Friends of Man lodge and subdued the Young Carbonari, the police worried about a regional coordinating society.[34] For half a year after June 1849, the Parisian Republican Solidarity had been chastened; once the state of siege was over in Paris, the Solidarity reactivated its campaign to capture the rural and military vote. The stunning success of democratic-socialist candidates in the March 1850 supplementary elections prompted the conservative majority in the Assembly to limit the national franchise. The law of 3 May 1850 introduced a three-year residency requirement which excluded and estimated 2,809,000 voters, many of them workers. Overall the law eliminated twenty-nine per cent of the previous electorate and nearly halved the electorate in large industrial cities like Lyon. In short, the law virtually taunted the Solidarity into conspiracy. Most of the Mountain, including most of the Rhône deputation, sensibly resisted temptation, but a minority, including Greppo, Faure, and Fond from the Rhône, formed a New Mountain to coordinate the secret societies proliferating in the provinces.[35]

The New Mountain inspired the attorney for the Lyonnais insurgents, Alphonse Gent, to travel through the southeast. During the summer and autumn of 1850, Gent took a series of trips from his home base in Lyon to other departments and Switzerland. His visits stimulated the clandestine organizations in the semi-rural departments and attracted the attention of the secret police. As excitement grew, secret police throughout the Sixth Military Division reported preparations for an insurrection. The Lyonnais police opened all letters addressed to Gent's inn until they had four letters which justified the arrest of Gent, his innkeeper, and three other local residents. Next, other police apprehended the correspondents, who were scattered all over the southeast. Searches of their homes implicated more people. By 6 November, sixty-three people had been indicted and twenty-three had been imprisoned in what was now designated the "Lyon Plot." Nine months later, Lyon's military court tried fifty-three: the original four, the journalist P. Delescluze from Paris, and the rest from cities and towns in the southeast.[36]

At the trial, the prosecution presented two sets of inconclusive evidence. One set consisted of letters and papers seized at defendants' homes. These documents indicate that Gent had received money from secret societies in the southeast, that these *chambrées* and *cercles* corresponded with one another, and that a few correspondents anticipated a struggle with the government. Accepting most of this evidence, the defence argued that the money was destined for political prisoners and exiles, that the societies corresponded in order to reconstitute the Mountain's electoral machine, and that their goals were to elect democratic-socialists and defend the constitution from "attack" by the authorities.[37]

The linchpin of the prosecution case was testimony from witnesses claiming that the network was plotting rebellion. The star witness had belonged to the Marseilles *chambrée* and had turned informer after losing his job, yet his damaging disclosures were second-hand. A less satisfactory witness was a professional police spy with hearsay revelations. Other witnesses were deserters from the army who had given depositions on their arrest; almost all the deserters recanted on the stand. Aware that the testimony could be challenged in civilian courts and distrustful of juries, Attorney-General Gilardin transferred the trial to the military courts. Michel de Bourges and the other Mountain deputies who made up the defence team objected to introducing this evidence, to no avail. When the colonel presiding over the court prevented them from cross-examining a key witness, the defence lawyers quit in disgust (and, since they publicized their resignations, scored a political point). Although the court appointed other attorneys, all but one defendant refused them. The verdicts were understandably severe: Gent and six others drew deportation; thirty-four received prison terms of up to fifteen years; only fourteen – including three from Lyon – were acquitted. The appeal procedure did not substantially alter the original decisions.[38]

From the trial records it seems clear that Gent was interested in maintaining an electoral machine for the Mountain, but that some of the secret societies in his network, and especially the *chambrées* of the Marseilles and the Alpine region, were prepared to resist the Bonapartist or monarchical coup that they, and many others, expected if the reds won the Assembly elections scheduled for 1852. Further proof of preparation is their resistance to the coup of December 1851. Both Vigier's study of the Second Republic in the Alps and Ted Margadent's investigation of the sources of the peasant revolt of 1851 accord Gent an important role in the diffusion of republican ideology and the extension of geographic links among the far-flung communities that rose in arms in 1851.[39]

For our purposes, though, the trial is significant because it reveals that Lyonnais societies did not participate in the network. The two Lyonnais prisoners who had had connections with local radical groups were acquitted. The concentration of troops in the city had dispelled or discouraged Lyonnais radicals – and, paradoxically, the authorities' preoccupation with the insurrectionary city had diverted the security forces away from the towns and left smaller centres free to develop conspiratorial societies. Only because the authorities wanted to smash an already battered democratic-socialist movement did they seek a Lyonnais conspiracy in a body of evidence that offered little proof of Lyonnais complicity. Because they preferred the "rigour" of the military tribunals in Lyon, they continued to refer to the Lyon Plot after they had admitted, privately, that the evidence did not warrant such a label.

In yet another twist in the contradictory relationship between repression and resistance, the trial stimulated the radicals to demonstrate their support for the defendants. As in less radical parts of France,[40] five to eight hundred mourners marched in funeral processions for two defendants who died in prison. As long as the defence lawyers remained on the case, escorts of several hundred people accompanied them to and from court. Even when the attorneys tried to evade their escorts to avoid confrontations with the troops, people assembled at the courthouse and Michel de Bourges' hotel to cheer the famous Montagnard. Long before the "plot," General Castellane had a comprehensive riot plan. When the demonstrations began, Castellane had confidentially ordered troops to defend themselves *à outrance*, to treat even columns of women and children as "advance guards of the enemy." Now he imposed a limit of 300 mourners in funeral cortèges and his soldiers ruthlessly dispersed the crowds around the courthouse.[41]

The firm military and judicial response to the mere possibility of protest ensured that Lyonnais radicals remained passive after the trial. The exile, imprisonment, or surveillance of virtually everyone in the democratic-socialist infrastructure robbed the movement of the leadership and organization needed to protest this coercive regime. True, the Young Carbonari who had contacted Gent now corresponded with Greppo and the Central Resistance Committee in Paris. Aware of the troop build-up as well as the soldiers' devotion to Louis Napoleon, they did not even hint about a resort to force at any time in the foreseeable future.[42] By 1851, it was Montagnards in the bourgs and villages of the southeast who were erecting paramilitary structures.[43]

In the calm before the storm, Lyonnais political discourse reverted to polite debates about Parisian initiatives (notably which municipality would be awarded the railway station on the Paris-Marseilles lines). Despite the restrictive electoral law, despite the prosecution of conspirators, conservatives worried about democratic-socialist gains in the Legislative Assembly and presidential elections of 1852. All over France, Bonapartists and Orleanists lobbied for a revision of the constitution to prolong the president's term of office, beginning in September 1850 with motions in the conservative General Councils. Although Chaley, Edant, Laforest, Morellet, and all the Lyonnais representatives elected to the Rhône Council in the autumn of 1848 voted against the motion, the council, like most of the councils, passed it. The next year, Bonapartists and Orleanists sponsored a petition for revision and accumulated 4,000 signatures. The legitimists, who initially opposed any revision as the first step toward a "Napoleonic monarchy," ultimately accepted "total and legal revision" as "monarchical revision." Only *La Gazette de Lyon* seriously criticized the controversial dismissal of the conservative military commander, Changarnier, and the Bonapartists' demagogic proposals to abrogate the electoral law of 31 May 1850.[44]

COUP D'ÉTAT, DECEMBER 1851

After the Legislative Assembly failed to give the two-thirds majority required to revise the constitution, rumours of a projected coup d'état spread. In October 1851, Louis Napoleon appointed a new ministry of nonentities to abrogate the unpopular electoral law – and to prepare the coup. The next month in Lyon, the inaugural address of the new and devotedly Bonapartist prefect played on conservative anxieties about revolution: "We will perhaps have to experience some difficult days together; ... you can count on my administration rivalling the zeal of your courageous army and its illustrious commander in assuring public tranquillity, on all decent men ... gathering around the flag of order raised on 10 December ... the flag that Louis Napoleon ... will never lower in the face of anarchy."[45]

On the morning of 3 December, telegrams announced the coup, or in the government's terms, the "counterinsurgency" in the capital. At this time, General Castellane dispatched "the largest deployment of troops ever seen in Lyon" to their riot stations. The artillery converged on Croix-Rousse. Not surprisingly, no disturbances occurred, though the news was received with "some emotion." That evening, Castellane reported that the metropolis was "calm," but secret societies were holding emergency sessions. A regiment each of dragoons and infantry, a battery of mobile artillery, and countless companies of cavalry patrolled all night. When small crowds gathered on the 4th, they mainly expressed curiosity; some even expressed approbation. Learning that one clandestine organization had entertained a motion to march down from Croix-Rousse to City Hall, Castellane ordered all units to their battle stations and the group desisted, if it ever intended to demonstrate. After the arrest of several members of the Guillotière council, the army resumed battle formation. By the 7th, though, Castellane had relaxed enough to disarm half the troops and relieve two-thirds of the soldiers in key locations. Within ten days, the stock market rallied, the faltering silk market enjoyed "an extraordinary rise," and the silk weavers returned to their looms. Within two weeks, the regiments bivouacked in the main squares reentered their barracks.[46]

The local newspapers tried to explain why the city known for insurrections did not rebel, while elsewhere (as subsequently established) 27,000 men from 270 communes fought the army and nearly 70,000 men from 775 communes mobilized in arms. Their explanations emphasized the surprise element in the coup d'état and General Castellane's advance preparations. The military commander also stressed the long-term coercive measures, and hence the absence of leaders and the "will" to foment rebellion. Neither the newspapers nor the general mentioned that the remaining democratic-socialist leaders had long ago forsworn armed resistance for electoral politics. Taking into account Ted Margadent's conclusions about the army's slow response and an underground network as essential elements in the making of the country-wide revolt, and his observation about the passive acceptance of the coup in all but one of the departments that elected democratic-socialist slates in May 1849,[47] the answer to the enigma of Lyon's acquiescence may be found in the combination of the army's anticipation of resistance, the virtual suppression of the democratic-socialist movement, and the democratic-socialist success in the May 1849 elections.

General Castellane's realistic evaluation of the democratic-socialists' strength did not prevent him from having 840 people arrested in the Rhône, "mostly for security reasons." While this figure hardly compares with the average of 1,389 arrests in the departments with major revolts, it far exceeds the average of 112 arrests in the seventy-two other departments (excluding the Seine). The repression followed the nation-wide pattern: for two months, preemptive arrests continued and military tribunals handed out hasty and often harsh penalties. Next, the judicial confusion was partly resolved by creating mixed commissions composed of prefects, attorneys-general, and military commanders to speed up the disposition of the cases involving "politically-suspect" prisoners, defined loosely as "pernicious elements" considered to be a danger to society. These commissions could either refer alleged murderers to military courts and minor offenders to civilian courts, or recommend deporta-tion, surveillance, or liberation. The disposition of cases in the Rhône differed in only two particulars from the disposition in most of the unrebellious departments. On the dark side, the Rhône was the only department to transfer ordinary political suspects to a War Council. On the lighter side, the Rhône, like the Seine, quickly released over half the prisoners.[48]

More precisely, the Rhône military commission and mixed commis-sion disposed of 548 cases by transferring seventy-six to other courts and dropping charges in the remaining cases. The military commission discharged 311 prisoners and imposed the severest sanction, deportation, on nineteen, and the intermediate sanction, surveillance, on 197. The mixed commission reduced these to sixteen deportations, fourteen expulsions from France, one hundred and one surveillances outside of Lyon, and sixty-three general probations. In the spring of 1852, the three commissioners sent by Louis Napoleon to review the mixed commissions' decisions further reduced the sentences and granted some pardons.[49]

Following precedent, Castellane and the two commissions focused on punishing democratic-socialists, especially those in secret societies. Of the 170 arrested men who can be identified, over 100 were democratic-socialists,[50] but only three (and one fugitive) had belonged to the New Mountain. The military commission condemned the fugitive and two other members of the New Mountain to deportation. Happily, the mixed commission commuted the last two sentences to surveillance and both commissions agreed on probation for the third member of the New Mountain. One of the two men apprehended for corresponding with Greppo when he was on the Central Resistance Committee got probation; the other correspondent was discharged without "trial."[51] These judgments confirm that neither the New Mountain nor the Central Resistance Committee was implicated in efforts to resist the coup or, for that matter, in any threat to the goverment.

Eighteen members of the Reformed Carbonari and Young Carbonari were also detained. Of the thirteen detained on the basis of police information, five never faced "trial," five drew surveillance, and three had their penalties lifted by the mixed commission.[52] Military prosecutors also pursued three Carbonari who allegedly met on 6 December to discuss resistance to the coup. The commissions first ordered them deported, then commuted their sentences to surveillance. Because two Carbonari who belonged to an Avengers' Society disappeared, they were automatically condemned to transportation. Another Avenger, the ex-editor of *Le Peuple Souverain*, received the same sentence although he was present.[53] Apparently the commissions wanted to punish Faures for "socialist propaganda" in the past – and to remove him in the future. The verdicts in these cases imply that only one or possibly two tiny offshoots of the Carbonari contemplated protesting the overthrow of the republic.

Still suspicious of the innocent cooperatives, Castellane dissolved all but the government-funded Brosse and Company and took out warrants for the arrest of at least fourteen members because of their political antecedents. Two who were also Croix-Rousse city councillors escaped to Switzerland and so were sentenced in absentia to deportation. Edant was released immediately, no doubt due to his political position as a Lyon city councillor and his social standing as a merchant.[54] The humbler members of cooperatives were less fortunate. After weeks of incarceration, Naudé and three others who had belonged to the radical masonic lodge were put on probation. Five members who had belonged to clubs and secret societies received the same penalty. The old militant of the 1830s and 1840s, Pierre Millet, and his protégé from the dissident Icarian society of 1844, Etienne Bacot, were ordered deported, then pardoned.[55]

Hereafter, the arrests become more and more arbitrary. Although the War Councils had already ruled that the Voraces had disintegrated, police rounded up twenty Voraces. Half were not detained for lack of evidence and six drew surveillance. The one who was transported had committed another "crime."[56] At least fifteen other arrests can be attributed to police accusations that the "suspects" belonged to unspecified secret societies. Eight who had committed other "crimes" such as hiding arms or making "seditious remarks" were condemned to be deported, but four won pardons and three, reduced penalties. Six were discharged without trial.[57] Having exhausted the supposedly active societies, police brought in eighteen as "known socialist," "socialist propagandist," or "militant socialist." Since most of their socialist endeavours dated back to 1848, few faced trial. Five were placed on probation, while one escapee drew deportation.[58]

But the arrests and convictions were not haphazard, for they were designed to punish democratic-socialists who had slipped through the previous repressive net and to prevent them from becoming leaders of a new opposition. The prison log lists twenty representatives of the clubs and committees of 1848–9, not counting those subsumed under another category. Sixteen spent weeks in jail before being released without trial. Incarcerated longer was Jean-Marie Perret, whose political career had begun in the Flowers Society of 1836.[59] Two of the Voraces had presided over the Voraces Society and the one deported had been *père* at the time of the unsuccessful case against the Voraces. Similarly, three of the "known socialists" had been implicated in the insurrection of June 1849 and two had served time for that "crime."[60]

While the authorities preferred "known socialists," they also apprehended twenty-seven men merely because they frequented radical cafes. The military commission discharged them as soon as it had reviewed their dossiers. Twelve (or more) jailed for "seditious remarks" returned home almost as quickly. Denunciations by personal enemies resulted in the brief imprisonment of a handful of people for making "seditious remarks," sometimes months before, in the privacy of their homes! One over-zealous police officer brought in two bakers from Mâcon who did not have their passports, because bakers were "full of bad ideas."[61]

Given the speed and magnitude of the arrests, it is not surprising that we can pinpoint only one person, a clerk, deported for participating in the one demonstration that did occur. The attorney-general's report implies, however, that many more were arrested for attending the small demonstration (Gilardin estimated the crowd at 600 to 800) on the evening of 3 December.[62] Presumably they were the artisans and silk weavers whose names are recorded on the prison log but whose "offences" cannot be identified because they were not radical leaders and therefore did not have formal hearings. By the evening of the 3rd, the few radical leaders still at liberty were thoroughly intimidated by the arrests of their colleagues.

If the repression was arbitrary and occasionally absurd, it served a purpose. To gain release from prison, dismissal of charges, or probation in Lyon, the prisoner had to convince the commissions not only that he had not committed a crime, but that he would not cause trouble in the future. Many humbled themselves in this way or asked the intercession of a Bonapartist official. Years later, members of their families begged the authorities to allow them to return to Lyon.[63] As Douglas Hays has shown for eighteenth-century England, dependence on patrons in an arbitrary and unpredictable legal system encourages deference and discourages challenges to the system.[64]

Within a month of the coup, the democratic-socialists' institutional bases had crumbled. All but one cooperative liquidated or dissolved into loose purchasing agencies; the only secret society that had survived succumbed. Their official political strongholds, the suburban councils, were first thinned by arrests and voluntary exiles, then replaced by retractable councils, and finally integrated into a metropolitan committee. Even the Lyon council lost members, usually through resignation, for instance, that of Laforest. Although the rump council took the first opportunity to thank Louis Napoleon for preserving France from "socialism" and to promise "most loyal and eager cooperation," an appointed committee replaced it in March 1852 (though twenty-seven of the thirty appointees came from the preceding council). Even the legitimists, who had offered a right-wing critique of the Bonapartists, now slavishly praised Castellane for "saving society."[65]

The tidal wave of repression and the flood of antisocialist propaganda did not sweep every form of opposition aside. In the plebiscite on the overthrow of the constitution held on 21 December, 22 per cent of the registered voters in the metropolis abstained, which can be interpreted, under the circumstances, as a sign of disapproval. Thirty-five per cent (17,623) of the ballots were marked nay. These figures fall slightly below the 27 per cent abstentions and 37 per cent negative vote in Paris and considerably below the proportions in the proletatian textile towns of Limoges and Mulhouse. However, the more homogenously working-class suburbs of Lyon (and Paris) provided higher proportions: 28 per cent of the registered Croix-Rousseans refrained from voting and 51 per cent (3,271) of the voters were opposed. In the electoral section where the Democratic Society/Jandard Club had met, 35 per cent of the eligible electors did not exercise their franchise, perhaps because so many were in jail or Switzerland. The department as a whole, with 20 per cent abstentions and 23 per cent nays, had a higher than average disapproval rate. As the prefect noted, 99 per cent of the nays came from the textile manufacturing communes, both urban and proto-urban.[66] Many of the proto-urban communes had established ties with Lyonnais radicals in 1848, when they were visited by delegates from the Central Democratic Club. In the only way left to them, the democratic-socialists of the Rhône expressed their displeasure with the assault on the republic.

However, abstaining or voting nay were only token gestures, for the French electorate had accepted the coup d'état by an overwhelming majority. The Second Republic and the democratic-socialist movement that it first engendered, then exterminated, were over.

Conclusion

For a year after the coup d'état, the police kept a close watch on the few remaining militants. Early reports of an Avengers' plot to assassinate the prince-president and of the Young Mountain's 970 affiliates throughout the south exaggerated the danger, though later accounts of individual democratic-socialists infiltrating mutual aid societies seem credible. In July 1852, the arrest of a Croix-Rousse radical drew so many people into the streets to jeer the police that the infantry had to load and take aim at the crowd to end the uproar. Shortly thereafter, the new municipal committee unanimously requested four more regiments of cavalry, which would have meant more cavalry billeted in the city than had been deployed in the insurrection of 1849. The committee was worried about an "infernal machine" allegedly being built in Croix-Rousse and set to explode during Louis Napoleon's visit in September 1852. The quiet but enthusiastic reception of the president and an aggressive campaign for ratification of the empire in the November plebiscite did not keep the prefect from fretting about the "incorrigible class in the metropolis," who, he felt, would follow the republicans' order to abstain from voting. Although more electors shunned the polls than the year before, a higher proportion of those who did vote, even in Croix-Rousse and Guillotière, favoured the empire. The prefect deduced that "the people" had been "disengaged from the pernicious influence of a destructive press and the despotism of demagogues."[1]

After the drastic suppression of 1852, the imperial authorities added subtler types of social control. From 1853 through 1864, the prefect of the Rhône, Vaisse, sponsored an urban renewal program similar to Haussmann's in Paris, which, supplemented by a railway building boom in the 1850s, employed thousands of unskilled workers. The imperial court also created "real" work for silk weavers by purchasing fabrics during depressions in the *fabrique*. To institutionalize workers' dependence on the government, the authorities approved and patronized their most docile associations, the mutual aid societies. All but one of the silk weavers' societies sought official recognition.[2] As early as 1853, master silk weavers reverted to the prerevolutionary tactic of petitioning the prefect for democratization of the *Conseil des Prud'hommes* and publication of a *tarif*.[3] As late as 1860, weavers reiterated prerevolutionary demands for codification of the customs of the *fabrique* and even preinsurrectionary demands for government intervention in disputes with merchants. The authorities were not responsive, but their liberal policy in the 1860s, including the legalization of strikes, appealed to many workers. At the same time the government supported cooperatives to "occupy" workers' minds. In the prefects' opinion, cooperatives did divert them from political theories "as being powerless to improve the condition of the class of workers."[4]

Thus the carrot-and-stick approach of encouraging economic dependence and discouraging political opposition, initiated under the Second Republic and elaborated under the Second Empire, seemed to have extinguished the radical movement of Lyon. Ironically, the movement had been kindled by the unmitigated repression of the mid-1830s, when workers learned to distrust government and consider radical solutions to their economic problems. Shocked by the bombardment of their neighbourhoods and mass arrests of their neighbours in 1834, workers refused to cooperate with judicial officials prosecuting the insurgents. Construction of a fortified wall around Croix-Rousse left a permanent reminder of the regime's willingness to use the army against workers. The Orleanists' hostility toward workers associations only increased alienation from the ruling elite. A few workers formed illegal societies to study and disseminate the new democratic, socialist, and communist theories. By the mid-1840s, there were hundreds of neobabouvists and dissident Icarians, whose propaganda societies had evolved their own democratic brand of socialism and had introduced it to thousands of workers. Well before the revolution, Lyonnais workers had local leaders familiar with democratic-socialist theory and accustomed to political organization. Much of the sophistication shown by Lyon's democratic-socialists in 1848 – and their persistence and success in 1849 – sprang from their leaders' long apprenticeship during the repression of the 1830s.

If the repression of the 1830s and the state of siege of the republic were unusual, they do suggest some generalizations about the relationship between repression and resistance, government and governed. The armed attack of 1834, show trial of 1835, expanded police force, and restrictive association law of the mid-1830s actually provoked working-class political opposition. It would take the more systematic preemptive arrests of 1849 through 1852, plus the substitution of martial for civil law, to eliminate the resulting radical movement. Up to a point, then, police and military pressure can promote resistance. The turning-point came with the massive troop build-up and military courts of the state of siege. Louis Napoleon, who pioneered plebiscitory "democracy" as well as the totalitarian police state, realized that coercion does not win support and wooed workers with government patronage. The Orleanists who governed Lyon during the July Monarchy, indifferent to the disenfranchised and dedicated to laissez-faire, did not leaven coercion with patronage *or* paternalism. In conservative cities like Toulouse, where legitimist notables practised traditional charity, the politics of deference prevailed longer. Clearly, one key to the emergence of a democratic movement is a reliance on repression unsweetened by paternalism.

Political miscalculations provided the tinder, but social, geographic, and economic conditions fuelled radicalism. One glaring feature of the militants' social base is the overrepresentation of immigrants (though native Lyonnais were present, sometimes prominently, as in the case of the Voraces). Militants recruited among immigrants who had been uprooted from their villages, then had found work in the silk industry and settled down in working-class suburbs. This pattern confirms Agulhon's argument about the importance of a break with tradition, William Sewell's thesis about the significance of a trade open to newcomers, and Joan Scott's insistence on the need for workers to establish a permanent residence in order to organize.[5]

More originally, this study has indicated that the demonstrations of 1848, the clubs and cooperatives of 1848–9, and the insurrection of 1849 started in the *suburban* communities of Lyon. The geographic isolation and social homogeneity of the suburbs ensured a high degree of community cohesion; the concentration of silk workers in the suburbs and merchants in the city enhanced class consciousness and conflict; the independence of the suburban communes facilitated grass-roots political organization. Historians of other metropolitan areas may wish to examine more closely the role of suburbs in the development of democratic-socialism.

Economic uncertainty fanned the flame of Lyonnais radicalism. The movement attracted workers in the *fabrique* and other manufactures that were expanding and modernizing without "industrializing" (i.e., mechanizing and concentrating production into factories); this evidence extends Christopher Johnson's discovery that most Icarians were employed in manufactures undergoing nonmechanical yet capitalistic change.[6] In Lyon, proletarianization was exacerbated by the silk merchants' callous practice of passing on the risks of an unstable market to the *chefs d'atelier*. The clash between silk merchants and their dependent weavers lay at the heart of Lyonnais radicalism, while fluctuations in the essential silk market set the pulse of economic activism. As early as 1831, weavers held strikes in periods of full employment, a strategy commonly associated with late nineteenth-century workers.[7] The revolutionary authorities, with a more tolerant attitude toward strikes, temporarily reversed this trend, but by the autumn of 1848, velours weavers returned to the tactic of delaying negotiations with merchants until velours weavers were in demand.

The revolution of 1848 found the Lyonnais politically, socially, and economically receptive to a democratic and social republic. At its very inception, secret societies arranged for radical, working-class representation on local councils. Sooner than other provincials, the Lyonnais democratic-socalists recognized that clubs had to indoctrinate the new electorate, including the peasantry. Their prompt and perceptive response can be attributed to their long experience in secret societies. Although they had the largest representation on any government agency except the Luxemburg Commission and the largest club network outside the capital, they were not immediately successful. In the municipal committee, they were outwitted by liberals and moderate republicans who were better versed in formal parliamentary politics. The abstention of radicals who understood that local government could not enforce fundamental change and the diversion of many radicals into organizing republican security forces reduced the democratic-socialists' civic political clout. In the National Assembly election, they simply could not compete, that quickly, with the "natural leaders" in the countryside. Still, this typical failure should not overshadow their atypical feat of electing four democratic-socialist workers to the National Assembly.

While politicized workers reacted in a "modern" manner, other workers acted in more transitional, even traditional ways. The Voraces' seizure of military installations is so singular that it is difficult to classify. On the one hand, the Voraces' prerevolutionary status as a communal recreational group of young, single men recalls the Abbeys of Misrule of early modern Europe. Their large size as a tolerated association and their antipathy toward the forts as residents of Croix-Rousse account for their capture of the fortifications. On the other hand, the Voraces had associated with communists and, during their occupation of the forts, reorganized on strict military lines to operate as a semiofficial paramilitary unit. Although the government commissioners tried to coopt the Voraces, they were never able to control the unit. The new authorities had to indulge an irregular corps that interfered in police, military, and foreign affairs, because the Voraces had guns and community support. When they antagonized the essentially electoral clubs and most of the public by kidnapping a judicial official, the corps was summarily dissolved. A rump group survived for a year by assuming the form of a secret society; this society then precipitated an insurrection.

Luddism was the most traditional, and transitory, response to the revolution. Like peasants and other workers, Lyonnais silk and ribbon workers believed in a moral economy that justified wrecking machinery that threatened their livelihoods. Many had the equally naïve, but more political notion that the republic had legalized luddism – a notion "validated"by the new authorities' tardiness in halting machine-breaking. While the crowds were exceptionally destructive, they were disciplined in selecting their targets. The methodical destruction of machines and charitable workshops that undercut weavers' rates was organized, informally, by men who shared an occupational problem and neighbour-hood ties. Soon workers organized formally, in unions. Many unions won favourable settlements, thanks to the intervention of a sympathetic work committee.

If Lyonnais crowds were hard on property, they spared human life. One reason for the nonviolent quality of the Lyonnais revolution was the radicals' control from the first appearance of the orderly columns descending to the Hôtel de ville on 25 February through the calm debates of the June Days. Very early in the revolution, Lyonnais radicals decided to demonstrate against the new government but not to use physical force against the democratic republic. The parallel explanation for nonviolence is the authorities' healthy regard for the population's insurrectionary potential. Both Provisional Government commissioners to the Rhône were willing to negotiate with demonstrators and make timely conces-sions. Both lobbied for a government silk order, so that they could provide "suitable" work for unemployed silk weavers. And both restrained an army command smarting from the humiliation of its capitulation in the early days of the revolution. By postponing piece-work in the National Workshops, announcing an infusion of money into the silk industry, and limiting the resort to force, Commissioner Martin-Bernard saved Lyon from a bloodletting in June 1848.

After the revolution, Lyon's democratic-socialists resisted the increas-ingly reactionary regime's efforts to regulate or restrict all voluntary associations. Since Lyonnais workers had formulated cooperative theory in the 1830s, many welcomed government aid to cooperatives but more eschewed government funds (and supervision) because they objected to the policy of including "capitalists." The objectors founded twenty independent producers' cooperatives without private investment capital. The Central Democratic Club exploited loopholes in the new club law, and frequent elections, to sustain their network. Learning from their mistakes in the December 1848 presidential election, they unified around one slate in the spring 1849 Legislative Assembly elections and cam-paigned vigorously among the peasants, who held the balance of power in the Rhône. Their slate's triumph was complemented by the election of democratic-socialists in surrounding departments, where Lyonnais radicals had also campaigned among the peasantry.

By blocking the avenues to open political activity, the reactionaries diverted radicals seasoned in the secret societies of the monarchy into covert activities. A few took cover in consumer cooperatives which they used as "fronts" for political groups and, in June 1849, as rendez-vous for insurgents. Others revived classic secret societies like the Rights of Man and distributed democratic-socialist propaganda. Perhaps because they had not suffered the trauma of class war a year earlier, as Parisians had, members of the clandestine associations overreacted to government provocations and created an impression of impending threats to the republic – and of their own capacity to withstand these threats. The supercharged atmosphere incited the Voraces and other, recently radicalized Croix-Rousse workers into the largest insurrection of June 1849. Older radicals and more generally people who remembered the conflict in 1834, refrained from fighting. Of course, the army retaliated by shelling the rebel suburb, just as it had done fifteen years before. Responsibility for the second devastation of Croix-Rousse in one generation lies on the shoulders of a few naïve radicals, an army anxious for revenge, and, most fundamentally, a government that deprived political opponents of legal outlets to express their discontent.

The state of siege permitted the outright prohibition of voluntary associations and the prosecution of hundreds of insurgents in military courts which admitted more questionable evidence and administered a more punitive kind of justice than civil courts. Retaining martial law for two and a half years allowed the government to avoid jury trials for political societies and suspects. In that two and a half years, the military authorities dismantled every democratic-socialist institution except the suburban councils and eliminated or subdued radical leaders by imprisonment or intimidation through surveillance, arrest, and trial. (However, their fixation on the Lyonnais movement caused them to underestimate the New Mountain network spreading through the adjacent departments.) By now, resistance was strictly defensive and symbolic: legal defence funds, escorts for defence attorneys, funeral cortèges for dead comrades. Lyon's passive acceptance of the coup d'état proved that the democratic-socialist movement was prostrate before the coup.

Inevitably a movement so precocious and persistent left traces. In the full employment economy following the Crimean War (1854–6), many workers' *corporations* struck to restore gains won in 1848 but lost in the intervening years. All failed due to harsh repression. In the next outburst of strike activity, from 1863 to 1867, many of these *corporations* stopped work for the same reason, but failed due to the rationalization of production and increased competition from the unskilled. Some of the last job actions of the empire also resembled the revolutionary job actions in so far as they involved the same *corporations*, organizational forms, and tactics and they were successful again. However, the participation of factory workers, who were peripheral in 1848, and the First International, which did not exist then, distinguished this wave of occupational activism from its predecessor.[8] After the relaxation of the association law in 1863, six "forty-eighters" set up dozens of cooperatives that imitated the cooperatives of 1848–9 in their concern for the education and welfare of their members. Nevertheless, their small membership, decentralized format, and lack of interest in the emancipation of the entire working class owed more to the circumspect cooperatives of the later republic.[9]

Political militants resurfaced periodically. The irrepressible Pierre Millet and two other prisoners of December 1851 were convicted of reconstituting secret societies in 1852, 1853, and 1854. Despite a ban on electoral meetings and no opposition organ, a secret society elected three moderate "forty-eighters" in the national elections of 1857. Perret of Guillotière's revolutionary council and four other working-class, republican politicians were deported or incarcerated for this feat under the new law on general security. Two founders of Naudé and Company and another activist of 1848–9 belonged to the clandestine republican committee[10] which sponsored the former Representative Commissaire, two other democratic-socialists of the Second Republic, and other radical, working-class candidates in the 1863–4 local elections.[11] Murat of *Le Censeur* and two other "forty-eighters" joined the Lyon branch of the First International when it formed in 1864. Gandy, Grinand, and Perret of the Central Democratic Club and its successors (not to mention the neobabouvist societies of the July Monarchy) sat on the Committee of Public Safety in the Lyon Commune of 1870.[12]

Nevertheless, the human links between the democratic-socialists of the Second Republic and the socialists of the late empire must not be exaggerated. Industrial workers began organizing in the late 1860s; the state supervised the cooperatives. New militants with an anarchist ideology dominated the Lyonnais branch of the International and the Lyonnais Commune.[13] Lyon's experience under the Second Republic had been not so much the beginning as the end of an era.

Notes

ABBREVIATIONS

ACCL Archives de la Chambre de Commerce de Lyon
ADR   Archives Départementales du Rhône
AML   Archives Municipales de Lyon
AN   Archives Nationales, Paris
BML   Bibliothèque Municipale de Lyon

INTRODUCTION

1 For example, J. Dautry, *1848 et la Seconde République* and L. Girard, *La IIe République*.

2 For example, J. Vidalenc, "La province et les journées du juin," *Etudes d'histoire moderne et contemporaine* 2 (1948).

3 For example, *Actes du Congrès historique de Centennaire 1848*; J. Godechot, ed., *La Révolution de 1848 à Toulouse et dans la Haute Garonne*; *La Révolution de 1848 à Moulins et dans le Département de l'Allier*; *Le Département de la Marne et la Révolution de 1848*; E. Reynier, *La Seconde République dans l'Ardèche*.

4 F. Dutacq, *Histoire politique de Lyon pendant la Révolution de 1848*.

5 J. Godart, *A Lyon, en 1848, les Voraces*.

6 P. Amann, *Revolution and Mass Democracy: The Paris Club Movement in 1848*.

7 R. Gossez, *Les ouvriers de Paris*, vol. 1, *L'Organisation, 1848–52*.

8 For example, J. Dommanget, *Auguste Blanqui et la Révolution de 1848*.

9 For instance, Tchernoff, *Associations et sociétés secrètes sous la deuxième République*.

10 M. Agulhon, *Une ville ouvrière au temps du socialisme utopique: Toulon de 1815 à 1851*.

11 C.H. Johnson, *Utopian Communism in France: Cabet and the Icarians*.

12 W.H. Sewell, *Work and Revolution in France: The Language of Labor from the Old Regime to 1848*.

13 ADR, M, Police générale, Rapports journaliers, 1835–49, and Police générale, 1835–48 (Rapports du Commissaire spécial); ADR, R, 6me Division militaire, Conseils de Guerre, 1849–51, Dossiers individuels, Saisie des journaux ..., Sociétés secrètes; AML, I^2 40, 41, Documents relatifs aux suspects politiques, sociétés et clubs, I^2 51–4, Lettres, enquêtes, instructions ... se rapportant à des particuliers, and I^2 63, Suspects et condamnés politiques.

14 J. Benoit, *Confessions d'un prolétaire*, presented by M. Moissonnier, and *Souvenirs de la République de 1848*; S. Commissaire, *Mémoires et souvenirs*.

15 M. Agulhon, "Les chambrées en Basse-Provence; histoire et ethnologie," *Revue historique* 245 (1971); Agulhon, "Vers une histoire des associations," *Esprit* 46 (1978).

16 R. Bezucha, "Masks of Revolution: A Study of Popular Culture during the Second French Republic," in *Revolution and Reaction*, ed. R. Price.

17 G. Rudé, *The Crowd in History, 1730–1848*; J. Scott, *The Glassworkers of Carmaux*.

18 J. Godard, *L'Ouvrier en soie*, especially pp. 206–8, 229–54, 273–82; A. Soboul, "Problems of Work in Year II," in *New Perspectives on the French Revolution*, ed. J. Kaplow, 211–25; L. Trénard, "The Social Crisis in Lyon on the Eve of the French Revolution," in ibid., 68–100.

19 C. Riffaterre, *Le mouvement antijacobin et antiparisien à Lyon ... en 1793*, in *Annales de l'Université de Lyon*, n.s., 2, no. 24 (1912): 334–54.

20 G. Ribe, *L'Opinion publique et la vie politique à Lyon lors des premières années de la Seconde Restauration*, in ibid., 3rd ser., 15–16 (1957): 25–72; P. Truchon, "La vie ouvrière à Lyon sous la Restauration," *Revue de l'histoire de Lyon* 11 (1912): 212–22.

21 R.J. Bezucha, "The Revolution of 1830 and the City of Lyon," in *1830 in France*, ed. J.M. Merriman, 119–38.

22 F. Rude, *L'insurrection lyonnaise de novembre 1831: Le mouvement ouvrier à Lyon de 1827–1832*; M. Moissonier, *La révolte des canuts, Lyon, novembre 1831*, 102–3.

23 Bezucha, *The Lyon Uprising of 1834*.

24 AN BB³⁰ 294, dos. 2, Tableau ... des Accusés d'avril; ADR, R, Fortifications entre Saône et Rhône; M, Police générale, Commissaire spécial, 1835–48.

25 P. Stearns, "Patterns of Industrial Strike Activity in France during the July Monarchy," *American Historical Review* 70 (1964–5); Johnson.

26 Agulhon, *Toulon*, pp. 94–9; W. Sewell, "La Classe ouvrière de Marseilles sous la Seconde République: Structure social et comportement politique," *Le Mouvement Social* 70 (1971); Scott.

27 R. Arminzade, "Breaking the Chains of Dependency: From Patronage to Class Politics, Toulouse, France, 1830–1872," *Journal of Urban History* 3 (August 1977).

28 F.A. De Luna, *The French Republic under Cavaignac*; H.C. Payne, "Preparation of a Coup d'Etat," in *Studies in Modern European History in Honor of Franklin Charles Palm*.

29 P. Vigier, *La Seconde République dans la région alpine*, 2 vols.

30 T.W. Margadant, *French Peasants in Revolt: The Insurrection of 1851*.

31 L. Loubère, *Radicalism in Mediterranean France, 1848–1919*, 45, 50, 53, 55, 56; Margadant, passim; R. Price, *The French Second Republic: A Social History*, 203–4, also notes the role of these agents.

32 P. Vigier, *La Seconde République*, 67.

33 J.M. Merriman, *The Agony of the Republic: The Repression of the Left in Revolutionary France, 1848–1851*.

34 T.R. Forstenzer, *French Provincial Police and the Fall of the Second Republic*.

CHAPTER ONE

1 Descriptions derive from A. Combe and G. Charavey, *Guide de l'étranger à Lyon*, and T. Ogier, *La France par cantons et par communes, Département de Rhône, Arrondissement de Lyon*, unless otherwise indicated.

2 F. Rivet, *Le Quartier Perrache, 1766–1946; Etude d'histoire et de géographie urbaine*, 8–60.

3 A. Audiganne, *Les populations ouvrières et les industries de la France*, 2:

224–5, 233, and J.F. Bunel, *Tableau historique, administratif et industriel de la ville de la Croix-Rousse*, 11–16.

4 J.B. Monfalcon and A.P.J. Polinère, *Hygiène de la Ville de Lyon, ou Opinions et Rapports de Conseil de Salubrité*, 41–52.

5 *L'indicateur commercial, industriel, administratif et judiciaire de la ville et des faubourgs de Lyon.*

6 L.V. Parisel, "Revue des établissements de Lyon, Rive gauche de Rhône," *Revue de lyonnais* 4 (1836): 369–77.

7 J. Arminjon, *La Population du département du Rhône: Son évolution depuis le début du XIXe siècle*, 34–5, and C. Pouthas, *La population française pendant la première moitié du XIXe siècle*, 101, 143.

8 Pouthas, 102, and *Annuaire de la ville de Lyon et du département du Rhône.*

9 G. Rudé, *The Crowd in History*, 198ff; C., L., and R. Tilly, *The Rebellious Century, 1830–1930*, 78 ff; L. Chevalier, *Classes laborieuses et classes dangereuses*, and Savey-Casarde, "La Criminalité à Lyon de 1830 à 1834," *Revue historique du droit français et étranger* 7 (1962): 249.

10 The number tried by the Correctional Court rose from 793 in 1831 to 2,520 in 1847. See Savey-Casarde and ADR, U, Tribunal Correctionnel, 1847. Twenty-nine of the fifty insurgents whose birthplaces are recorded were migrants. See ADR, R, Conseil de Guerre, Dossiers individuels, Insurrection de 1849. Of the 423 radicals in the file whose birthplaces were recorded 290 were migrants.

11 AML, Croix-Rousse, Garde Nationale, Recensement, 1841.

12 AN BB^{30} 1287–90. Etat des individus jugés pendant l'année 1834 (–1851) et precedemment condamnés pour crimes, délites ou contraventions.

13 Quote from J. Augier, *Le Canut*, 291; see also L. Strumingher, "The Artisan Family: Traditions and Transition in Nineteenth Century Lyon," *Journal of Family History* 2 (1977). According to samples of approximately 500 households in representative quarters and suburbs in the 1836, 1841, 1846, and 1851 censuses, the overwhelming majority of men over twenty-six were married. See ADR, M, Dénombremont de la population, 1836, 1841, 1846, 1851.

14 ADR, M, Dénombrement, 1851, and *Annuaire*, 1838 and 1847. The old quarters averaged 7 persons a household; the suburbs 3.3. There were 3 single men for every married man in the old city; the ratio was 1.14 to 1 in the suburbs.

15 For instance, M.R.L. Reybaud, *Etudes sur le régime des manufactures: Conditions des ouvriers en soie*, and L.R. Villermé, *Tableau de l'état physique et moral des ouvriers employés dans les manufactures de coton, de laine et de soie.*

16 Of the 3,507 men surveyed for the Croix-Rousse National Guard, 57 per cent had been born in the ring of departments around Lyon. See AML, Croix-Rousse, Garde Nationale, Recensement, 1841. On the tradition of migration, see A. Chatelain, "La formation de la population lyonnaise. L'Apport d'origine montagnarde (XVIIe–XXe siècles)," *Revue de géographie de Lyon* 24 (1954): 91–115.

17 My interpretation has been informed by M. Anderson, *Family Structure in Nineteenth Century Lancashire* (Cambridge: Cambridge University Press, 1971).

18 On the influence of temporary migration on the dissemination of radicalism, see A. Chatelain, "Les migrations temporaires et la propagation des idées révolutionnaires en France au XIXe siècle," *Revue des révolutions contemporaines* 188 (1951): 6–11.

19 Of the 463 (known) radical migrants 163 can be traced to the departments that resisted. Twelve of the 22 came from towns or cities with unarmed mobilizations. For data on these departments and towns, see T.W. Margadant, *French Peasants in Revolt* 11–21.

20 Arminjon, 34–6; on *octrois*, see Conseil Général du Département du Rhône, *Rapport sur l'administration du département ... 1839*, 97.

21 Twenty per cent of the men surveyed for the Croix-Rousse National Guard had moved from Lyon or other suburbs. Most arrived in Croix-Rousse in their early to mid-twenties and married shortly afterward, in their mid- to late twenties.

22 In 1851, 85 per cent of the people over twenty-five in Croix-Rousse were married. A sample of 490 households found that 83 per cent of the households contained nuclear families; about half of them also had relatives or workers living with the family. ADR, M, Dénombrement 1851.

23 J. Benoit, *Confessions d'un prolétaire* 35 ff.

24 There were 1,906 Savoyards in Croix-Rousse in 1851. The sample cited above found that every household headed by a Savoyard contained an older relative or younger worker or apprentice from Savoy.

25 ADR, M, Sociétés de secours, 1810–51, 14 February 1845, 5 October 1847.

26 In 1851, in Croix-Rousse, 15,021 of 19,080 inhabitants with occupations were in textiles; in Guillotière, 11,258 of 23,925 with nonagricultural occupations were in textiles and clothing. ADR, M, Dénombrement, 1851. The sample of 490 Croix-Rousse households revealed silk workers in over two-thirds.

27 See my article, "Consciousness and Community: The Workers of Lyon, 1830–1850," *Journal of Social History* 12 (1978): 129–45. Some of the statistics in this article differ from the figures cited here because here I am including all radicals, not just workers.

28 AML, Croix-Rousse, D, Liste des Electeurs, 1846, listed 460 *propiétaires*, but most of them were very modest *propriétaires*. There were only eight *négociants* in this silk weaving centre.

29 AML, Croix-Rousse, 1¹, Police, Commissaires de Police; and S. Commissaire, *Mémoires et souvenirs*, 1: 97–8.

30 For income figures, see C. Beaulieu, *Histoire de commerce, de l'industrie et des fabriques de Lyon* 144–6. For employment figures, see AML, Documents Gasparin, vol. 1, "Situation industrielle de la ville de Lyon ... (52,000 weavers). Since sources like the *Statistique de la France*, ser. 1, vol. 2, *Industrie*, 132–5, include all silk workers, their figures exceed 100,000. For the number of looms, see the *Annuaire*, 1849, vol. 2, "Dénombrement ... 1846."

31 *L'Indicateur*, 20 June 1835.

32 The average annual weight of silk thread conditioned (dried prior to sale) rose from 441,558 kgs in 1815–24 to 905,132 kgs in 1835–44: ACCL, "Procès-verbaux et délibérations," 1849–50, pp. 160–1.

33 Beaulieu, 123–4; Conseil générale du Rhône, *Rapport sur l'administration ... 1844–1845*, 6.

34 ADR, M, Situation industrielle, "Rapport à M. le Ministre de Commerce ... 1835" (12,917 looms) and Police générale, Rapports journaliers, 9 September 1848.

35 *L'Avenir*, 11 November 1846; *L'Echo de la Fabrique de 1841*, 20 April, 15 May 1843, 15 March 1845; *La Tribune prolétaire*, 12 October 1834.

36 ADR, M, Statistique industrielle, "Statistique des arts et metiers, 26 mars

1847"; Beaulieu, 172–4; Kauffmann, *Des causes locales qui nuisent à la fabrique de Lyon...*, 38–43.

37 Beaulieu, 176; Cour des Pairs, *Affaire du mois d'avril 1834*, vol. 1, *Rapport...par M. Girod*, 169; *L'Echo des Ouvriers*, October 1940; *La Tribune prolétaire*, 16 November 1834, 8 February 1835.

38 *Statistique de la France*, ser. 1, vol. 3, *Commerce extérieur*, 468–75; Exposition universelle de 1889, *La Fabrique lyonnaise de soieries et l'industrie de la soie en France, 1789–1889*, App. J.

39 ADR, U, Tribunal de Commerce, Dossiers des faillites, 1837–8, 1840, 1843, 1846–7.

40 ACCL, "Procès-verbaux et délibérations, 1849–1850," p. 159.

41 General Poncelet, "Machines et outils appliqués aux arts textiles," in Exposition de 1851, *Travaux de la Commission française*, vol. 3, *Machines, outils et constructions*, pt. 2, 346–60; C. Ballot, *L'Introduction du mécanisme dans l'industrie française*, 375–81.

42 *Annuaire*, 1849, vol. 2, "Dénombrement... 1846."

43 ACCL, "Compte-rendu des travaux de la Chambre de Commerce, 1846–1847," 16–18, and 1847–8, 8–10; J. Buret, *Exposition de l'industrie française année 1844*, vol. 1, pt. 3, *Tissus* (Paris: Challand, n.d.), 25–6; M. Laferrère, *Lyon: Ville industrielle*, 165–6.

44 Conseil général, *Rapport... 1845–1846*, 26.

45 Beaulieu, 179; Cour de Pairs, *Affaire du mois d'avril 1834* 1: 169; Villermé, 354–5.

46 The 30,000 figure may be low, since it appeared in Girod's report to the Cour des Pairs (*Affaire du mois d'avril 1834* 1: 171).

47 Audiganne, 7; Beaulieu, 180–1; Reybaud, 151–9.

48 *Le Journal de Commerce*, 26 March 1837; ADR, M, Ouvriers sans travail (1838–40), letters dated 9 December 1839 and 16 April 1840; AML, Q², Ouvriers sans travail, Prefect's report, November 1842; *L'Echo de l'Industrie*, 6 December 1845.

49 M. Perrot, "Grèves, grévistes et conjoncture," *Le Mouvement Social* 63 (1968).

50 F. Rude, *L'Insurrection lyonnaise de novembre 1831*, and R.J. Bezucha, *The Lyon Uprising of 1834*.

51 AN BB¹⁸ 1357, 1358, 1474ᴮ; BB³⁰ 396; AML, I² 47ª Compagnonnages; and my "Experiments in Organization, Workers' Societies in Lyon, 1830–1850," in *Proceedings of the Eighth Annual Conference of the Western Society for French History*.

52 AN BB¹⁸ 1420, 1421, 1423, March through June, October, and November 1844; ADR, M, Police générale, Commissaire spécial, 3 March 1845, and U, Tribunal Correctionnel, Jugemens, 6 August, 6 November 1844.

53 ADR, U, Conseil des Prud'hommes, "Résultat des travaux... 1846"; analysis of the cases is based on the president's reports published in *L'Echo de la Fabrique de 1841*, 31 January 1843, 31 March 1844, 5 February 1845; for weavers' attitudes, see ibid, 30 September, November 1841, 15, 31 August 1843, 15 October 1844; *L'Echo des Ouvriers*, November 1840–February 1841.

54 AN, BB¹⁸ 1358, 13 February 1835; ADR, U, Tribunal Correctionnel, Jugemens, 9 January 1835. See note 52.

55 AN F¹² 2409, 1841–2; ADR, M, Travail des enfants, 1847; AML, Croix-Rousse, I¹, Police, October 1847; *L'Echo des Ouvriers*, August 1840–May 1841; *L'Echo de la Fabrique de 1841*, 15 November 1841–28 February 1842; *Le*

Censeur, April–December 1847; and *La Tribune Lyonnaise*, July 1847–January 1848.

56 ADR, M, Statistique industrielle, Statistique des arts et metiers, 26 March 1847, and Dénombrement, 1851.

57 AN BB[18] 1239, 1366, 1368, February, May, and November 1836 and August through October 1838; ADR, M, Police générale, Commissaire spécial, 5 May 1835, March, August, and October 1837, October–November 1838; AML, I[1] 74, no. 4, 4 June 1836, I[2] 45, 49, May–July 1835, 24 September 1838.

58 F. Rivet, *La navigation à vapeur sur la Saône et le Rhône*, passim, and *Perrache*, 38–71.

59 R. Price, ed., *Revolution and Reaction* (1975), 3–5; P. Stearns, *Paths to Authority*, 197.

60 C. Aboucaya, *Les structures sociales et économiques de l'agglomeration lyonnais à la veille de la Révolution de 1848*, 19–24; G. Garrier, *Paysans de Beaujolais et du Lyonnais, 1800–1970*, 137–9; P. Léon, *Géographie de fortune et structures sociales à Lyon au XIXe siècle*, 66, 70, 90, 95.

61 M. Jal, "Lyon en 1835," *Revue du Lyonnais* 3 (1836): 21 (quote); J.B. Monfalcon, *Souvenirs d'un bibliothèquaire*; A.J. Tudesq, *Les grands notables en France* 1: 43–4, 166, 284.

62 Aboucaya, 19–20; Léon, 66, 70, 75, 176, 180.

63 A. Latreille, *Histoire de Lyon et du Lyonnais*, 340–5; Léon, 41; Tudesq, 1: 167.

64 Abbé Bez, *La ville des aumônes*; J. Rivet, *Les œuvres de charité et les établissements d'enseignement libre de 1789 à 1945*, 71–2, 133–41, 145; Stearns, 133.

65 R. Arminzade, "Breaking the Chains of Dependency: From Patronage to Class Politics, Toulouse, France, 1830–1872," *Journal of Urban History* 3 (August 1977).

66 Aboucaya, 19–20; M. Garden, *Lyon et les lyonnais au XVIIIe siècle*, 52; Léon, 396.

67 ADR, U, Conseil des Prud'hommes, Procès-verbaux de l'élection ... 1840–1848; *La Tribune prolétaire*, March 1835; N. Truquin, *Mémoires et aventures d'un prolétaire*, 216.

68 Rude, 733.

69 Aboucaya, 17. Of 8,000 deceased workers in 1847, only 985 left goods of any value.

70 AN C 963, Lyon; ACCL, Procès-verbaux et délibérations, 1849–50, p. 169.

71 *l'Avenir*, 4 December 1846; Benoit, *Confessions*, 63, 72–3; *Le Censeur*, 1 August 1848; Conseil général, *Rapport ... 1845–1846*, 5; *L'Echo de l'Industrie*, 10 January 1846.

72 *Statistique de la France*, ser. 1, vol. 11, *Prix et salaires*, 190.

73 Ibid., 99; Kauffmann, 74; Villermé, 388.

74 ADR, M, Mercuriales générales, 1833–4, 1843–7; *Statistique de la France*, ser. 1, 11: 127.

75 House of Commons, *Reports from Committees*, vol. 19, number 678, *Report from the Select Committee on the Silk Trade*, 556; *Le Censeur*, 15 October 1845; *L'Echo de l'Industrie*, 1, 15 November 1845, 5 January 1846.

76 Augier, 290; Conseil général, *Rapport ... 1838–1839*, 95, 97; *L'Echo de l'Industrie*, 14 March 1846; Reybaud, 154. In 1846, over two-thirds of the suburban looms wove fancy silks, while more than two-thirds of the urban looms wove simple silks (*Annuaire*, 1849, vol. 2, "Dénombrement ... 1846").

77 AN BB[18] 1362, 10, 14 January 1836; M. Derrion, *Constitution de l'industrie et organization pacifique du commerce et du travail*; J. Gaumont, *Le Commerce Veridique et Social (1835–1838) et son fondateur Michel Derrion (1803–1850)*; *L'Indicateur*, December 1834–May 1835.
78 *L'Avenir*, 6 November 1846. In Lyon, Fourierists published *L'Harmonie*, December 1837–March 1838; *La Revue sociale*, September 1844–September 1845; *L'Echo de l'Industrie*, October 1845–October 1846; *L'Avenir*, November 1846–January 1847. For the Fourierists' impact, see AN BB[18] 1451, 8 April 1847; ADR, M, Police générale, Rapports journaliers, 5 December 1847; *La Tribune lyonnaise*, February, March, and December 1847.
79 AML, Croix-Rousse, D, Procès-verbaux du Conseil municipal, 21 August 1850, p. 189; *L'Echo de l'Industrie*, 10 January, 14 March, 20 June, 5 September 1846.
80 ADR, J, Caisse de ₁ rêts pour chefs d'atelier, and X, Mont de Piété and Caisse d'épargne; AML, F², Fabrique des soies, Affairs diverses, Caisse de prêts; *Annuaires*, 1839–49 (tables on the Mont de Piété); *Le Censeur*, 18 May 1839, 10 July 1843, 22 September 1844; *L'Echo de la Fabrique de 1841*, 15 October 1841, on the loan bank's decision to cut back the number of loans.
81 ADR, M, Sociétés de secours, 1810–51, "Etat des Sociétés de Secours, 1847, 1848 and 1850," and "Sociétés ... ayant un livret à la Caisse d'épargne, 1845." Weavers' societies had between 200 and 5,200 francs in the savings bank and dispensed up to 1,500 francs annually.
82 AML, Q¹, Bureau de bienfaisance, Organisation; *Le Censeur*, 3–4 May 1843; C. Dufour, "L'assistance à Lyon de 1838 à 1851" (DES, Université de Lyon, 1960), 314–15.
83 AML, Q², Ouvriers sans travail, Commission du travail, "Compte général des Recettes et Dépenses," 1837, "Rapport ... sur le résultats des ses travaux pendant ... 1837," and minutes, 15 January, 5 March 1840; ADR, M, Ouvriers sans travail, 1839–42, enrolment lists.
84 ADR, M, Mercuriales générales, 1845–7; AML, D, Procès-verbaux du Conseil municipal, 1846–7; *L'Avenir*, 8–20 November 1846; *Le Censeur*, 8 October 1846–16 February 1847; *Le Courrier de Lyon*, October–December 1846; *L'Echo de l'Industrie*, 31 January, 15 August 1846; Rivet, *Navigation*, 397–401.
85 R. Price, *The French Second Republic*, 84–5; G. Créveuil, "La condition ouvrière et la crise de 1847 à Nantes," *1848* (1948): 40–58.
86 ADR, M, Police générale, Rapports journaliers, 9, 31 October, 16 November 1846, 3 January–15 February, 20 March, 5 April, 30 May 1847.
87 M. Agulhon, "Les chambrées en Basse-Provence," *Revue historique* 245 (1971): 337–68, and "Vers une histoire des associations," *Esprit* 46 (1978): 13–18.
88 AML, I¹ 245 Carnavale, 1806–63, and AML, Croix-Rousse, I¹ Police, Carnavale.
89 AML, I² 47^A Compagnonnage, especially documents numbered 13, 16, 94, 95; ADR, M, Police générale, 18 August 1835, 11 April 1839, 23 May 1843; 15 July 1846; AN BB[18] 1425, 18 August 1846.
90 ADR, M, Sociétés de secours.
91 AML, Croix-Rousse, Elections, Liste des électeurs, 1846, lists twenty-six *cafetiers* and forty-one *cabaretiers*; for police attitudes, see ADR, M, Police générale, Rapports journaliers, passim.
92 Agulhon, *La République au village*, 266–77; also Bezucha, "Masks of Revolution," in *Revolution and Reaction*, ed. Price, 237.

93 *L'Echo de la Fabrique de 1841*, 15 March 1841; AML, Croix-Rousse, D, Procs-verbaux du Conseil municipal, 4 March 1848.

94 Names of shareholders are found in *L'Indicateur*, 8, 15, 22 February, 1, 8, 22, 29 March, 5 April 1834.

95 AML, Croix-Rousse, 1¹ Police, Carnavale, 3 February 1837; ADR, M, Police générale, Rapports journaliers, 6 March 1840, 3 March, 14 April 1841; N.Z. Davis, "The Reasons of Misrule," *Society and Culture in Early Modern France*, 100, 109 ff.

96 AML 1⁵ 10; ADR, X, Dispensaire and Vaccine; Monfalcon and Polinière, 156-9.

97 ADR, M, Police générale, Rapports journaliers, January, 27 March, 13 July, 29 August 1838, and Sociétés de secours, "Règlement du Cercle Philanthropique et Industriel"; AML, Croix-Rousse, Ecoles Primaires, Reports, December 1842, December 1843, February 1844; *Annuaire*, 1849, 2: 339-41; Monfalcon, *Code moral des ouvriers*, 293-4; *L'Echo de la Fabrique de 1841*, 28 February, 30 June, 15, 31 July, 31 August, 15 December 1842.

98 Monfalcon, *Code moral*, 289-93, and *Histoire des insurrections lyonnais*, 26-7; Reybaud, 130-41, 145; Villermé, 364-6, 371, 373.

99 R. Gossez, "Presse parisiènne à destination des ouvriers, 1848-1851," *la presse ouvrière, 1819-1950*, 130.

100 *L'Echo des Travailleurs*, 23 November 1835; *L'Echo de la Fabrique*, 9 March 1834; *L'Indicateur*, 21 September, 16 November 1834; *La Tribune prolétaire*, 12 October, 23 November 1834; *L'Echo des Ouvriers*, August-October 1840, June 1841; *Le Travail*, Prospectus and September 1841; *L'Echo de la Fabrique de 1841*, 15 September 1841, 15 October 1842, 15 February 1844.

101 *L'Echo de la Fabrique*, 28 October 1832, 9 March 1834; *L'Echo des Travailleurs*, 22 February 1834; *La Tribune prolétaire*, 5 October, 23 November 1834, 8 February 1835; *L'Indicateur*, 12 October, 2, 9 November, 14 December 1834; *L'Echo des Ouvriers*, July and October 1840, February 1841; *Le Travail*, August 1841; *L'Echo de la Fabrique de 1841*, 15 October 1842, 15 December 1843.

102 *La Tribune prolétaire* was subtitled *Journal de Progrès social*; see also 21 September 1834, 26 July 1835; *L'Echo des Ouvriers*, September 1840; *Le Travail*, June 1841; *L'Echo de la Fabrique de 1841*, 31 December 1843.

103 *L'Echo des Ouvriers*, December 1840, May and June 1841; *L'Echo de la Fabrique de 1841*, 30 September, 31 December 1841; the latter's reform petition was signed by over half (5,000) of the masters.

104 *L'Echo de la Fabrique*, 26 February, 25 March, 8, 15 April, 23 November 1832; *L'Indicateur*, 28 September 1834, 31 May 1835; *L'Echo des Ouvriers*, July 1840, June and August 1841; *L'Echo de la Fabrique de 1841*, 15 April, 1 May 1842.

105 A.J. Tudesq, *Les grands notables en France* 1: 284; Bezucha, *The Lyon Uprising*.

106 G. Perreux, *Au temps des sociétés secrètes: La propagande républicaine au début de la Monarchie de Juillet, 1830-1835*, 99.

107 M. Buffenoir, "Le Fourierisme à Lyon de 1834 à 1848," *Revue d'histoire de Lyon* 12 (1913): 444-55.

108 AN BB¹⁸ 1415, 1420.

109 *L'Echo de la Fabrique de 1841*, 15 April 1842; *L'Echo de l'Industrie*, 3, 17 January 1846; *L'Avenir*, 15 November 1846.

110 AN BB³⁰ 294, Tableau des accusés d'avril; ADR, M, Police générale 1835-48,

and R, Fortifications; AML, I¹, Police, Commissaires et Commissaire Central, and M¹ Fortifications.

111 Tudesq, 1: 284.

112 AN BB¹⁸ 1230, 14 March 1835; ADR, M, Police générale, Rapports journaliers, March–August 1835; AML, I¹ 74, Correspondance du commissaire spécial, 6 April 1837; *Le Censeur*, January–March 1835.

113 ACCL, Compte-rendu des travaux, 1846–7, pp. 24–9; *Le Courrier de Lyon* and *Le Journal de Commerce*, passim.

114 *L'Echo des Ouvriers*, July and August 1840; *L'Echo de la Fabrique de 1841*, 15 April, 30 June 1843, 31 August 1844; *La Tribune lyonnaise*, May 1845, January and April 1846, March 1847; *L'Echo de l'Industrie*, 3 January, 14 March 1846; *L'Avenir*, 4 November 1846.

115 Tudesq, 1: 285–7.

116 *La Gazette de Lyon*, 5 April 1845, 8 July–2 August, 11 and 13 September 1846, 2, 13, 27 June 1847.

117 H. de Riancy, *Compte-rendu des elections de 1846*, includes Mortemart's campaign promises. See also AN C 1286 A, Rhône 133, Elections, 1848, and *Le Courrier de Lyon*, 20 January 1848.

118 AN C 1286 A Rhône 133, Elections 1834–48; Tudesq, 1:285.

119 ADR, M, Police, Affaires diverses, 1838–45, July 1841; *Le Courrier de Lyon*, 11–31 July 1846.

120 *Le Courrier de Lyon*, 22 27 August 1846; *La Gazette de Lyon*, 25 August 1846.

121 *Le Courrier de Lyon*, 16 July 1846; *Le Censeur*, 18 September 1846.

122 *Le Censeur*, 9 December 1847, 16–20 January, 2–7 February 1848; BML, Fonds Coste, Affiches 11497–501.

123 Bezucha, *The Lyon Uprising*, passim; "Les Carbonari en France sous la Restoration," *La Révolution de 1848* 9 (1912–13): 413; G. Weill, *Histoire du parti républicain en France*, 77.

124 *Le Censeur*, 1834–9; AN BB¹⁸ 1240, 1241, 1252, 1386, 1387; ADR, M, Police, Affaires diverses, 1838–45, July 1841.

125 ADR, M, Police générale, Commissaire spécial, 24 October 1838, 28 September 1844; F. Rude, "Le mouvement ouvrier à Lyon," *Revue de Psychologie des Peuples* 12 (1958): 223–46.

126 ADR, M, Police générale, Commissaire spécial, 29 August 1840; AN BB¹⁸ 1388, 16, 23 December 1840, 20 March 1841; BB²⁰ 112, 20 March 1841; *Le Censeur*, 14 June 1839; Cour des Pairs, *Attentat du 15 octobre, Rapport ... Girod*, 60–1.

127 AN BB¹⁸ 1387 and 1474ᴮ, October 1840, 20 September 1849; ADR, M, Police générale, Rapports journaliers, October 1840; Benoit, *Confessions*, 71; Commissaire, 1: 79; *Le Censeur*, 12–13 October 1840.

128 *Le Censeur*, 14 October–27 December 1838; 7 August–28 October 1840; 1 March, 4 June 1841; 18 June–8 July 1842; 13 November 1847, 11 July 1848; Benoit, *Confessions*, 75; J.J. Baughman, "The French Banquet Campaign of 1847–1848," *Journal of Modern History* 31 (March 1959): 10.

129 *Le Censeur*, 26 October 1839, 12 December 1844–30 July 1845; *La Tribune lyonnaise*, December 1847, February 1848.

130 Benoit, *Confessions*, 79–82, and *Souvenirs de la République de 1848*, 22.

131 AN BB¹⁸ 1246, 1248, 1360, 1397, 1421, 8 October 1835, 6 May, 23 August 1837, 5 October, 17 December 1841, 8 February 1842, 26 October, 22 November 1844, 8, 11 July, 27 August 1845; ADR, M, Police générale, Commissaire spécial, 4 August, 31 October, 23 November, 1 December 1837; AML, I² 40, pieces 17 and 18.

132 ADR, R, Conseils de Guerre, Insurrection du ... 1849, Saisie des journaux and Dossiers individuels, "Ami de l'homme loge"; *Le Conseil central aux loges maçonniques de Lyon*; *Simples explications* by "Deux Frères de l'Asile du Sage"; *L'Echo de la Fabrique de 1841*, 31 December 1842.

133 ADR, M, Police générale, Rapport journaliers, 13 December 1837, 8–26 January, 27 March, 13 July, 29 August 1838; U, Tribunal Correctionnel, Jugemens, 12 July 1838; Benoit, *Confessions*, 57–9, 61, 71–2.

134 Benoit, *Confessions*, 73–5; E. Cabet, *Utile et franche explication avec les Communistes lyonnais*, 1, 20; C.H. Johnson, *Utopian Communism in France*, 79 and passim.

135 ADR, M, police générale, Commissaire spécial, 7 May, 3 August 1841; *Le Travail*, June–September 1841.

136 Cabet, 2–4, 12–15; Johnson, "Deux lettres inédites de cinq ouvriers lyonnais à Cabet et à Dézamy," *Revue d'histoire économique et sociale* 47 (1969): 529–39.

137 AN BB^{18} 1415, September–October 1843; *Addresse de la Commission Parisienne pour le Populaire au Communistes lyonnais, suivie d'un Addresse des Communistes lyonnais*; Cabet, 26; Commissaire, 1:97–108; *Le Populaire*, 22 August 1844.

138 P.J. Proudhon, *Correspondance* 2: 136.

139 AN BB^{18} 1421 and 1423, July–November 1844, 14, 17 January 1845; ADR, U, Tribunal Correctionnel, 19 September 1844, Jugemens, 9 April, 23 August 1845; ADR, M, Police générale, Rapports journaliers, 30 August, 6 December 1847.

140 AML, I^2 40, no. 9; *L'Echo de l'Industrie*, 16, 23 May 1846; Poncet, Meurgé, Mamessier, and Racine, *Réponse communiste icarienne à La Tribune lyonnaise*; *La Tribune lyonnaise*, August and October 1845; May 1846; March, September, and November 1847.

141 Davis.

142 AN BB^{18} 1458, 8 December 1846, 21 January 1847; ADR, M, Police générale, Rapports journaliers, 3 November 1846, 31 January 1848; Benoit, *Souvenirs*, 76.

143 AN BB^{18} 1441, 22 September 1846; ADR, U, Tribunal Correctionnel, Jugemens, 18 January 1848; AML, I^2 47^A, Compagnonnages, no. 33; Agulhon, *Une ville ouvrière au temps du socialisme utopique*, 131–6.

144 AN BB^{18} 1460, 3 February 1848; BB^{30} 361, 23 February 1848; ADR, M, Police générale, Rapports journaliers, 20 October 1847, 21–30 January, 2, 4, 18, 19 February 1848; *Le Censeur*, 20 February 1848.

CHAPTER TWO

1 L. Loubère, *Radicalism in Mediterranean France, 1848–1919*, 9; R. Price, *The French Second Republic*, 99.

2 G. Fasel, "Urban Workers in Provincial France, February-June 1848," *International Review of Social History* 14 (1977): 644–7.

3 J. Bergier, *Le journal d'un bourgeois de Lyon en 1848*, ed. J. Godart, 10; A.J. Tudesq, *Les grands notables en France*, 2: 1008.

4 AML, I^2 40, 27; J. Benoit, *Souvenirs de la République de 1848*, 20; Bergier, 10–13; *Le Censeur*, 26 February 1848; M. Treillard, *La République à Lyon sous le gouvernement provisoire*, 6–8.

5 Benoit, *Confessions d'un prolétaire*, 79–81 and *Souvenirs*, 21–2; *Le Censeur*, 22 May 1848.

6 Bergier, 13–14; *Le Censeur*, 27 February, 10, 16, 22 March 1848; Treillard, 8; *Le Tribun du Peuple*, 3 March 1848.

7 Bergier, 16; F. Blanc, "Le Comité éxécutif de Lyon en 1848," *Révolution de 1848* 9–19 (1912–13): 342–7, 350; *Le Tribun du Peuple*, 3 March 1848.

8 M. Agulhon, *Une ville ouvrière au temps du socialisme utopique*, 269–71; A. Armengaud, *Les populations de L'Est-Aquitain au début de l'époch contemporaine ...*, 346; A. Charles, *La Révolution de 1848 et la Seconde République à Bordeaux et dans le département de la Gironde*, 98, 101; G. Dupeux, *Aspects de l'histoire sociale et politique du Loir-et-Cher, 1848–1914*, 320–1; H. Fortin, *Contribution à l'histoire de la Révolution de 1848 dans le Pas de Calais*, 18–19; J. Godechot, ed., *La Révolution de 1848 à Toulouse et dans la Haute Garonne*, 140–4, 168–9; R. Levy, *Le Havre entre trois révolutions*, 110–11; Y.-H. Monceau, "Moulins en 1848," in *La Révolution de 1848 à Moulins et dans le département de l'Allier* (Moulin: Pottier et Cie., 1950), 111; E. Reynier, *La Seconde République dans l'Ardèche*, 29–31; L. de Tricaud, *Histoire du département de l'Ain du 24 février au 20 décembre 1848*, 21–2, 31–2; P. Vigier, *La Seconde République dans la région alpine* 1: 186.

9 P. Deyon, "Aspects industrielles de la crise, Rouen," in *Aspects de la crise et de la dépression de l'économie française ... XIXe siècle*, 154; G. Duveau, *1848: The Making of a Revolution*, 44–59; G. Laurent, "Les événements de l'année 1848 à Reims et dans le Marne," in *Le Département de la Marne et la Révolution de 1848*, 47–53; Vigier, 1: 188.

10 Benoit, *Confessions*, 83, and *Souvenirs*, 24; Bergier, 18–20; *Le Censeur*, 27 February, 22 May 1848; *Le Courrier de Lyon*, 27 February 1848; J.B. Monfalcon, *Histoire de notre temps*, 14; Treillard, 9.

11 Benoit, *Confessions*, 84, 86, and *Souvenirs*, 24, 26.

12 Benoit, *Confessions*, 83; Monfalcon, *Histoire de notre temps*, 19.

13 M. Dommanget, *Auguste Blanqui et la Révolution de 1848*, 2–16.

14 Benoit, *Confessions*, 85–6.

15 Ibid., 85; Bergier, 21; Blanc, "L'œuvre de Comité éxécutif de Lyon," *Révolution de 1848* 9–10 (1912–13): 175; *Le Censeur*, 27 February 1848; *L'Organisateur lyonnais*, 28 February 1848.

16 AML, I² 40, 31, 32; Benoit, *Confessions*, 88, 94; Blanc, "Le Comité éxécutif," 350, 359–61.

17 Blanc, "Le Comité éxécutif," 344–7, 349.

18 AML, I² 40, 30, 31, and "Affaire Crouzet, Pros et Cie."

19 AN BB³⁰ 361, 1 March 1848; M. Hodieu, *Rapport présenté au Conseil municipal de Lyon ... sur les demandes en indemnités formées contre la ville de Lyon*, 7; *La Sentinelle*, 4 April 1848.

20 Benoit, *Confessions*, 95; Blanc, "Le Comité éxécutif," 362; V. Chazelas, "Félix Blanc," *Révolution de 1848* 9–10 (1912–13): 158; Treillard, 22–3.

21 BML, Fonds Coste, 5314, Affiches, 9261, 9270, 9283; Benoit, *Confessions*, 90; Bergier, 24–6.

22 AML, D, Croix-Rousse, Guillotière, and Vaise, Procès-verbaux du conseil municipal, 25 February–10 March 1848; BML, Fonds Coste, 5314, Affiches, 9295, 9301; Blanc, "Le Comité éxécutif," 356; J. Lentillon, *Un page de l'histoire de Lyon en 1848: Administration de la Commune de Caluire*, 3.

23 BML, Fonds Coste, 5314, Affiches, 9265; Benoit, *Confessions*, 88; Bergier, 33; Blanc, "Le Comité éxécutif," 360–1.

24 Blanc, "Le Comité éxécutif," 360; *L'Organisateur lyonnais*, 1 March 1848.

25 ACCL, Compte-rendu des travaux de la Chambre de Commerce, 1847–8, pp.

22–3; AML, I² 40, 36, 40; Bergier, 22, 28, 33–6; Blanc, "Le Comité éxécutif," 361.

26 AML, Fonds Coste, 5314, Affiches, 9264, 9266–68, 9272, 9274–5, 9279; Blanc, "Le Comité éxécutif," 362; "L'œuvre de Comité éxécutif," 178.

27 BML, Fonds Coste, 5314, Affiches, 9278, 9280; Treillard, 17.

28 Le Tribun du Peuple, 3, 5, 12, 17 March 1848; E. Reveil, "Notice sur le jeton du Comité provisoire de Lyon en 1848," Révolution de 1848 7 (1910–11): 80–3.

29 A. Lamartine, History of the French Revolution of 1848 3: 29, 58, 162; Treillard, 18; AN BB³⁰ 361, dos. 3, 1 March 1848.

30 J.M. House, "Civil-Military Relations in Paris, 1848," in R. Price, Revolution and Reaction, 157; ADR, R, Garde nationale mobile, Correspondance, 4 April, 28 August 1848.

31 ADR, R, Garde nationale mobile, Correspondance, 24 April, 9, 11, 26, 29 May 1848, 31 March 1849, Arrêtés, 1, 4, 17, 18, 20, 22 April 1848, Régistre, 25 April–12 May 1848.

32 BML, Fonds Coste, 5314, Affiches, 9267, 9268, 9285, and unnumbered, "Ordre. Le Comité de Guerre et Police reste Comité de Police seulement"; La République, 7, 9 March 1848; Le Tribun du Peuple, 12, 17 March 1848.

33 Benoit, Confessions, 84, 93; Blanc, "Le Comité éxécutif," 357, 362, and "L'œuvre du Comité éxécutif," 169; Treillard, 20.

34 Benoit, Confessions, 84–5; Blanc, Le Comité éxécutif," 347; Chazelas, 158.

35 Agulhon, Une ville, 276; Charles, 130; Dupeux, 327–8; Fortin, 68; G. Frambourg, "Un Commissaire du Gouvernement Provisoire de la République, Guépin," Annales de Bretagne 46 (1954): 336; Godechot, 206; G. Laurent, "Les événements de l'année 1848 à Reims et dans le Marne," in Le Département de la Marne et la Révolution de 1848, 61; Levy, 111; G. Rougeron, "De la Révolution de février au 2 décembre," in La Révolution de 1848 à Moulins, 21–2; Vigier, 1: 230–5.

36 Benoit, Confessions, 91–2, Souvenirs, 27; Maurin-Béraud, Almanach démocratique et social des clubs lyonnais pour 1849, 30–1; Le Tribun du Peuple, 3 March 1848.

37 Blanc, "Le Comité éxécutif," 170.

38 P. McPhee, "The Crisis of Radical Republicanism in the French Revolution of 1848," Historical Studies 16 (1974): 73, 77–9.

39 AML, I² 40, 377; P. Montagne, Le comportement politique de l'armée à Lyon sous la Monarchie de Juillet et la Seconde République, 215–19; General M. Rey, M. Emmanuel Arago et les événements de Lyon au 24 février 1848, 7.

40 ADR, M, Police générale, Rapports journaliers, 17–18 March 1848; AML, D, Croix-Rousse, Procès-verbaux de Conseil municipal, 1 March 1848.

41 Montagne, 209–11; Rey, 3–4, 7–8, 12, 20, 29.

42 AML, D, Procès-verbaux de Conseil municipal, 1849, pp. 70, 113, 619, and I² 40, 289; Le Censeur, 19 March 1848; La République, 2 March 1848.

43 AML, D, Procès-verbaux de Conseil municipal, 1849, pp. 115, 618, 749, and Croix-Rousse, Procès-verbaux de Conseil municipal, 1847–9, p. 364.

44 AML, D, Procès-verbaux de Conseil municipal, 1849, pp. 113–14, and Croix-Rousse, Procès-verbaux de Conseil municipal, 1847–9, pp. 68–9; I² 40, 273, 340.

45 AML, Guillotière, D19, 334, and I² 40, 297, 301; Bergier, 27–8.

46 AML, I² 40, 273; La Feuille de Jour, 29 February 1848.

47 AML, I² 40, 273; Le Courrier de Lyon, 2 March 1848; Le Moniteur Judiciaire de Lyon, 3 June 1848.

48 AML, I² 40, 300, 304, 305; *Le Moniteur Judiciaire de Lyon*, 3 June 1848; *Résumé de plaidorie pour la Ville de Lyon, contre la Commune d'Oullins et M. l'Abbé Rey* 3, 35 ff.

49 Bergier, 34, 36, mentions the final raids. I have reckoned a total of 734,901 francs in damages from the claims and indemnities mentioned in the documents cited in notes 37–43. This sum excludes costs (e.g., repairs) for which claims were not filed. A total of 557,746 francs in damages occurred in church-run charities.

50 *La Gazette de Lyon*, 27 February 1848; AML, I² 40, 273, 300, 305, 332, 339, 340.

51 AN BB²⁰ 143, 1 June 1848. Only three of the thirteen men tried for their actions at Oullins were from Lyon. Six were manual labourers; three were metal workers; two were miners.

52 *L'Echo des Ouvriers*, March 1841; *L'Echo de la Fabrique de 1841*, 15 November, 15 December 1841, 28 February 1842.

53 AML, I² 40, 273; AN BB³⁰ 361, dossier 3, 1 March 1848; *L'Organisateur lyonnais*, 28 February 1848; P. de la Perrière et al., *Mémoire pour la Commune d'Oullins, appelante, contre le refuge de St.-Joseph et la Ville de Lyon, intimés*, 61.

54 Agulhon, *La République au village*, 279; E.P. Thompson, "The Moral Economy of the English Crowd in the Eighteenth Century," *Past & Present*, no. 50 (1972): 76–136.

55 AML, I² 40, 273; Perrière et al., 62–63.

56 AN BB³⁰ 361, dos. 3, 1 March 1848; *Le Courrier de Lyon*, 8 March 1848; *La Feuille du Jour*, 7 March 1848; *La Gazette de Lyon*, 2 March 1848; *Le Moniteur judiciaire de Lyon*, 9 March 1848; *L'Organisateur lyonnais*, 29 February 1848.

57 *Le Censeur*, 16 April 1844, 28 April–1 June 1847; *L'Echo de la Fabrique de 1841*, 15 April 1844; *L'Echo des Ouvriers*, July 1841; *Le Travail*, June 1841.

58 *Le Censeur*, 28, 29 February 1848.

59 AML, I² 40, 273.

60 AML, D, Vaise, Procès-verbaux de Conseil municipal, 1843–52, 11 November 1852, p. 270; Perrière et al., 69.

61 AML, I² 40, 297; Hodieu, 11.

62 Montagne, 215–18.

63 AML, Guillotière, D19, 506; Bergier, 23, 27.

64 *Le Moniteur*, 25 March 1848, 681.

65 *La Feuille de Jour*, 3 March 1848.

CHAPTER THREE

1 J. Balteau, M. Barroux, and M. Prevost, *Dictionnaire de biographie française*.

2 *Le Courrier de Lyon*, 30 April, 7 May 1848, 12, 21 February 1849; *La Gazette de Lyon*, 21 May 1848, mid-February 1849; *Le Salut Public*, 19, 21, 24 May 1848; General Le Pays de Bourjolly, *De l'armée et 40 jours de 1848 à Lyon*; General Rey, *M. Emmanuel Arago et les événements de Lyon au 24 février 1848*.

3 *Le Moniteur*, 15 February 1849.

4 ADR, M, Personnel, Préfets.

5 A.R. Calman, *Ledru-Rollin and the Second French Republic*, 109–11; P. Haury, "Les commissaires de Ledru-Rollin en 1848," *Révolution française*

57 (1909): 438–75; H. Machin, "The Prefects and Political Repression: February 1848 to December 1851," in *Revolution and Reaction*, ed. R. Price, 282–3.

6 P. O'Brien, "The Revolutionary Police of 1848," in *Revolution and Reaction*; Price, *The French Second Republic*, 112–39.

7 Rey, 7–9 (a letter from Arago).

8 AML, D, Croix-Rousse, Procès-verbaux de Conseil municipal, 4, 5 March 1848; BML, Fonds Coste, 5314, Affiches, 9296, 9299, 9306; *Le Tribun du People*, 5 March 1848; *La Feuille du Jour*, 6, 7 March 1848; *L'Organisateur lyonnais*, 8, 10 March 1848.

9 Bourjolly, 17–34; BML, Fonds Coste, 5314, Affiches, 9302.

10 BML, Fonds Coste, 5314, Affiches, 9312; AML, Croix-Rousse, D, Procès-verbaux de Conseil municipal, 6–13 March 1848.

11 AML, Croix-Rousse, D, Procès-verbaux de Conseil municipal, 17–25 March 1848; Le Pays de Bourjolly, 39–41; *Le Tribun du Peuple*, 26–27 March 1848; *L'Organisateur lyonnais*, 27 March 1848; ADR, M, Police générale, Rapports journaliers, 22, 24 March 1848.

12 ADR, M, Police générale, Rapports journaliers, 17–19 March 1848; AML, Croix-Rousse, D, Procès-verbaux du Conseil municipal, 6 March 1848; Rey, 29–30; *Le Tribun du Peuple*, 17 March 1848; *L'Organisateur lyonnais*, 18 March 1848.

13 M. Treillard, *La République à Lyon sous le gouvernement provisoire*, 48.

14 AML, I² 40, 341, 342, 345, 346; BML, Fonds Coste, 5314, Affiches, 9335; *Le Censeur*, 31 March 1848.

15 F. Lentacker, "Les ouvriers belges dans le département du Nord au milieu de XIXe siècle," *Revue du Nord* 38 (1956): 12–13.

16 *Le Censeur*, 12, 19, 24, 30 March 1848; *La Feuille du Jour*, 21 March 1848; *La Gazette de Lyon*, 20–1, 27–8, 29 March 1848; *La République*, 23 March 1848; *Le Salut Public*, 20, 22, 27–30 March 1848; BML, Fonds Coste, 5314, Affiches, 9314.

17 BML, Fonds Coste, 5314, Affiches, 9331, 9333; ADR, M, Police générale, Rapports journaliers, 28 March 1848; *La Feuille du Jour*, 5 March 1848; *L'Organisateur lyonnais*, 30 March 1848; *Le Tribun du Peuple*, 29–30 March 1848; *Le Vingt-Quatre Février*, 30 March 1848.

18 P. Reveyron, *Appreciation des principes qui ont dirigé et des faits qui ont accompagné le mouvement républicain des volontaires savoyards*, 1–39; BML, Fonds Coste, 5314, Affiches, 9334, 9339, 9340; Treillard, 44–5; all the Lyonnais newspapers, 30 March–2 April 1848; *La Gazette de Lyon*, 19 March 1849.

19 Reveyron, 39 ff.; *Le Censeur*, 16 April, 1–2 May 1848; *Le Courrier de Lyon*, 8, 12, 28 April, 3 May 1848; *Le Peuple Souverain*, 2, 5, 8, 17–18 April, 1–2, 9 May 1848; *Le Tribun du Peuple*, 13 April 1848; *Le Vingt-Quatre Février*, 6–7, 9–10, 11–12 April 1848.

20 P. Amann, *Revolution and Mass Democracy*, 169–170; M. Dessal, "Les Incidents franco-belges de 1848," *Actes du Congrès Historique du Centenaire 1848*; A. Gues, "Les Expeditions armées de 1848," *Ecrits de Paris* 344 (1975): 82–8; A. Lamartine, *History of the French Revolution of 1848* 2: 140, 141.

21 F. Rude, *L'Insurrection lyonnaise de novembre 1831*, 212–13; P. Stearns, *1848: The Revolutionary Tide in Europe*, 123–30.

22 M. Caussidière, *Mémoires* 1: 201–7.

23 J. Benoit, *Souvenirs de la République de 1848*, 62–3; Gues, 84–5; Lamartine, 2: 141; Treillard, 45; *La Gazette de Lyon*, 13 March 1849.

24 Le Pays de Bourjolly, 18–19; Treillard, 39; *Le Tribun du Peuple*, 19–20, 22–23, 29–30 March 1848.

25 Le Pays de Bourjolly, 44–5; *La Montagne*, special edition, "Jean-Marie Gigou, Fourrier au 4me d'artillerie"; *L'Organisateur lyonnais*, 2 April 1848; *Le Vorace*, May 1848; AN BB³⁰ 361, dos. 3, 31 March 1848.

26 AN BB³⁰ 361, dos. 3, 31 March 1848; J. Bergier, *Le Journal d'un bourgeois de Lyon en 1848*, 71–2; Le Pays de Bourjolly, 48–52; *La Montagne*, special edition; *L'Organisateur lyonnais*, 2 April 1848.

27 AN BB³⁰ 361, dos. 3, 31, March 1848; ADR, M, Police générale, Rapports journaliers, 30 March, 1 April 1848; BML, Fonds Coste, 5314, Affiches, 9337, 9343, 9347; Bergier, 73; Treillard, 40; *L'Organisateur lyonnais*, 2–3 April 1848; *Le Vingt-Quatre Février*, 2–3 April 1848.

28 Amann, 93–109.

29 *Le Censeur, Le Courrier de Lyon, La Gazette de Lyon, Le Salut Public*, 22–23 March 1848.

30 J. M. House, "Civil-Military Relations in Paris, 1848," in *Revolution and Reaction*, ed. R. Price, 154–5; W. Zaniewicki, "L'armée au lendemain de la Révolution de 1848," *Cahiers d'histoire* 14 (1969): 297–406.

31 P. Chalmin, "Les crises dans l'armée française, 1848," *Revue historique de l'armée* 18 (1962): 50.

32 Le Pays de Bourjolly, 54–9; J.B. Monfalcon, *Histoire de notre temps* 1: 61–2; Captain P. Montagne, *Le comportement politique de l'armée à Lyon sous le Monarchie de Juillet et la Seconde Républic*, 236–7; Rey, 4, 10; *L'Organisateur lyonnais, Le Salut Public*, and *Le Vingt-Quatre Février*, 13 April 1848.

33 Le Pays de Bourjolly calls the assailants Voraces but no other source mentions Voraces.

34 *La Liberté*, 12 April 1848.

35 ADR, M, Police générale, Rapports journaliers, 24 April 1848; AML, D, Croix-Rousse, Procès-verbaux de Conseil municipal, 28 April 1848.

36 *Le Patriote lyonnais*, 29 April 1848.

37 Ibid., 6, 15, 20 April 1848; *La Gazette de Lyon*, 5, 16, 20 April 1848; *L'Organisateur lyonnais*, 6, 15 April 1848; *Le Peuple Souverain*, 12, 19, 26 April 1848; *Le Salut Public*, 25 April 1848.

38 Bergier, 60; Monfalcon, *Histoire de notre temps*, 1: 58.

39 ADR, R, 2me Conseil de Guerre, Société dit les Voraces.

40 *La Sentinelle*, 4 April 1848.

41 *Details circonstanciés et très-curieux sur les Voraces, les Ventre-creux et les Vauteurs de Lyon*, par un affilié.

42 E. Labrousse, "Panorama de la Crise." in *Aspects de la crise et de la dépression de l'économie française au milieu de XIXe siècle*, xvii–xxi.

43 ADR, Banque Guérin, Correspondance expédiée, 24–28 February, 8–25 March, 4–11 April 1848; Bergier, 57–62.

44 ADR, M, Police générale, Rapports journaliers, 21 March, 28 July, 9 September, 17 November, 26 December 1848.

45 M. Agulhon, *Une ville ouvrière au temps du socialisme utopique*, 269, 274; A. Charles, *La Révolution de 1848 et la Seconde République à Bordeaux et dans le département de la Gironde*, 126; P. Deyon, "Aspects industrielles de la crise, Rouen," in *Aspects de la crise …*, 154–7; G. Fasel, "Urban Workers in Provincial France, February–June 1848," *International Review of Social History* 17 (1972): 661–74; R. Gossez, *Les Ouvriers de Paris*, vol. 1, *L'Organisation, 1848–1851*, 127; P. Vigier, *La Seconde République dans la région alpine*, 278–83.

46 *La Feuille du Jour*, 2–8 March 1848; *La Gazette de Lyon*, 3, 8 March 1848; Monfalcon, 37, 39; ADR, M, Police générale, Rapports journaliers, 13 March 1848.

47 ADR, M, Police générale, Rapports journaliers, 13, 15, 23 March 1848; *L'Organisateur lyonnais*, 4, 8, 15, 27 March 1848.

48 ADR, M, Police générale, Rapports journaliers, 10 April 1848; *Le Peuple Souverain*, 12 April 1848; *Le Censeur*, 6, 8 April 1848.

49 *Le Censeur*, 6, 8 April 1848; *Le Courrier de Lyon*, 23 March 1848; *L'Organisateur lyonnais*, 17, 23 March 1848.

50 *Règlement des maîtres et ouvriers peintres, plâtriers et vitriers* (Lyon: Nigon, 1848).

51 *Statuts de l'Association des Entrepreneurs Peintres-Plâtriers de la Ville de Lyon* (Lyon: Nigon, 1848); ADR, M, Police générale, Rapports journaliers, 1, 18 August, 21 September, 13, 25 October 1848; AML, Q², Ouvriers sans travail, Ateliers de Charité, "Liste des citoyens patrons et ouvriers peintres …"

52 E. Flotard, *Le Mouvement coopératif à Lyon et dans le Midi de la France*, 96–8.

53 Bergier, 53–63; *Le Censeur*, 18 March 1848; BML, Fonds Coste, 5314, Affiches, 9300, 9313; ADR, Banque Guérin, Correspondance expédiée, 1–18 March 1848.

54 ADR, Banque Guérin, Correspondance expédiée, 21 March–1 April 1848; *Le Moniteur*, 8, 9, 25, 26 March 1848; ACCL, *Compte-rendu des travaux*, no. 11, pp. 391–2.

55 BML, Fonds Coste, 5314, Affiches, 9297, 9298; *Le Censeur*, 6, 10 March 1848; *La Feuille du Jour*, 8, 10 March 1848; *L'Organisateur lyonnais*, 17 March 1848.

56 Benoit, *Confessions*, 101; *Le Tribun du Peuple*, 13, 17 March 1848.

57 *Le Tribun du Peuple*, 13 March 1848; Flotard, 153–4 (quote).

58 Gossez, 226, 242–66; Benoit, *Confessions*, 101.

59 Benoit, *Confessions*, 101; AML, D, Procès-verbaux de Conseil Municipal, vol. 39, 1848, p. 78, Fayolle's Report; *Le Censeur*, 29 February, 2, 3, 21 March 1848; *Le Tribun du Peuple*, 13 March 1848; *L'Organisateur lyonnais*, 10 March 1848.

60 *L'Organisateur lyonnais*, 16, 18, 21, 22 March 1848; BML, Fonds Coste, 5314, Affiches, 9315, 9322, 9326.

61 BML, Fonds Coste, 5314, Affiches, 9329, 9333.

62 AML, I², 40, no. 184; AML, D, Croix-Rousse, Procès-verbaux de Conseil municipal, 11 May 1848.

63 *Le Censeur*, 14 May, 9 June 1848; Treillard, 27–9; BML, Fonds Coste, 5314, Affiches, no number: "Arrête … la dissolution des chantiers nationaux … 15 juillet 1848."

64 BML, Fonds Coste, 5314, Affiches, 9372, 9377; AML, I² 40, no. 342; *L'Organisateur lyonnais*, 30 March 1848; Monfalcon, *Histoire de notre temps* 1: 66.

65 As of 9 March, they had collected 235,000 francs. Many companies, banks, and landowners donated 1,000 francs or more. *La Gazette de Lyon*, 9 March 1848.

66 Bergier, 56; *Le Censeur*, 22 March 1848; *Le Courrier de Lyon*, 28 March 1848.

67 *Le Moniteur*, 28 March 1848.

68 M. Agulhon, *La République au village*, 42, 107; J. Godechot, *La Révolution de 1848 à Toulouse et dans la Haute Garonne*, 196–7; D. Snyder

and C. Tilly, "Hardship and Collective Violence in France, 1830 to 1960," *American Sociological Review* 37 (1972): 520.

69 *Le Censeur, Le Courrier de Lyon, La Gazette de Lyon, Le Peuple Souverain*, and *Le Salut Public*, 23–31 March 1848.

70 According to AML, Guillotière, G1, Finances, only three-quarters of the tax revenue had been collected by July 1851.

71 *Le Moniteur*, "Commission d'enquête," II, p. 32, and 16 February 1848; *Le Censeur*, 20 February, 6 March 1849; Monfalcon, *Histoire de notre temps* 2: 65; *Revue de Lyon* (1849–50): 301.

72 *Le Moniteur.*

73 T.R. Christofferson, "The French National Workshops of 1848: The View from the Provinces," *French Historical Studies* 11 (1980): 507 ff.

74 Division of workshop costs and the extraordinary tax revenues plagued intragovernmental relations for months. The central government finally agreed to cover workshop and food relief expenses of 2,419,561 francs with the extraordinary tax receipts to keep the city from cutting off essential services. See AN F^6 11, Rhône, Comptabilité communale, 31, Lyon, 1847–9, "Chapitres additionnels ... 1848" and correspondence of 15 December 1848 and 18 January 1849.

75 BML, Fonds Coste, 5314, Affiches, 9344; Bergier, 72–3, *Le Peuple Souverain*, 2 April 1848.

76 *L'Organisateur lyonnais*, 7, 11 April 1848.

77 Ibid., 12 April 1848; BML, Fonds Coste, 5314, Affiches, 9356, 9362; AML Q², Ouvriers sans travail, Ateliers de charité, Commission pour la répartition du travail, Compte-rendu, Constitution, Emplois et fonctions.

78 AML, Q², especially correspondence with the minister of commerce, and proclamation, 8 May 1848.

79 Ibid., "Commande de 130,000 écharpes ... Répartition"; *Le Peuple Souverain*, 8 April 1848; *Le Spartacus*, April 1848; *Association Fraternelle des femmes ouvrières lyonnaises pour l'exploitation de toutes industries, fondée le 17 septembre 1848.*

80 ADR, Banque Guérin, Correspondance expédiée, 13 April–4 May 1848.

81 AML, D, Procès-verbaux de Conseil municipal, vol. 39, 22 June 1848, "Réclamation à l'état ...," and 29 July 1848, "Rapport ... sur le budget"; Bergier, 33, 43; Monfalcon, *Histoire de notre temps* 1: 41; *Revue de Lyon*, 1849–50, p. 48.

82 AML, Q², Souscriptions pour les ouvriers sans travail, 1848, complete lists for Bellecour, Perrache, and the Hospital quarter and incomplete lists for the old city and Croix-Rousse. Of the 1,022 persons whose places of birth were recorded, 672 (65.7 per cent) were immigrants. Half the people whose ages were recorded were between 38 and 60 years old. The lists include 2,479 heads of household and 7,345 dependents. Of the 1,097 listed with their profession, 582 (53 per cent) were silk workers; 330 (30 per cent) were *journaliers* or *manœuvres*.

83 AML, D, Croix-Rousse and Guillotière, Procès-verbaux de Conseil municipal, 25 February–28 April 1848; BML, Fonds Coste, 5314, Affiches, Faubourgs, Arretés, 5 March 1848.

84 R. Lacour, *La Révolution de 1848 dans le Beaujolais et la campagne lyonnaise*, 19–21.

85 AML, H, Garde Nationale, Lyon, 1838, Recensement, 10–21 March 1848; *Le Censeur*, 12 March 1848; BML, Fonds Coste, 5314, Affiches, 9290 and unnumbered, "Etat-Major ... Ordre," 9 March 1848.

86 BML, Fonds Coste, 5314, Affiches, 9323 and "Elections," 9 March 1848; ADR, R, Garde Nationale, Organisations.

87 Benoit, *Confessions*, 106–9, and *Souvenirs*, 55–6; Bergier, 78–88; *Le Courrier de Lyon*, 11, 13 April 1848; *La Gazette de Lyon*, 12, 16, 19 April 1848; *La Liberté*, 13 April 1848.

88 *La Liberté*, 7 April 1848; BML, Fonds Coste, 5314, Affiches, 9361, 9366, 9376; AML, H, Garde Nationale, Armement and Elections, 20 April 1848; AML, Croix-Rousse, Garde Nationale, Elections, 11–16 April 1848.

89 L. Girard, *La garde nationale, 1814–1871*, 293–8.

90 AML, D, Croix-Rousse, Procès-verbaux de Conseil municipal, 4, 8, 9, 13, 23, 27 March 1848; Benoit, *Confessions*, 92; *Le Tribun du Peuple*, 3, 12, 15 March 1848.

91 *Le Tribun du Peuple*, 15, 16, 21–27 March 1848; *Club de l'Egalité, Bulletin Hebdomodaire*, 11 April 1848; *Comité Général des Clubs, Bulletin*, 28 March 1848.

92 Sixteen of the forty-four activists mentioned in *Le Tribun du Peuple*, 3 March–23 April 1848, can be identified as members of radical secret societies.

93 *Le Tribun du Peuple*, 13, 15, 19–20 March 1848.

94 Gossez, 247–8.

95 *Le Censeur*, 17, 20, 22 March 1848; *La République*, 19–23 March 1848; *Le Tribun du Peuple*, 21–22, 29–30 March 1848.

96 Gossez, 226, 253–256.

97 In addition to the silk, clothing, and construction workers' circles and *compagnonnages*, there were two printers' groups. See ADR, R, Conseil de Guerre, Insurrection, Saisie des Journaux, poster dated 7 April 1848.

98 *Le Peuple Souverain, 23 April 1848*; *Le Comité Général des Clubs, Bulletin*, 28 March–17 April 1848.

99 Amann, 123, 135–6, 143–5, 153.

100 Benoit, *Confessions*, 79–82, 92; *Le Tribun du Peuple*, 15 March 1848; S. Wassermann, "Le Club de Raspail de 1848," *La Révolution de 1848* 5 (1908–9): 594.

101 AN C939, Rhône, correspondence, 8–22 April 1848.

102 Agulhon, *Une ville*, 276–8; Amann, 125–6; Charles, 131–5; Godechot, 206–8; Laurent, 61–73; Price, *Second Republic*, 114–39. Club of Clubs envoys had some influence in Grenoble (Vigier, 233–5) and Limoges (J.M. Merriman, "Social Conflict in France and the Limoges Revolution of April 27, 1848," *Societas* 4 [1974]: 30).

103 *La Tribune Lyonnaise*, 20 April 1848.

104 Amann, 34–5; 78–81.

105 *Le Tribun du Peuple*, 12, 15 March 1848.

106 Reports on sixteen local clubs appear in ibid., 3, 5, 13 April 1848, and *Le Peuple Souverain*, 12 April 1848; see also *Club de l'Egalité, Bulletin Hebdomodaire*, 31 March–11 April 1848.

107 *Le Tribun du Peuple*, 15, 16 March 1848.

108 Amann, 173–86.

109 *Le Tribun du Peuple*, 17, 21 April 1848; *Le Peuple Souverain*, 23 April, 1–2 May 1848; *La Gazette de Lyon*, 24–25 April 1848; *Le Salut Public*, 30 April–2 May 1848; ADR, M, Police générale, Rapports journaliers, 17 April, 1 May 1848.

110 *Le Censeur, Le Courrier de Lyon*, and *La Gazette de Lyon*, 30 April 1848.

111 Deyon, 158; Merriman, "Social Conflict," 31–4.

112 Amann, 134, 137, 141–3, 187–8.
113 *Le Tribun du Peuple*, 15, 19–20, 23–24, 26–27 March, 2, 5, 8, 12 April 1848.
114 Ibid., 21 April 1848; BML, Fonds Coste, 5314, Affiches, 9385. According to *Le Patriote lyonnais*, 16 April 1848, Laforest received 7,141 votes; Lortet 6,160; Benoit 5,446; Raspail 5,353; Doutre 5,226; Blanc 4,547; Pelletier 3,988; Greppo 3,816; Arago 3,390; Cabet 3,009; Proudhon 2,471. On Pelletier, see C.M. Lesaulnier, *Biographie des neuf cents députés à l'Assemblée nationale* (Paris: 1848), 381.
115 ADR, Conseil de Guerre, Insurrection, Saisie des journaux, *A mes amis d'enfance*, by J. Lentillon.
116 Ibid., plus all the electoral pamphlets in this dossier; BML, Fonds Coste, 111500–80.
117 According to S. Commissaire, *Mémoires et souvenirs*, 1: 99, Cabet and Raspail were the only men Lyonnais workers called *père*.
118 BML, Fonds Coste, 111502; *Le Censeur*, 27–28 March, 19 April 1848.
119 *Le Censeur*, 27–28 March, 19 April 1848.
120 A.J. Tudesq, *Les grands notables en France* 2: 1009–10.
121 *Le Courrier de Lyon*, 29 February–16 March, 12–14 April 1848; *La Gazette de Lyon*, 1, 12–25 March, 9–18 April 1848; *Le Salut Public*, 14–26 March, 10–17 April 1848; *Union Nationale*, 19–22 March, 8–14 April 1848.
122 *Comité Général des Clubs, Bulletin*, 28 March–14 April 1848.
123 *Le Tribun du Peuple*, 12, 15, 21–22 March, 3 April 1848; *Club de l'Egalité, Bulletin Hebdomodaire*, 31 March, 11 April 1848; the others were: *La Feuille du Jour*, *Le Franc-Parleur Lyonnais*, *La Montagne*, *L'Organisateur Lyonnais*, *Le Patriot Lyonnais*, *Le Peuple Souverain*, *Le Réformateur*, *La République*, *Le Reveil du Peuple*, *La Sentinelle*, *Le Spartacus*, *Le Vengeur*, *Le Vingt-Quatre Février*, *La Voix du Peuple*, *Le Vorace*, and *Le Vrai Républican*.
124 *L'Echo des Electeurs*, April 1848; *Journal des Electeurs Ruraux*, 22 March 1848.
125 *Le Courrier de Lyon*, 2 May 1848; *La Gazette de Lyon*, 24–25 April 1848; *Le Tribun du Peuple*, 17 April 1848.
126 *Le Censeur*, 30 April 1848; *Le Courrier de Lyon*, 30 April 1848; *Le Salut Public*, 29 April 1848.
127 S.B. Watkins, "The Working-Class Deputies of the French Constituent Assembly" (PHD diss., University of North Carolina, Chapel Hill, 1970), v–21; G. W. Fasel, "The French Election of April 21, 1848: Suggestions for Revision," *French Historical Studies* 5 (1968): 285–98, claims fewer than 300 moderate republicans, only 70–80 radicals (out of 900); *Le Moniteur*, 8 June, 29 July, 10 August 1848.
128 Benoit, *Confessions*, 118.
129 Treillard, 50–3.
130 *Le Tribun du Peuple*, 13 March 1848.

CHAPTER FOUR

1 ADR, M, Personnel, Préfets.
2 ADR, M, Police générale, Rapports journaliers, 10–11 May 1848; *Le Censeur*, 12 May, 9 June 1848; J. Bergier, *Le journal d'un bourgeois de Lyon en 1848*, 94–8; L. Levy-Schneider, "Correspondance de Martin-Bernard, Commissaire-Général de la République à Lyon," *Revue d'histoire de Lyon* 12 (1913):

179–80; J.B. Monfalcon, *Histoire de notre temps*, 1: 83–5; *La Statue de Louis XIV, place Bellecour* ..., 10–11.

3 *Le Courrier de Lyon, La Gazette de Lyon, La Liberté, Le Peuple Souverain, Le Salut Public*, and *L'Union National*, 10–15 May 1848.

4 AN BB³⁰ 361, dos. 3, 1, 2 June 1848; ADR, M, Police générale, Rapports journaliers, 13, 16 May 1848.

5 ADR, M, Police générale, Rapports journaliers, 16–17 May 1848; AN BB¹⁸ 1460, 17 May 1848; Levy-Schneider, 186–7; *Le Censeur*, 18 May 1848; *Le Peuple Souverain*, 19 May 1848.

6 ADR, R, Conseil de Guerre, Société dit les Voraces, letter, 17 May 1848.

7 AN BB¹⁸ 1480, 18, 20 May 1848; *Le Moniteur Judiciaire de Lyon*, 24 August 1848; *Le Peuple Souverain*, 26 May 1848.

8 *Le Peuple Souverain*, 26 May 1848; *Le Moniteur Judiciaire de Lyon*, 24 August 1848; Levy-Schneider, 195.

9 Bergier, 101–2; *Le Censeur, Le Peuple Souverain*, and *Le Salut Public*, 20–26 May 1848; ADR, M, Police générale, Rapports journaliers, 19, 22 May 1848.

10 BML, Fonds Coste, 5314, Affiches, 9420; Levy-Schneider, 187–190.

11 AN BB¹⁸ 1460, 22 May 1848; BB²⁰ 143, 21 August 1848; *Le Censeur*, 23 May 1848; *Le Moniteur Judiciaire de Lyon*, 24 August 1848. (The attorney-general, Alcock, was in Paris.)

12 P. Amann, *Revolution and Mass Democracy*, 205–40.

13 *Le Censeur*, 29 August 1848; *Le Courrier de Lyon*, 18 May 1848; *La Gazette de Lyon*, 14 May 1848; *Le Salut Public*, 12 May 1848; AN C939, Rhône, correspondence, 9, 18 April 1848; ADR, R, Conseil de Guerre, Société dit les Voraces, correspondence, 17 May 1848 and undated, signed by the Provisional Committee; M, Police générale, Rapports journaliers, 17 May 1848.

14 ADR, M, Police générale, Rapports journaliers, 10, 29 May 1848; R. Lacour, *La Révolution dans le Beaujolais et la campagne lyonnaise*, 78, 81, 83–7.

15 ADR, M, Police générale, Rapports journaliers, 24–25 May, 10 June, 21 October, 29 November 1848; ADR, R, Conseil de Guerre, Société dit les Voraces and Insurrection du 15 juin 1849; AN BB³⁰ 396, 2 December 1851, App. C.

16 AN C 2240; *Le Courrier de Lyon, La Gazette de Lyon, La Liberté, Le Salut Public*, and *L'Union Nationale*, 1–7 May 1848; A.J. Tudesq, *Les grands notables en France* 2: 1054–7, 1097–9.

17 AML, H, Garde Nationale, correspondence, 19 April–15 May 1848.

18 Ibid., reports, 9, 10 May 1848; BML, Fonds Coste, 5314, Affiches, unnumbered, "220 Cannoniers réunis à leurs concitoyens," 13 May 1848; *Le Courrier de Lyon, La Liberté*, and *Le Salut Public*, 12–17 May 1848.

19 AML, H, Garde Nationale, petition, 24 May 1848; ADR, R, Garde Nationale, Ordonnances, petition, 3 June 1848, and correspondence, 4, 20 June, 20 July 1848.

20 ADR, R, Garde Nationale, Ordonnances, 7 June 1848; BML, Fonds Coste, 5314, Affiches, 9460, 113149; *Le Courrier de Lyon, La Gazette de Lyon, La Liberté, Le Salut Public*, and *L'Union Nationale*, 20–25 May 1848.

21 Bergier, 105–6; *Le Censeur*, 25, 30 May 1848.

22 *Le Courrier de Lyon* and *L'Union Nationale*, 22–25 May 1848.

23 ADR, M, *Receuil des Actes administratives*, 24, 29 May 1848; AML, Croix-Rousse and Guillotière, Procès-verbaux du conseil municipal, 20–23 May 1848; *Le Courrier de Lyon* and *La Gazette de Lyon*, 30–31 May 1848.

24 AN BB[18] 1473, 20 September 1849; *La Tribune Lyonnaise*, March 1849.
25 *Le Courrier de Lyon*, *La Gazette de Lyon*, *La Liberté*, *Le Salut Public*, and *L'Union Nationale* 25 May–6 June 1848.
26 The same newspapers, 26 May–14 June 1848.
27 Ibid., 6, 8, 15, 27 May 1848; Amann, 197–204, 243–8.
28 *L'Union Nationale*, 6, 10 June 1848.
29 *Le Peuple Souverain*, 31 May 1848; ADR, M, Police générale, Rapports journaliers, 27–28 May 1848.
30 ADR, M, Police générale, Rapports journaliers, 7–13 June 1848; BML, Fonds Coste, 5314, Affiches, 9424, 9436, 9441, 9442.
31 *Le Peuple Souverain*, 1, 5 June 1848.
32 *Le Censeur*, 30 May–6 June 1848; *La Tribune Lyonnaise*, 1, 10 June 1848.
33 *Le Courrier de Lyon*, *La Liberté*, *Le Salut Public*, and *L'Union Nationale*, 31 May–12 June 1848.
34 BML, Fonds Coste, 5314, Affiches, 9435, 9445; *Le Censeur*, 14–16 June 1848; *L'Union Nationale*, 17 June 1848.
35 All Lyonnais newspapers, 15–20 June 1848.
36 Amann, 249–64.
37 *Le Courrier de Lyon*, 17 June 1848; *Le Salut Public*, 21 June 1848.
38 Even *Le Censeur* favoured administrative regularization and fiscal responsibility (30 May 1848).
39 AML, D, Procès-verbaux du Conseil municipal, 19 June–17 July 1848.
40 AML, Croix-Rousse and Guillotière, Procès-verbaux du conseil municipal, 13 May–14 July 1848.
41 Bergier, 107; *Le Censeur*, *Le Courrier de Lyon*, *La Liberté*, and *Le Salut Public*, 5, 14–18 May 1848.
42 AN BB[30] 361, dos. 3, 1, 2 June 1848; ADR, M, Police générale, Rapports journaliers, 31 May 1848; ADR, U, Tribunal Correctionnel, Jugemens, 4 July 1848.
43 *Le Peuple Souverain*, 2 June 1848.
44 *Le Moniteur*, 4 June 1848, p. 1253; *Le Salut Public*, 16 June 1848; *Le Censeur*, 2–3 June 1848.
45 *Le Censeur*, 22 June 1848; AML, D, Procès-verbaux de Conseil municipal, 22 June 1848.
46 AN BB[30] 361, dos. 3, 2 June 1848; Bergier, 114; *Le Censeur*, *Le Courrier de Lyon*, and *Le Salut Public*, 4–7, 9–16 June 1848.
47 The same newspapers, 22–24 June 1848; ADR, M, Police générale, Rapports journaliers, 20–22 June 1848.
48 ADR, M, Police générale, Rapports journaliers, 24–27 June 1848; AN BB[30] 361, dos. 3, 27 June 1848.
49 AN BB[30] 361, dos. 3, 27 June 1848; F. Dutacq, *Histoire politique de Lyon pendant la Révolution de 1848*, 421–8.
50 J. Vidalenc, "La province et les journées de juin," *Etudes d'histoire moderne et contemporaine* 2 (1948): 99–112.
51 Ibid., 129–30; AN BB[30] 361, dos. 3, 27 June 1848; *Le Censeur*, 29 August 1848; *Le Courrier de Lyon*, 3 July 1848; Monfalcon, *Histoire de notre temps*, 1: 107–8.
52 Amann, 292–305.
53 *Le Censeur*, 27–28 June 1848.
54 G. Fasel, "Urban Workers in Provincial France, February-June 1848," *International Review of Social History* 14 (1977): 672–3.
55 *L'Organisateur lyonnais*, 19 March 1848; AN C934, Relevé des petitions adressés à la commission … pour l'organisation du travail par les ouvriers.

56 *Le Censeur,* 26 June 1848.

57 Bergier, 108.

58 *Le Moniteur,* 5 April 1848, p. 765; 3 July 1848, p. 2282.

59 Levy-Schneider, 203–4; AN BB³⁰ 361, dos. 3, 27 June 1848; BB³⁰ dos. 1, 2–3 July 1848.

60 AN BB³⁰ 333, dos. 1, 2–3 July 1848; ADR, M, Police générale, Rapports journaliers, 3–5 July 1848; Bergier, 137–41; *Le Censeur, Le Courrier de Lyon,* and *La Gazette de Lyon,* 1–8 July 1848; Monfalcon, *Histoire de notre temps* 1: 106–7; Vidalenc, 136–9.

61 ADR, M, Personnel, Préfets, T.R. Forstenzer, "Bureaucrats under Stress: French Attorneys General and Prefects and the Fall of the Second Republic" (PH D diss., Stanford University, 1973), 182–3, 185–6.

62 BML, Fonds Coste, 5314, Affiches, 9460; *Le Censeur, Le Courrier de Lyon, La Gazette de Lyon, La Liberté, Le Peuple Souverain,* and *Le Salut Public,* 4–10 July 1848.

63 F. De Luna, *The French Republic under Cavaignac, 1848,* 200–1.

64 AML, I² 40, nos. 65, 66; Monfalcon, *Histoire de notre temps,* 1: 109–12.

65 ADR, R, Garde Nationale, Armement, 18–20 June, 16, 29 July 1848; *La Gazette de Lyon,* 20 July 1848.

66 Bergier, 143; *Le Censeur,* 23 July 1848; *Le Peuple Souverain,* 15, 18 July 1848.

67 *Le Courrier de Lyon, La Gazette de Lyon, La Liberté, Le Salut Public,* and *L'Union Nationale,* 29 June–18 July 1848; *La Verité,* 5–9 July 1848; Vidalenc, 133–4.

68 Vidalenc, 133n; *Le Censeur, Le Peuple Souverain,* and *La Tribune Lyonnaise,* 28 June–25 July 1848.

69 AML, D, Procès-verbaux du conseil municipal, Lyon, Guillotière and Croix-Rousse, 28 June–17 July 1848; *Le Censeur* and *Le Peuple Souverain,* 29–30 June 1848; Bergier, 132–3; Monfalcon, *Histoire de notre temps* 1: 103–6.

70 AN BB³⁰ 361, dos. 2, 24, 28 July 1848; ADR, M, Police générale, Rapports journaliers, 20, 27 July 1848; *Le Courrier de Lyon, La Liberté, Le Peuple Souverain,* and *Le Salut Public,* 15–17 July 1848.

71 ADR, M, Police générale, Rapports journaliers, 23, 27 September, 9, 12, 17 October, 16 December 1848; AML, H, Garde Nationale 1848, petition, October 1848; BML, Fonds Coste, 351167, 351169; *Le Censeur,* 4, 8, 24 September, 2–11 October 1848; *Le Peuple Souverain,* 27–28 September, 3–9 October 1848.

72 AN BB³⁰ 361, dos. 2, 27 July 1848; *Le Censeur* and *Le Courrier de Lyon,* 17, 18 July 1848; *Le Salut Public,* 9 July 1848; Monfalcon, *Histoire de notre temps* 1: 93–8.

73 ADR, Banque Guérin, Correspondence expédiée, 16 August, 14 September, 5, 24, October, 3 November 1848; *La Tribune Lyonnaise,* November 1848.

74 Dutacq, 449–52.

75 *Le Censeur* and *Le Peuple Souverain,* 28 June, 6 July 1848; ADR, M, Police générale, Rapports journaliers, 11, 18 July 1848.

76 ADR, M, Police générale, Rapports journaliers, 1 August 1848; *Le Peuple Souverain,* 31 July, 2, 5 August 1848.

77 *Le Peuple Souverain,* 2, 8, 10 August 1848; AML, Croix-Rousse and Guillotière, K4, Elections municipales, July 1848.

78 *Le Courrier de Lyon, La Gazette de Lyon, La Liberté, Le Salut Public,* and *L'Union Nationale,* 2–19 August 1848.

CHAPTER FIVE

1 AN F¹² 4617, Etat des demandes par départements, and 4618, Etat général des demandes soumises au Conseil d'Encouragement.

2 F. De Luna, *The French Republic under Cavaignac, 1848*, 319–35.

3 AN F¹² 4618; B. Schnapper, "Les sociétés ouvrières de production pendant la Seconde République: l'exemple Girondin," *Revue d'histoire économique et sociale* 43 (1965): 162–4.

4 *Le Censeur, Le Courrier de Lyon*, and *La Liberté*, 3–11 July 1848; also *Le Salut Public*, 23–25 July, 4–5 September 1848.

5 A. Blanqui, *Des classes ouvrières en France pendant l'année 1848*, 157; R. Gossez, *Les ouvriers de Paris*, vol. 1, *L'Organisation*, 319, and "La presse parisiènne à destination des ouvriers, 1848–1851," in *La presse ouvrière, 1819–1850*, 133.

6 AN F¹² 4618, Etat général des liquidations, 4619, Procès-verbaux, 23 January 1849, 4626, Contrat de prêt... Martin et Cie; *Le Peuple Souverain*, 23 September 1848; O. Festy, "Les deux associations ouvrières lyonnaises encouragées par application du décret du 5 juillet 1848," *Revue d'histoire de Lyon* 11 (1912): 342–4.

7 B. Moss, "Parisian Producers Associations (1830–51): The Socialism of Skilled Workers," in *Revolution and Reaction*, ed. R. Price, 82.

8 Festy, 344–9.

9 A. Covillard, *Projet d'organisation pour la fabrique des étoffes de soie*, and *Statutes de la Société dite l'Union des Veloutiers*.

10 AN B¹² 4620, Correspondance, September 1848, April and July 1849; Exécution du décret, 23 January 1849, and Acte de prêt, 3 July 1849.

11 AML, I² 45, no. 191, and I² 63, no. 208.

12 AN F¹² 4620, Correspondance, January–March 1850 and 1851.

13 Ibid., May and September 1853, February–July 1856, July and December 1857, September 1859, January and June 1862, March 1863, July 1868; also AML, I² 45, nos. 192–4.

14 AN F¹² 4618, Correspondance, 27 June 1856; Gossez, *Ouvriers*, 317, 319; Schnapper, 188–9.

15 BML, Fonds Coste, 351392; AN F¹² 4618, Correspondance, 30 September, 21 October 1848; 4619, Procès-verbaux, 19 April 1849, 4629, Correspondance, 24 July, 16 August, 26 October 1849, 4630, Correspondance, from "Fraternal Association of Mechanical Workers," 4631, Correspondance, from "Fraternal Society of Silk Printers," and Exécution du décret, 3 May 1849, 4635, Correspondance, 14 January, 6, 7 February 1849, and Exécution du décret, 20 March 1849.

16 ADR, M, Police générale, Rapports journaliers, 5 September, 13 October 1848; *Le Peuple Souverain*, 28 October 1848; *Le Censeur*, 2–3, 14, 20 November 1848.

17 P. Deyon, "Aspects industrielles de la crise, Rouen," in *Aspects de la crise et de la dépression de l'économie française au milieu de XIXe siècle*, 159; A.M. Gossez, *Le Département du Nord sous la Deuxième République*, 351.

18 ADR, M, Police générale, Rapports journaliers, 14 June, 1, 9–21 August, 21 September, 13–28 October, 2–15 November 1848, also 22, 27 February, 5, 12 March 1849.

19 R. Gossez, *Ouvriers*, 334–8; Moss, 80.

20 Commission pour l'organisation du travail, *Projet d'association libre et volontaire entre les chefs d'industrie et les ouvriers et de réforme commerciale; Le Peuple Souverain*, 3, 7, 15 June, 2, 3, 10, 24 July, 15 August 1848.

21 *Le Peuple Souverain*, 3 June–21 November 1848.

22 Gossez, *Ouvriers*, 321; Moss, 80; Schnapper, 168, 171–5.

23 *Le Peuple Souverain*, 19 August 1848; C. Lecompte, "Trois Fraternelles dans la région lilloise en 1848 et 1849," *1848* 44 (1951).

24 E. Flotard, *Le mouvement coopératif à Lyon et dans le Midi de la France*, 114–17, 122–8; *Acte d'association des Ouvriers tailleurs du département du Rhône* (Lyon: n.p., 1 April 1849); AN BB^{18} 1474^B, 23 January 1850.

25 AN BB^{18} 1474^B, 23 January 1850; "Association fraternelle des Ouvriers menuisiers de … Lyon, Statuts," Articles 30 and 31.

26 Ibid.; Flotard, 98–100.

27 Flotard, 100–1; ADR, M, Police générale, Rapports journaliers, 14, 25, 27 October 1848; *Le Peuple Souverain*, 30 December 1848, 1 January 1849.

28 AN F^{12} 4635, Correspondance, 15 January, 6, 7 February, 1849, and Exécution du décret, 20 March 1848; BB^{18} 1474^B, 15 November 1850; *Le Censeur*, 20 February 1849; Flotard, 101–10.

29 Flotard, 128–9; *Le Peuple Souverain*, 5 November 1848, 16 April 1849; AN BB^{30} 396, 2 December 1851, p. 34.

30 Flotard, 104–11.

31 *Le Moniteur*, 29 July, 9 August 1848; ADR, *Receuil des Actes administratifs*, no. 45, 1848, pp. 320–1.

32 AN BB^{18} 1468, 3 August 1848; ADR, M, Police générale, Rapports journaliers, 1–3 August 1848.

33 ADR, M, Police générale, Rapports journaliers, 11–31 August, 7 September 1848; *Le Peuple Souverain*, 22–31 August, 2 September 1848.

34 *Le Peuple Souverain*, 23, 31 August, 3–15 September 1848.

35 AML, Croix-Rousse and Guillotière, Elections, August–September 1848; *Le Courrier de Lyon*, *La Gazette de Lyon*, *La Liberté*, *Le Salut Public*, and *L'Union Nationale*, 8–15 September 1848.

36 A.J. Tudesq, *Les grands notables en France* 2: 1136.

37 AML, Croix-Rousse, D, Procès-verbaux de Conseil municipal, 30 September, 7 October, 6 November 1848; Guillotière, D, Procès-verbaux de Conseil municipal, 2, 13 November, 29, 30 December 1848, 15, 30 January, 3, 8, 12 February 1849; AN F^{17} 10321, Correspondance, 29–31 December 1848, 1, 29 January 1849. See also L. de Vaucelles, "La querelle scolaire sous la Seconde République à la Guillotière," *Cahiers d'histoire* 4 (1965): 365–78.

38 *Le Courrier de Lyon*, *La Gazette de Lyon*, *Le Salut Public*, and *L'Union Nationale*, 12–20 September, 15 November 1848–15 February 1849; ADR, IN, Conseil général, 2–5 December 1848.

39 *Le Censeur* and *Le Peuple Souverain*, 7–17 September 1848; ADR, M, Police générale, Rapports journaliers, 11–15 September 1848.

40 Ibid., 14, 16 September 1848; *L'Union Nationale*, 20 September 1848; AN F^{1C} III, Rhône 4^1, 13 September 1848.

41 AN F^{1C} III, Rhône 4^1, 21 September 1848; *La Tribune Lyonnaise*, October 1848; De Luna, 323. In "L'Election d'un réprésentant du Rhône à l'Assemblée Nationale," *Revue d'histoire de Lyon* 7 (1908): 460–2, Dutacq refers to irregularities, but no record of anyone contesting the results survives.

42 AN BB^{30} 327, dos. 1, 19–21 September 1848; BB^{30} 361, dos. 3, 3, 4 October 1848; ADR, M, Police générale, Rapports journaliers, 18–22 September 1848.

43 ADR, M, Police générale, Rapports journaliers, 11–20 August, 14 September–3 October 1848; ADR, R, Garde Nationale Mobile, Arrêtés, 26 September 1848; Conseil d'administration, 27 September 1848; Service-Discipline, Registre, especially 14–26 August, 24–26 September 1848. See

also F. Dutacq, "Un episode de la Révolution de 1848 à Lyon: La dissolution de la Garde Nationale mobile," *Revue d'histoire de Lyon* 11 (1912): 103–17.

44 ADR, M, Police générale, Rapports journaliers, 22, 25 September 1848; De Luna, 323–4; *Le Peuple Souverain*, 21, 26 September, 3 November 1848.

45 *Le Peuple Souverain*, 21 November 1848, ADR, M, Police générale, Rapports journaliers, October–November 1848; Maurin-Béraud, *Almanach démocratique et social des clubs lyonnais pour 1849*, 66.

46 AN BB[18] 1469, 22 October 1848; BB[30] 327, dos. 1, 29 September–18 November 1848; BB[30] 331, petition of April 1848.

47 De Luna, 372; AN BB[30] 327, dos. 1, 9–18 November 1848; ADR, M, Police générale, Rapports journaliers, 9–14 November, 8 December 1848.

48 ADR, M, Police générale, Rapports journaliers, 1, 2, 4, 8 December 1848; *Le Peuple Souverain*, 3, 19, 22–23, 27–29 November, 1–12 December 1848.

49 *Le Censeur, Le Courrier de Lyon, La Gazette de Lyon, La Liberté, Le Salut Public*, and *L'Union Nationale*, 4 November–10 December 1848; *Le Président*, 1–10 December 1848; Tudesq, 2: 1190, and *L'élection présidentielle de Louis-Napoleon Bonaparte*, 113–98.

50 Tudesq, *L'élection présidentielle*, 210–17; R. Price, *The French Second Republic*, 221–2; *La Tribune Lyonnaise*, January 1848.

51 Tudesq, *L'élection présidentielle*, 210; De Luna, 393–4.

52 AML, Guillotière, K1, Election du président, Correspondance, 28 November, 1 December 1848; AN BB[18] 1469, 19 November 1848.

53 AN BB[30] 333, dos. 1, 18 December 1848; ADR, M, Police générale, Rapports journaliers, 5–12, 16–27 December 1848; *Le Peuple Souverain*, 18–27 December 1848; N. Zastenker, "La Montagne en 1849," *Questions d'histoire* 2 (1954): 109–14.

54 AML, I[2] 40, nos. 352, 355; H. Machin, "The Prefects and Political Repression: February 1848 to December 1851," in *Revolution and Reaction*, ed. Price, 285.

55 F. Dutacq, "Le dernier commandement du maréchal Bugeaud," *Révolution de 1848* 23 (1925): 705–7, 714; J.B. Monfalcon, *Histoire de notre temps* 2: 18–25.

56 *Le Censeur*, 22 February, 11–13 March 1849; AN BB[30] 361, dos. 3, February 1849; ADR, M, Police générale, Rapports journaliers, 7, 14, 19–21 February, 9 March 1849; AML, I[2] 40, no. 354.

57 *La Constitution*, 3, 8 February 1849; AN BB[18] 1740, 18 March 1849, and Registre spécial des poursuites en matière de presse; 1470[C], 14, 19, 26 February, 5 May, 22 June 1849; 1474[B], 2 March 1849; BB[20] 147, 15, 22 June, 25 August 1849; ADR, M, Police générale, Rapports journaliers, 13–28 February, 2–3 March 1849; T.R. Forstenzer, "Bureaucrats under Stress" (PHD diss., Stanford University, 1974), 362, 384, 441–3.

58 Forstenzer, "Bureaucrats under Stress," 106–7; Merriman, 25–54, 106–37.

59 ADR, M, Police générale, Rapports journaliers, 12 February–1 May 1849; AML, I[2] 40, nos. 359 and 360; *Le Républicain*, 25 February–13 May 1849; *Le Peuple Souverain*, 24 February–8 May 1849.

60 *Le Peuple Souverain*, 3 February–16 March 1849.

61 A third democratic-socialist organ, *La Commune Sociale*, appeared from December 1848 until May 1849. It demanded "the democratic and social republic," the right to work, state ownership and direction of production, and decentralization of government. It did not discuss daily politics, but tried to disseminate "communist ideas."

62 ADR, R, Conseil de Guerre, Insurrection, Saisie des journaux; *Le Républicain*, 25, 27, 28 February, 2, 24, 31 March, 14, 22 April 1849; J. Bouillon,

"Les Démocrates-socialistes aux élections de 1849," *Revue français de Science politique* 6 (1956): 71; Forstenzer, "Bureaucrats under Stress," 293–4; G. Génique, *L'élection de l'Assemblée Législative en 1849*, 20–1; Zastenker, 124–5.

63 ADR, M, Police générale, Rapports journaliers, 26 February, 10–20 March, 23–26 April, 1 May 1849; *Le Censeur*, 8 May 1849; *Le Peuple Souverain*, 17 March, 1 April, 1, 8 May 1849; *Le Républicain*, 16–29 March, 1, 6, 8 April, 1, 8 May 1849; Zastenker, 105–6.

64 The slate was published in *Le Peuple Souverain* and *Le Républicain* on 1 May 1849. For the history of the Rhône representatives, see *Le Moniteur*, 1, 6, 15 August, 13 September, 3, 5, 16 November 1848, 30, 31 January 1849; J. Benoit, *Souvenirs de la République de 1848*, 107, 137–81.

65 AN BB^{18} 1470^C, 27–29 April 1849; ADR, M, Police générale, Rapports journaliers, 13 March, 4, 10, 14, 20–30 April 1849; *Le Peuple Souverain*, 25–30 April, 6 May 1849; *Le Républicain*, 24, 31 March, 3, 21–30 April 1849.

66 ADR, M, Police générale, Rapports journaliers, 11 May 1849 (quote); J.P. Charnay, *Société militaire et suffrage politique en France depuis 1789*, 183.

67 AN BB^{18} 1469, 9 May 1849; ADR, M, Police générale, Rapports journaliers, 15, 24 March, 3, 10 April, 7, 8 May 1849; *La Commune Sociale*, December 1848; *Le Peuple Souverain*, 18, 21, 24, 27 April 1849; *Le Républicain*, 10, 20, 23, 24, 31 March, 17 April, 1, 13 May 1849; Maurin-Béraud, 22–7; L. Loubère, "The Emergence of the Extreme Left in Lower Languedoc, 1848–1851: Social and Economic Factors in Politics," *American Historical Review* 73 (1968): 1036, 1050; R.W. Magraw, "Pierre Joigneaux and Socialist Propaganda in the French Countryside, 1849–1851," *French Historical Studies* 10 (1978): 599–640; Zastenker, 136–7.

68 *Le Peuple Souverain*, 16–19 May 1849; F. Dutacq, "Les élections législatifs du 1849 à Lyon," *Révolution de 1848* 25 (1927): 195–6; Loubère, 1020–3, 1038.

69 *Le Courrier de Lyon*, *La Gazette de Lyon*, and *Le Salut Public*, 2 March–12 May 1849; *Le Démon Socialiste, Journal Populaire et Anti-Communiste*, 22 April 1849; Monfalcon, *Histoire de notre temps* 2: 30–1.

70 Monfalcon, *Histoire de notre temps* 2: 32; *Le Censeur*, 21 May 1849; *Le Peuple Souverain*, 16–19 May 1848.

71 Bouillon, 81.

72 Ibid., 78–9, 83, 87–9; Loubère, 45, 50, 55–6; Vigier, 2: 207, 209, 217–18, 220, 224. Nearly forty per cent of those migrants in the radical movement whose place of birth can be identified came from these six nearby departments. On the correspondence, see chapter 6.

CHAPTER SIX

1 AN BB^{18} 1472, 29 July, 2 August 1848; ADR, Police générale, rapports journaliers, 12 July 1848, 8 January 1849.

2 A.J. Tudesq, *Les grands notables en France* 2: 992–1072.

3 T.R. Forstenzer, "Bureaucrats Under Stress" (PH D Stanford University, 1974): 255 ff.; J. Merriman, *The Agony of the Republic*, passim; P. Vigier, *La Seconde République dans la région alpine* 2: 224 ff.

4 Cited in Merriman, 64.

5 Ibid., 68–78.

6 ADR, M, Police générale, Rapports journaliers, 11, 17, 28, 30 August 1848; *Le Peuple Souverain*, 13, 27 August, 1 September 1848.

7 AN BB^{18} 1474^B, 23 January 1850.

8 Ibid., 22 August 1849; ADR, M, Police générale, Rapports journaliers, 3 September–17 October, 15 November 1848; *Le Peuple Souverain*, 19–26 October, 25 November 1848, 5 January 1849.

9 AN BB^{18} 1474^B, 23 January 1850, Statuts.

10 Ibid., also 22 August 1849; AN BB^{30} 379, 7 February 1850; 396, 2 December 1851; AML, I^2 41, nos. 158–250; ADR, R, Conseil de Guerre, Dossiers individuels and Commission militaire, 1851–2.

11 E. Flotard, *Le mouvement coopératif à Lyon et dans le Midi de la France*, 139; J. Gaumont, *Le mouvement ouvrier d'association et de coopération à Lyon*, 33–4.

12 G. Laurent, "Les événements de l'année 1848 à Reims et dans la Marne," in *Le Département du Marne et la Révolution de 1848*, 73–5; Merriman, 68–78.

13 J. Lacroix, *La deuxième République à Vienne*, 55–67.

14 AN BB^{18} 1474^B, 22 August 1849, 23 January 1850; ADR, M, Police générale, Rapports journaliers, 9 April 1849; *Le Peuple Souverain*, 9 April 1949.

15 AN BB^{18} 1474^B, 22 August 1849; ADR, R, 2me Conseil de Guerre, Insurrection, Dossiers individuels, Charpy et al; ADR, M, 6me Division militaire, Jugemens, 2me Conseil de Guerre, 5 September, 20 November 1849.

16 AN BB^{30} 396, 2 December 1851.

17 Flotard, 130–1.

18 *Le Peuple Souverain*, 23 December 1848; AN BB^{18} 1474, Statuts de la Société des Travailleurs Unis; ADR M, Police générale, Rapports journaliers, 23 December 1848.

19 ADR, M, Police générale, Rapports journaliers, 3 March, 7, 14, 16 April 1849; ADR, R, 1er Conseil de Guerre, Insurrection, Saisie des journaux, lease dated 18 March 1849; *Le Républicain*, 15, 20 April, 4, 13 May 1849.

20 AN BB^{18} 1474^B, 31 July 1849; ADR, R, Conseils de Guerre, Insurrection, Dossiers individuels, Bacot, Choppe, Leclerc, Perret *dit Sans Rancune*; ADR, M, 6me Division militaire, Jugemens, 1er Conseil de Guerre, 30 October, 4, 21 December 1849, 10 September 1850, 2me Conseil de Guerre, 26 November 1849; AML, I^2 63, nos. 140, 180.

21 AN BB^{18} 1474^B, 22 August 1849; *Le Censeur*, 5 August 1849; *Le Républicain*, 15 June 1849; Flotard, 135.

22 AML, I^2 45, nos. 225–8; ADR, M, 6me Division militaire, Jugemens, 2me Conseil de Guerre, 1 October 1850; *Le Censeur*, 20 August, 7 December 1849; Flotard, 133, 137–40.

23 N. Zastenker, "La Montagne en 1849," *Questions d'histoire* 2 (1954): 107.

24 ADR, M, Police générale, Rapports journaliers, 12, 22 July, 17–28 August 1848.

25 Ibid., 18 July–28 December 1848.

26 *Le Censeur*, 18 May 1848; ADR, R, Insurrection, Dossiers individuels, Société des Droits de l'Homme, Ordre du jour, 27 May 1848; also Saisie des journaux, Statuts.

27 ADR, R, Saisie des journaux, Ordre du jour, 30 October 1848, and Compte-rendu, 27 January 1849; AML, I^2 52, no. 49.

28 G. Charavey, *Le projet de la Constitution jugé au point de vue démocratique.*

29 Maurin-Béraud, *Almanach démocratique et social des clubs lyonnais pour 1849*; *Le Républicain*, 18 March 1849.

30 ADR, R, 1er Conseil de Guerre, Insurrection, Saisie des journaux, Acte d'association, 20 February 1849 (eighteen of the twenty-six members of the *Républicain's* editorial board belonged to the Rights of Man); ADR, M, Police générale, Rapports journaliers, 15, 28 December 1848, 4–29 January, 7–22 February 1849.

31 Cf. Forstenzer, "Bureaucrats under Stress," 293–4 (on Nîmes); E. Reynier, *La Seconde République dans l'Ardèche*, 67; G. Rougeron, *La Révolution de 1848 à Moulins et dans le département de l'Allier*, 43; Vigier, 183–214; Zastenker, 110–25.

32 AN BB^{18} 1474^B, 19 February 1849; ADR, R, 1er Conseil de Guerre, Insurrection, Saisie des journaux, Séance du cercle électoral du démocrats-socialistes, 21 February 1849, and "Nous sousignés, membres du Comité électoral central démocratique," 28 March 1849; *Le Censeur*, 25 February 1849.

33 AN BB^{18} 1474^B, 17 July 1850; ADR, M, Police général, Rapports journaliers, 15 March–15 May 1849.

34 ADR, M, Police générale, Rapports journaliers, 6 March, 9, 10 May 1849; *Le Censeur*, 8 March, 18 April 1849; *Le Républicain*, 18 March 1849.

35 F. Dutacq, "Le dernier commandement du maréchal Bugeaud," *Révolution de 1848* 24 (1926): 841–4; J.B. Monfalcon, *Histoire de notre temps* 2: 34.

36 ADR, R, 1er Conseil de Guerre, Insurrection, Saisie des journaux, Ordre du jour, 16 May 1849; *Le Républicain*, 18 May 1849.

37 ADR, M, Police générale, Rapports journaliers, 16–22 May 1849.

38 Monfalcon, *Histoire de notre temps* 2: 33–4; ADR, Banque Guérin, Correspondance expediée, 16–23 May 1849.

39 ADR, Banque Guérin, Correspondance expediée, 25 May–8 June 1849; ADR, M, Police générale, Rapports journaliers, 25 May 1849.

40 ADR, R, 1er Conseil de Guerre, Insurrection, Saisie des journaux, letters from soldiers, 10 April–7 June 1849; *Le Peuple Souverain*, 22 May 1849; *Le Républicain*, 23–26 May 1849.

41 *Le Républicain*, 2, 4 June 1849; *Le Peuple Souverain*, 9–13 June 1849; ADR, M, Police générale, Rapports journaliers, 24 May–11 June 1849.

42 R. Price, *The French Second Republic*, 248–9.

43 *Le Censeur*, special edition, 13 June 1849; *Le Courrier de Lyon*, 14 June 1849; Monfalcon, *Histoire de notre temps* 2: 37; ADR, M, Police générale, Rapports journaliers, 13 June 1849.

44 ADR, M, Police générale, Rapports journaliers, 14 June 1849; *Le Peuple Souverain* and *Le Républicain*, 14 June 1849; *Le Censeur*, 16 June 1849.

45 ADR, R, 1er Conseil de Guerre, Insurrection, Saisie des journaux, Burel dossier; *Le Peuple Souverain* and *Le Républicain*, 16 June 1849.

46 ADR, R, Conseils de Guerre, Insurrection, Dossiers individuels, Arrestay, Berger, Cerdon, and Choppe; AML, I^1 116, no. 263, 20 June 1849.

47 ADR, R, 2me Conseil de Guerre, Insurrection, Affaire de l'école veterinaire, Désarmement des postes; *La Démocratie*, 10 November 1849; Monfalcon, *Histoire de notre temps* 2: 40–1.

49 Monfalcon, *Histoire de notre temps* 2: 44–45, and "Rapports de M.M. les généraux Gemeau et Magnin," 150–3; *Evénements de Lyon du 14 au 17 juin 1849*, 2–3.

49 *Evénements de Lyon*, 4; ADR, M, Police générale, Rapports journaliers, 27 June–25 July 1849; AML, I^2 40, no. 474; *Le Courrier de Lyon*, 17, 18 June 1849; Monfalcon, *Histoire de notre temps* 2: 49–51, 150–3.

50 ADR, R, Conseils de Guerre, Insurrection, Dossiers individuels, J. Berger et

al., Bonnabrit et al., Gazet et al., Messonet et al., and Viricel et al., and the large dossier entitled Environs; *Le Courrier de Lyon*, 17 June 1849; Monfalcon, *Histoire de notre temps* 2: 47–8; Vigier, 2: 225–6.

51 ADR, M, 6me Division militaire, Conseils de Guerre, Jugemens, 1849–51; ADR, R, Conseils de Guerre, Dossiers individuels; AML I² 63.

52 J. Benoit, *Souvenirs de la République*, 193–203; S. Commissaire, *Mémoires et Souvenirs* 1: 217 ff.; *Le Moniteur*, 13, 14 June 1849.

53 *La Tribune Lyonnaise*, January and June 1850.

54 ADR, R, Insurrection du 15 juin 1849, Dossiers individuels, Bert(h)ault, Cerdon, and Durand.

55 Ibid., Berger, Choppe, and Travers (in Charpy et al. dossier).

56 Ibid.; see also Affaire de l'Ecole Véterinaire, Désarmement des Postes.

57 Of the ninety-one convicted insurgents whose occupations can be identified (another eight were absent and their occupations cannot be identified), thirty-six were silk workers, twenty-nine were other workers (mainly construction workers from Guillotière and Vaise), and sixteen were petty bourgeois. For sources, see note to table 1.

58 Monfalcon, *Histoire de notre temps* 2: 42.

CHAPTER SEVEN

1 *Le Moniteur*, 15 June 1849.

2 ADR, M, 6me Division militaire, Conseils de Guerre, Jugemens, 1849–51; AN BB³⁰ 379, 11 January, 2 February, 2 July 1850.

3 ADR, Receuil des Actes administratifs, 1849, pp. 167–75, and M, Personnel, Préfecture, Darcy; AML, I² 40, nos. 271, 273, 274, 477, 479; *Le Censeur*, 20 June 1849.

4 T.F. Forstenzer, "Bureaucrats under stress" (PHD diss., Stanford University, 1974); J. Merriman, *The Agony of the Republic* 44–6.

5 AN BB³⁰ 379, 22 May 1850; ADR, M, Personnel, Préfecture, De la Coste, and Receuil des Actes administratifs, 1850, January; AML, I² 41, nos. 2–3, 5, 8, 11, 24, 45, 54; Forstenzer, "Bureaucrats under Stress," 198–9.

6 ADR, Banque Guérin, Correspondance expédiée, 16 June–31 July 1849, and ADR, M, Police générale, Rapports journaliers, 23 June, 14, 21 July 1849; J.B. Monfalcon, *Histoire de notre temps* 2: 109–10.

7 Forstenzer, "Bureaucrats under Stress," 239; AN BB³⁰ 379, 11 January, 14 March, 20 August 1850, 5, 13 February, 26 March, 9 April, 20 May 1851.

8 AN BB³⁰ 379, December 1849; ADR, M, 6me Division militaire, Conseils de Guerre, Jugemens, 1849–51, and R, Conseils de Guerre, Insurrection, Dossiers individuels, Champagne, Chapelain, Henry, Jacquet fils, Koskow, J.-B. Laloge, Ledère, J. Maréchal, Maurepin, Pupier et al., and Razin.

9 ADR, R, Conseils de Guerre, Insurrection, Dossiers individuels, Grandperrin *dit* Laurier; *Le Censeur*, 8, 16–17 August 1849.

10 *La Tribune Lyonnaise*, July, August, October, and December 1849; January, February, and April–June 1850; AML, I² 59, no. 63.

11 AN BB¹⁸ 1470ᶜ, 11 December 1849, and BB³⁰ 379, December 1849; *Le Censeur*, 27–31 August, 14–19 September, 4 October, 2, 11, 16–30 November, 6 December 1849.

12 *L'Esope*, 21 July 1849 (also datelined "46th day of Year One of the State of Siege"); *Le Niveau Social*, August and September 1849; AML, I² 59, no. 65; ADR, U, Tribunal Correctionnel, Jugemens, 29 August, 11 December 1849; AN BB²⁰ 147, 150, 22 June, 25 August 1849, 23 January 1850, and BB¹⁸ 1470ᶜ, 21 November 1849.

13 *Le Monde Républicain*, 14–17 August 1849; *L'Homme du Peuple*, 22 August 1849; *La Revue Démocratique*, 27 August 1849; *L'Egalité*, 30 August 1849; *Le Travail*, September 1849; *L'Espoir*, 21 September 1849; *Le Démocrate*, 4 October 1849; *La Démocratie*, 10–18 November 1849; AN BB²⁰ 150, 23 January 1850; AML, I² 59, no. 67.

14 AML, Croix-Rousse, I², Police générale, Crieurs publics, 5 October, 5 December 1849; ADR, U, Tribunal Correctionnel, Jugemens, October–November 1849; Forstenzer, "Bureaucrats under Stress," 413–15.

15 ADR, Receuil des Actes administratifs, 1850; AN BB³⁰ 379, 11 January 1850; AML, I² 59, no. 72; I¹ 115, nos. 30–2.

16 AN BB¹⁸ 1470ᶜ, 30 April 1850; ADR, U, Tribunal Correctionnel, Jugemens, 21 May, 21 August 1850; see also Merriman, *Agony of the Republic*, 37.

17 *Le Censeur*, 25 September 1849; *La Tribune Lyonnaise*, October 1849, January 1850; AN BB³⁰ 379, December 1850; ADR, M, 6me Division militaire, Jugemens, 2me Conseil de Guerre, 26 November 1849, 9 March 1850; 1er Conseil de Guerre, 7 May 1850.

18 ADR, Receuil des Actes administratifs, 1849, pp. 177–86; ADR, M, Police générale, Rapports journaliers, 30 June, 2, 5 July 1849; AML, I¹ 115, no. 271.

19 *Le Courrier de Lyon*, *La Gazette de Lyon*, and *Le Salut Public*, 29 June–7 July 1849.

20 Ibid., 12, 15 July 1849; *La Tribune Lyonnaise*, July 1849; AN BB¹⁸ 1468, 2 August 1849.

21 AN BB¹⁸ 1468, 13 August 1849; ADR, M, Police générale, Rapports journaliers, 11, 17 July 1849; AML, Croix-Rousse, Elections au Conseil municipal, 1849; *Le Censeur*, 6, 20 August 1849; *Le Monde Républicain*, 15 August 1849.

22 AML, D, Procès-verbaux de Conseil municipal, Lyon, 21 September 1849, 12 June, 13 November 1851, and Guillotière, 21 September–4 October 1849.

23 *Le Courrier de Lyon*, *La Gazette de Lyon*, and *Le Salut Public*, August–September 1849, May–June and September 1850, May–June 1851.

24 AML, Guillotière, D, Procès-verbaux de Conseil municipal, 6–10 August, 9 November–29 December 1850; 7 January–20 February 1851, also K2, Conseil municipal, Nominations, 18 November 1850, Tableaux des Conseilleurs municipals, and Elections, 21 April 1851; AN BB³⁰ 379, 26 October 1850, 12 May 1851.

25 AN BB³⁰ 379, December 1849, 11 January, 20 August 1850.

26 Ibid., 2 June, 3 July, 8 September 1851.

27 AN BB¹⁸ 1474ᴮ, 19 December 1849, and BB³⁰ 396, p. 34; *Le Censeur*, 27 April, 10 December 1849; E. Flotard, *Le mouvement coopératif à Lyon et dans le Midi de la France*, 110–21.

28 AN BB¹⁸ 1474, Statuts de l'Union des Travailleurs and letter, 5 January 1850, and BB³⁰ 379, 7 February 1850; ADR, R, 1er Conseil de Guerre, Commission militaire, 1851, Association fraternelle des Travailleurs unis de la ouest de la ville de Lyon; Statuts; J. Gaumont, *Le mouvement ouvrier d'association et de coopération à Lyon*, 33–4.

29 Gaumont, *Le mouvement ouvrier*, 36–7; Flotard, 142–50.

30 ADR, M, Police générale, Rapports journaliers, 3–16 April 1849, and U, Tribunal Correctionnel, Jugemens, 1, 13 May, 6 September 1850, 6 August 1851.

31 Forstenzer, "Bureaucrats under Stress," 375–9; AN BB³⁰ 379, 11 January, 26 November 1850.

32 AN BB¹⁸ 1488, 23 September, November 1850; *La Tribune Lyonnaise*, August 1850–February 1851.

33 AN BB³⁰ 379, 2 July, 26 October 1850, 1 February 1851; ADR, M, 6me Division

militaire, Jugemens, 1er Conseil de Guerre, 16 May 1851, 2me Conseil de Guerre, 1 October 1850, and Dossiers individuels, 1850–1, Mouvements insurrectionnels, Sociétés secrètes, Carbonari, Boirivant et al.; AML, I² 41, nos. 36–7.

34 AN BB³⁰ 379, 1–2 February, 14 March, 20 August, 26 November 1850.

35 J. Benoit, *Confessions d'un prolétaire*, 189–202, and *Souvenirs*, 212–13, 240–3; Merriman, *Agony of the Republic*, 127, 135; R. Price, *The French Second Republic*, 258–9.

36 AN BB³⁰ 394, Travail sur le mouvement démagogique, Groupe de Centre, Groupe de Midi, and BB¹⁸ 1488, 22 September, 23–27 October, 6, 19, 20 November 1850, 17 March 1851.

37 *Complot de Lyon*, 2me Conseil de Guerre de la 6me Division militaire, *Audiences du 5 et 27 août 1851*, a special edition of *Le Salut Public*, 28 August 1851.

38 Ibid.; AN BB¹⁸ 1488, 28 January, 31 March, 17 May, 19, 24–30 August, 15 October 1851, also Lombard's deposition, 30 December 1850, 6 January 1851; AN BB³⁰ 391, Rapport du Procureur-Général du Jura, 14–23 November 1850, and resumé of Sentenac's testimony; AML, I² 41, nos. 322–6.

39 See M. Dessai, "Le Complot de Lyon et la résistance au coup d'état dans les départements du Sud-Est," *1848*, *Revue des révolutions contemporaines* 44 (1951): 83–96; T. Margadent, *French Peasants in Revolt*, 124, 130, 189; E. Tenot, *La provence en décembre 1851*; P. Vigier, *La Seconde République dans la région alpine* 2: 285–93, 307–37.

40 Margadent, 117–19, 131; Merriman, *Agony of the Republic*, 141.

41 *Le Courrier de Lyon* and *Le Salut Public*, 19–20 March, 6–31 August 1851; AN BB³⁰ 379, 1, 18 March, 8 September 1851; Maréchal de Castellane, *Journal*, *1804–1862*, 283–8; Captain P. Montagne, *Le comportement politique de l'armée à Lyon sous la Monarchie de Juillet et la Seconde République*, 300–2, 307–12.

42 AN BB³⁰ 379, 26 October, 27 December 1850; 1 February, 20 May, 8 September 1851; AN BB¹⁸ 1488, 10, 11 November 1850, 16, 29 August 1851; Castellane, 291, 305–9, 341.

43 Margadent, 164–5.

44 *Le Courrier de Lyon* and *Le Salut Public*, July 1850–November 1851; *La Gazette de Lyon*, 30 August–November 1851; ADR, IN, Conseil général, 5–7 September 1850.

45 Price, *Second Republic*, 272–82; ADR, Receuil des Actes administratifs, 9 November 1851.

46 AN F⁷ 12654, 3–12 December 1851; *Le Courrier de Lyon*, *La Gazette de Lyon*, and *Le Salut Public*, 4–12 December 1851; Castellane, 346–51.

47 Castellane, 348–51; AN F⁷ 12654, 1, 4 December 1851; Margadent, 8, 10 (figures), and passim.

48 AN BB³⁰ 396, 31 December 1851; AN BB³⁰ 401, 17 March 1852; R. Arnaud, *Le 2 décembre*, 125, 130; Margadent, 309–21; V. Wright, "The Coup d'Etat of December 1851; Repression and the Limits of Repression," in *Revolution and Reaction*, ed. R. Price, 303–14.

49 ADR, R, 1er Conseil de Guerre, Commission militaire, Dossiers individuels, Mis en liberté, Renvoi à Cayenne, Renvoie à Zembésa; ADR, M, Victimes du 2 décembre; AN F⁷ 2587, 2591.

50 I have checked the names derived from the preceding sources and from AML I² 41, nos. 158–250, against AML I² 51–54, 63.

51 ADR, M, Victimes …, André, Cornu, Mingat, Morel, and Vincent; AN F⁷ 2587, Durand.

191 Notes to pages 150-5

52 AN F⁷ 2587, Gros-Piron, Huche, Joannin, and Millet-Mangin; AN F⁷ 2591, Roussy; ADR, R, 1er Conseil de Guerre, Commission militaire, Transportations, and M, Victimes ..., Blain, Grégoire, Richard, and Venture.
53 ADR, M, Victimes ..., Gandy, Gantet, Garin, L'Hôpital, and Michalon.
54 AN BB³⁰ 396, p. 34; AML, I² 52, 53, Edant, Guillermin, and Manigot.
55 ADR, M, Victimes ..., Bacot, Blache, Bouveyron, Démard, Crevet, Millet, Naudé, Pascot, and Rivay, and R, 1er Conseil de Guerre, Commission militaire, Dossiers individuels, Mis en Liberté, and Transportations; AN F⁷ 2587, Bacot and Démard.
56 AN F⁷ 2587, Bonjour, Jailloux, and Jaud; AN F⁷ 2591, Goyet and Valland; ADR, R, 1er Conseil de Guerre, Commission militaire, Dossiers individuels, nos. 319-21, 325, 338, 340; ADR, M, Victimes ..., Carret, Charpeno, Lautaud, Magnolle, Sarrobert, Sanlaville; AML, I² 51, 54, Carret, Richard, and Robert.
57 AN F⁷ 2587, Clapot, Ducotte, Leboulbin, Longuet, Grivaud, Heitzman, and Koenig; AML I² 53, 54, Poulard and Raton; ADR, M, Victimes ..., Berthelier and Maquaire; ADR, R, 1er Conseil de Guerre, Commission mixte, Dossiers individuels, Belin, Mayer, Oblin, and Sigaud.
58 ADR, R, 1er Conseil de Guerre, Commission mixte, Dossiers individuels, Gracias and Verdelat, also Insurrection du 6 et 7 décembre 1851, Individus mis en liberté, Joannin and Jourdon, and M, Victimes ..., Arnaud, Berard, Berthet, Bois, Bony, Gros, Mangue, Martinière, and Pabiou; AML, I² 52, 54, Durand, Grinand, Robert, and Roland.
59 ADR, M, Victimes ... Bois, Martinière, and Pabiou; AML, I² 63, Barbécot.
60 AML I² 63, Pallud, Perret, Thomas, and Vallier; I² 41, nos. 75, 137, 158-250.
61 AML, I² 41, nos. 59, 81; I² 51-3, Cachet, Diochene, Ferrand, Lacroix, Laurent, and Perrot; I¹ 117, nos. 274, 275; ADR, R, 1er Conseil de Guerre, Commission militaire, Dossiers individuels, Insurrection du 5 et 7 décembre 1851, Individus mis en liberté, Gardon and Monnier.
62 ADR, R, 1er Conseil de Guerre, Commission militaire, Etat nominatif des individus ... renvoies à Cayenne, Rebuffat; AN BB³⁰ 396, p. 37.
63 ADR, M, Victimes ..., passim.
64 D. Hays, "Property, Authority and the Criminal Law," in *Albion's Fatal Tree*, ed. E.P. Thompson.
65 AML, D, Croix-Rousse, Guillotière and Lyon, Procès-verbaux du Conseils municipals, December 1851, March 1852; *La Gazette de Lyon*, 18, 19 December 1851.
66 AN BB¹¹ 1114, 27 December 1851, and the minutes of the electoral committees; Price, *Second Republic*, 321-3.

CONCLUSION

1 AN BB³⁰ 379, 4-5 July 1852; AN F¹ᶜ III Rhône 4¹, 2, 26 November 1852; Maréchal de Castellane, *Journal, 1804-1862*, 359-77; F. Dutacq, "La Police politique et les parties d'opposition à Lyon et dans le Midi en 1852," *Révolution de 1848* 20 (1923): 240-50, 316-27.
2 G. Sheridan, "The Political Economy of Artisan Industry: Government and the People in the Silk Trade of Lyon, 1830-1870," *French Historical Studies* 2 (1979): 222-5.
3 AML, F², Fabrique des soies, Affaires diverses, Rapport sur la petition presenté à M. le Préfect par M.M. les chefs d'ateliers ... 1853.
4 Sheridan, 226-35.
5 M. Agulhon, *Une ville ouvrière au temps du socialisme utopique*, 94-9; J.

Scott, *The Glassmakers of Carmaux*; W. Sewell, "La classe ouvrière de Marseilles sous la Second République," *Le Mouvement Social* 70 (1971).

6 C. Johnson, "Communism and the Working Class before Marx," *American Historical Review* 76 (1971).

7 M. Perrot, "Grèves, grévistes et conjoncture," *Le Mouvement Social* 63 (1968).

8 S. Maritch, *Histoire du mouvement social sous le Second Empire à Lyon*, 99–100, 217–56.

9 Ibid., 117–41; E. Flotard, *Le mouvement coopératif à Lyon et dans le Midi de la France*, 198–9, 251, 374–7; J. Gaumont, *Le mouvement ouvrier d'association et de coopération à Lyon*, 39–41, 87–9.

10 AML, I² 53, no. 27; I² 54, nos. 346–7; I² 63, no. 18; ADR, M, Victimes de 2 décembre, Bacot, Cornu, Démard, Garin, Millet, Mingat, Pascot, and Pallud.

11 Maritch, 85–95.

12 J. Maitron et al., *Dictionnaire biographique du mouvement ouvrier français, première partie: 1789–1864*, Gandy, Grinand, Murat, Perret, Seux, and Vincent.

13 A. Kleinclaus, *Histoire de Lyon et du lyonnais* 3: 206–15; Maritch, 143–71.

Bibliography

MANUSCRIPT SOURCES

Archives Nationales

Series	Carton and Description
BB[11]	1114 Results, plebiscite December 1851
BB[18]	1230, 1239–41, 1246, 1248, 1252, 1358, 1360, 1362, 1366, 1386–8, 1397, 1415, 1420–1, 1423, 1441, 1451, 1458, 1460, 1468–70, 1472–4, 1488: Attorney-Generals' Reports, Lyon, 1834–52
BB[20]	74, 80, ... 154: Comptes-rendus d'assises, Lyon, 1834–51
BB[30]	294 Tableau synoptique des accusés d'avril jugés par la cour des pairs, 1837
	327 Rapport de Jouve Dubor ... chargé de diriger la police politique dans les départements du Rhône ... 1848
	331, 333, 335, 361, 379, 391, 392[a]: Affaires politiques, Rhône, 1848–50
	394 Travail sur le mouvement démogogique antérieur au 2 décembre 1851
	396 Evénements du décembre 1851
	397 Affaires politiques, Rhône, December 1851–January 1852
	401 Rapports sur les Commissions mixtes, Rhône
	1287–90: Etat des individus jugés dans le ressort de la cour d'appel de Lyon et précédemment condamnés pour crimes ... 1836–52
C	934 Relevé des petitions adressés à la commission du gouvernement pour l'organisation du travail par les ouvriers
	936[B] and 939: Enquête dans les départements, May–June 1848
	1286[A] Rhône 133, Elections, 1834–48
F[1a]	10 Proclamations ... December 1851 and January 1852
F[1c]	111 4[1] Esprit publique et élections–Rhône
	11 Comptabilité communale, 1847–9, Rhône, Lyon

F⁷   2587 Individus transportés en Afrique, December 1851
       2591 Décisions des Commissions mixtes
       12654 Dépêches des préfets, December 1851
F⁹   1072 Rapports, Garde nationale mobile
F¹²   2409 Tissus de soie, 1767–1836
       4617–19: Association ouvrières: loi du 5 juillet 1848
       4620 and 4626 Associations ouvrières: demandes de prêts rejetés
       4637 Associations ouvrières: état des demandes par département
F¹⁷   10321 Ecoles primaires, 1849–50

Archives Departementales du Rhône

Series	Carton and Description
Banque Guérin	Correspondance expédiée, 1847–9
IN	Conseil général, Rapports et déliberations, 1848–50
J	Caisse des Prêts pour les chefs d'ateliers, 1832–46
M	Dénombrement, 1851
	Mercuriales générales, 1833–4, 1843–7
	Ouvriers sans travail, 1839–42
	Personnel, Préfets, 1848–52
	Police, Affaires diverses, 1838–45
	Police générale, 1835–48 (Rapports de Commissaire spécial)
	Police générale, Rapports journaliers, 1835–6, 1840–9
	Recueil des actes administratifs de la Préfecture du Rhône, 1848–51
	Situation industriel
	6me Division militaire, Jugemens prononcés par le 1er et 2me Conseils de Guerre, 1849–51
	Sociétés de secours, 1810–51
	Statistiques industrielles
	Travail des enfants dans les manufactures
	Victimes du deux décembre, 1851
R	Fortifications entre la Saône et le Rhône, 1831–48
	Garde nationale mobile
	Garde nationale sedentaire
	6me Division militaire, 1er et 2me Conseils de Guerre, 1849–51, Dossiers individuels; Insurrection du 15 juin 1849; Affaire de l'école vétérinaire; Insurrection … dans les environs de Lyon; Saisie des journaux *Le Peuple Souverain* et *Le Républicain*; Mouvements insurrectionnels, Sociétés secrètes, Carbonari; Société secrète *dit* les Voraces; Commission militaire, 1851–2

U   Conseil des Prud'hommes de Lyon, 1806–1919
           Tribunal de Commerce, Dossiers des faillites, 1835–47
           Tribunal Correctionnel de Lyon, Jugemens 1834–51
X   Caisse d'épargne, 1818–50
           Dispensaire de Lyon

Archives Municipales de Lyon

Series   Carton and Description
Croix-Rousse   Ecoles primaires, 1842–4
                Elections au Conseil municipal, 1840–52
                Garde nationale, Election des officiers, 1831–48, and Recense-
                ment, 1841
                1¹ Police
                1² Police générale, 1790–1852
Guillotière   D¹⁹ Contentieux–damages, February 1848
                G¹ 111 Contributions extraordinaires, 1848
                K¹ Election du Président de la République
                K² Conseil municipal, Nominations, 1793–1851
                K⁴ Elections municipales, 1842–51
D   Procès-verbaux de Conseil Municipal, Croix-Rousse, Guillo-
                tière, Lyon, and Vaise, 1846–51
F²   Fabrique des soies, Affaires diverses, 1810–52
H   Garde nationale, Lyon
I¹   Police locale
I¹ 74   Copie de la correspondance du Commissaire spéciale, 1835–8
I¹ 115–17   Rapports, enquêtes, procès-verbaux des commissaires de police:
                arrondissement Palais-des-Arts, 1846–52
I²   Police générale; Police politique, 1816–70
I² 40   Documents relatifs aux suspects politiques, sociétés et clubs …;
                agitation politique, mouvements populaires de février 1848;
                émeute du 15 juin 1849
I² 41   Documents relatifs aux suspects politiques …; Coup d'état du 2
                décembre: arrestations 1850–4
I² 45   Sociétés coopératives de production et de consommation,
                1849–70
I² 49   Revendications et manifestations ouvrières, 1806–70
I² 51–4   Lettres, enquêtes, instructions … se rapportant à des particuliers
I² 59   Presse périodique, 1791–1870
I² 63   Suspects et condamnés politiques, 1849–58.
M¹   Croix-Rousse fortifications

Q¹   Bureau de Bienfaisance, Year VII–1890
Q²   Ouvriers sans travail, Ateliers de charité, 1790–1866
           Souscriptions pour les ouvriers sans travail, 1848
Documents Gasparin, Vols. 1 and 4

Bibliothèque Municipale de Lyon

Fonds Coste (a collection of documents)
11031 *Règlement des maîtres et ouvriers peintres, plâtriers de la ville de Lyon et des communes suburbaines* (Lyon 1848)
11032 *Statuts de l'Association des entrepreneurs peintres-plâtriers de la ville de Lyon et des communes suburbaines ... des 4 et 12 juillet 1848*
11034 *L'Union des Travailleurs, Association entre patrons et ouvriers* (Lyon: Leon Boitel, 1848)
11035 *Acte d'Association des ouvriers tailleurs du département du Rhône* (Lyon: n.p., 1 April 1849)
5314 Affiches, numbers 9257–465
Elections, 111497–580

Archives de la Chambre de Commerce de Lyon

Procès-verbaux et déliberations, Régistre no. 12, 1849–50
Compte-rendu des travaux de la Chambre de Commerce, 1846–7

PRINTED SOURCES

Workers' Press

L'Avenir, 1846–7
L'Echo de la Fabrique, 1831–4
L'Echo de la Fabrique de 1841, 1841–5
L'Echo de l'Industrie, 1845–6
L'Echo des Ouvriers, 1840–1
L'Echo des Travailleurs, 1833–4
L'Indicateur, 1834–5
Le Travail, 1841
La Tribune Lyonnaise, 1845–51
La Tribune Prolétaire, 1834–5

Democratic-socialist Press

Club de l'Egalité, Bulletin Hebdomadaire, March–April 1848
La Commune Sociale, December 1848–May 1849
L'Esope, followed by *Le Niveau Social*, July–September 1849

La Feuille du Jour, February–March 1848

Le Franc-Parleur Lyonnais, March 1848

Le Monde Républicain, followed by *La Revue Démocratique, L'Homme du Peuple, L'Egalité, Le Travail, L'Espoir, Le Démocrate, La Démocratie*, August–November 1849

La Montagne, March–April 1848

L'Organisateur Lyonnais, February–April 1848

Le Patriote Lyonnais, April 1848

Le Peuple Souverain, March 1848–June 1849

Le Réformateur, 1848

Le Républicain, February–June 1849

La République, March 1848

Le Reveil du Peuple, 1848

La Sentinelle, April 1848

La Spartacus, April 1848

Le Tribun du Peuple, March–April 1848

Le Vengeur, 1848

Le Vingt-Quatre Février, March–April 1848

La Voix du Peuple, 1848

Le Vorace, May 1848

Le Vrai Républicain, March 1848

Other Newspapers and Periodicals

Le Censeur, 1834–49

Comité Général des Clubs, Bulletin, March–April 1848

La Constitution, 1849

Le Courrier de Lyon, 1834–52

Le Démon Socialiste, Journal Populaire et Anti-Communiste, April 1849

L'Echo des Electeurs, April 1848

La Gazette de Lyon, 1845–52

L'Harmonie, 1837–8

Le Journal de Commerce, 1834–44

Journal des électeurs ruraux, 1848

La Liberté, 1848–9

Le Moniteur, 1848–51

Le Moniteur Judiciaire de Lyon, 1841–9

Le Président, December 1848

La Revue de Lyon, 1848–50

La Revue Sociale, 1844–5

Le Salut Public, 1848–51

L'Union Nationale, 1848–9

La Verité, 1848

Contemporary Works

Addresse de la Commission Parisienne pour le Populaire au Communistes Lyonnais, suivie d'une Addresse des Communistes Lyonnais. Lyon: n.p., 1844.

Annuaire de la Ville de Lyon et du Département du Rhône. Lyon: Pelagaud, Lesne et Crozet, 1837–50.

Association Fraternelle des Femmes Ouvrières Lyonnaises pour l'exploitation de toutes industries. Lyon: Chanoine, 1848

Audiganne, A. Les populations ouvrières et les industries de la France. 2nd ed. Vol. 2. Paris: Capelle, 1862.

Beaulieu, C. Histoire du commerce, de l'industrie et des fabriques de Lyon. Lyon: A. Baron, 1838.

Benoit, J. Confessions d'un prolétaire, presented by Maurice Moissonier. Paris: Editions Sociales, 1968.

– Souvenirs de la République de 1848. Geneva: Duchamp et Cie., 1855.

Bergier, J. Le journal d'un bourgeois de Lyon en 1848. Edited by J. Godart. Paris: Presses Universitaires de France, 1924.

Bez, Abbé. La ville des aumônes. Lyon: Librairie Chrétiene, 1840

Blanc, F. "Le Comité éxécutif de Lyon en 1848." Révolution de 1848 9–10 (1912–13): 342–66.

– "L'Oeuvre du Comité éxécutif de Lyon en 1848." Révolution de 1848 9–10 (1912–13): 165–78.

Blanqui, A. Des classes ouvrières en France pendant l'année 1848. Paris: Pagnerre, 1848.

Bunel, J.F. Tableau historique, administratif et industriel de la ville de la Croix-Rousse. Croix-Rousse: Lepagnez, 1842.

Bureau de la Statistique Générale. Statistique de la France. 1st ser., vols. 2 and 3.

Cabet, E. Utile et franche explication avec les Communistes lyonnais. Paris: Breton, 1842.

Castellane, Maréchal de. Journal, 1804–1862. Paris: n.p., 1895–7.

Caussidiere, M. Mémoires. Paris: Michel Levy Frères, 1849.

Charavey, G. Le projet de Constitution jugé au point de vue démocratique. Lyon: Boursy, 1848.

Chipier, aîné. Mémoire sur l'impôt des 55 centimes, sur les chantiers nationaux et sur les secours extraordinaires avancés par la Ville de Lyon. Lyon: Nigon, 1849.

Combe, A., and Charavey, G., Guide de l'étranger à Lyon. Lyon: Charavey frères, 1847.

Commissaire, S. Mémoires et souvenirs. Vol. 1. Lyon: Meton, 1888.

Commission pour l'organisation du travail. Projet d'association libre et voluntaire entre les chefs d'industrie et les ouvriers et de réforme commerciale. Lyon: n.p., 2 July 1848.

Conseil central aux loges maçonniques de Lyon. Lyon: L. Boitel, 1891.

Conseil Général du Département du Rhône. Rapport sur l'administration du département, présenté par M. le Préfet. Lyon: Ayné, 1839–45.

Cour des Pairs. *Affaire du mois d'avril 1834.* Vol. 1. *Rapport fait à la cour par M. Girod, Les Faits généraux.* Vol. 10. *Réquisitoire.* Paris: Imprimerie royale, 1835.

– *Attentat du 15 octobre 1840: Rapport ... par M. Girod de l'Ain.* Paris: Imprimerie royale, 1841.

Covillard, A. *Projet d'organisation pour la fabrique des étoffes de soie.* Lyon: Boursy, 1848.

Derrion, M. *Constitution de l'industrie et organisation pacifique du commerce et du travail.* Lyon: Durval, 1834.

Details circonstanciés et très-curieux sur les Voraces, les Ventre-Creux et les Vauteurs de Lyon, par un affilié. Montmartre: Pillay Frères, 1848.

Evénements de Lyon du 14 au 17 juin 1849. Guillotière: Bajat, 1849.

Exposition universelle de 1889. *La Fabrique lyonnaise de soieries et l'industrie de la soie en France, 1789–1889.* Lyon: Imprimerie Pitrat, 1889.

Flotard, E. *Le Mouvement coopératif à Lyon et dans le Midi de la France.* Paris: Librairie des Sciences Sociales, 1867.

Greppo, L. *Réponse d'un socialiste à M. le Maréchal Bugeaud.* Paris: Bautriche, 1848.

Histoire de l'Académie de Lyon. Lyon: Begerton et Brun, 1839.

Hodieu, M. *Rapport présenté au Conseil Municipal de Lyon ... sur les démandes d'indemnité formée contre la ville de Lyon.* Lyon: Nigon, n.d.

House of Commons. *Reports from Committees.* Vol. 19, no. 678 (1832). *Report from the Select Committee on the Silk Trade.*

Indicateur commercial, industriel, administratif et judiciaire de la ville de Lyon. Lyon: Lusy, 1845.

Jal, M. "Lyon en 1834." *Revue du Lyonnais* 3 (1836): 18–25.

Kauffmann, *Des causes locales qui nuisant à la Fabrique de Lyon, des moyens de les faire cesser ou au moins d'en atténuer les effets.* Lyon: n.p., 1846.

Lamartine, A. de. *History of the French Revolution of 1848.* Boston: Phillips, Sampson, 1849.

Lentillon, J. *Un page de l'histoire de Lyon en 1848, Administration de la Commune de Caluire.* Lyon: Mougin-Rusand, 1863.

Le Pays de Bourjolly, General. *De l'armée et quarante jours de 1848 à Lyon.* Paris: Libraire Militaire de J. Dumaine, 1853.

Lesaulnier, C. M. *Biographie des neuf cents députés à l'Assemblée nationale.* Paris: n.p., 1848.

Maurin-Béraud, Président du Club des Petit-Pères. *Almanach démocratique et social des clubs lyonnais pour 1849.* Lyon: Charavey, 1849.

Monfalcon, J.B. *Code morale des ouvriers.* Paris and Lyon: Pelagaud, Lesne et Crozet, 1836.

– *Histoire de notre temps.* 2 vols. In *Annuaire de Département du Rhône,* 1849, 1850.

– *Histoire des insurrection de Lyon.* Lyon: n.p., 1834.

– *Souvenirs d'un bibliothèquaire.* Lyon: n.p., 1853.

– and Polinière, A.P.J. *Hygiène de la Ville de Lyon, ou Opinions et Rapports de Conseil de Salubrité.* Paris: Bailliere, 1845.

Ogier, T., Poncet, P., and Dubouchet, J. *La France par canton et par commune, Département du Rhône.* Lyon: Ogier, 1849–51.

Parisel, L.V., "Revue des établissements industriels de Lyon, Rive gauche du Rhône," *Revue du lyonnais* 4 (1836): 369–84.

Perrière, P. de la, et al. *Mémoire pour la commune d'Oullins, appelante, contre le refuge de Saint-Joseph et la Ville de Lyon.* Lyon: Perrin, 1850.

Poncelet, General. "Machines et outils appliqués aux arts textiles." In Exposition de 1851, *Travaux de la Commission française sur l'industrie.* Vol. 3, pt. 1. *Machines, Outils et Constructions.* Paris: Imprimerie impérial, 1852.

Poncet, Meurgé, Mamessier, and Racine. *Réponse communiste-icarienne à la Tribune lyonnaise.* Lyon; n.p., 1845.

Porter, G.R. *Treatise on the Origin, Progressive Improvement and the Present State of Silk Manufacture.* London: n.p., 1831.

Procès du complot de Lyon (compte-rendu et jugement rendu par le 2me Conseil de Guerre ... le 19 août 1851). Lyon: n.p., 1851.

Proudhon, P.J. *Correspondance.* Vol. 2. Paris: Librairie internationale, 1857.

Résumé de plaidorie pour la Ville de Lyon, contre la Commune d'Ouillins et M. l'Abbé Rey. Lyon: Nigon, 1850.

Reveyron, P. *Appreciation des principes qui ont dirigé et des faits qui ont accompagnés le mouvement républicain des volontaires savoyards.* Lyon: L. Boitel, 1848.

Rey, General M. *M. Emmanuel Arago et les événements de Lyon au 24 février 1848.* Grenoble: Barnel, n.d.

Reybaud, M.R.L. *Etudes sur le regime des manufactures, Conditions des ouvriers en soie.* n.p.: n.p., 1859.

Riancy, H. de. *Compte-rendu des élections de 1846.* Paris: P.J. Lecoffre, 1848.

Simples explications by "Deux Frères de l'Asile du Sage." Lyon: Nigon, 1843.

La Statue de Louis XIV, place Bellecour. ... Lyon: Buyot, 1848.

Statuts de la Société dite l'Union des Veloutiers. Lyon: Boursy, 1 September 1848.

Treillard, M. *La République à Lyon sous le gouvernement provisoire.* Lyon: Charavey, 1849.

Truquin, N. *Mémoires et aventures d'un prolétaire.* Paris: Librairie des Deux-Mondes, 1888.

Villermé, L.R. *Tableau de l'état physique et moral des ouvriers employés dans les manufactures de coton, de laine et de soie.* Paris: J. Remouard et Cie., 1840

Later Works

Aboucaya, C. *Les structures sociales et économiques de l'agglomeration lyonnais à la veille de la Révolution de 1848.* Paris: Recueil Sirey, 1963.

Actes du Congrès historique de Centennaire 1848. Paris: Presses Universitaires de France, 1948.

Agulhon, M. "Les chambrées en Basse-Provence; histoire et ethnologie." *Revue historique* 245 (1971): 337–68.

– *La République au village*. Paris: Plon, 1970.

– "Vers une histoire des associations." *Esprit* 46 (1978): 13–18.

– *Une ville ouvrière au temps du socialisme utopique: Toulon de 1815 à 1851*. Paris: Mouton, 1970.

Amann, P. *Revolution and Mass Democracy: The Paris Club Movement in 1848*. Princeton: Princeton University Press, 1975.

Armengaud, A. *Les populations de l'Est-Aquitaine au début de l'époche contemporaine. ...* Paris: Mouton, 1961.

Arminjon, J. *La population du département du Rhône: Son évolution depuis le début du XIXe siècle*. Lyon: Bosc Frères, 1940.

Arminzade, R. "Breaking The Chains of Dependency: From Patronage to Class Politics, Toulouse, France, 1830–1872." *Journal of Urban History* 3 (August 1977): 485–505.

Arnaud, R. *Le 2 décembre*. Paris: Hachette, 1967.

Ballot, C. *L'Introduction du mécanisme dans l'industrie française*. Paris: Rieder, 1923.

Balteau, J., Barroux, M., and Prevost, M. *Dictionnaire de biographie française*. Paris: Letouzet et Ane, 1939.

Baughman, J.J. "The French Banquet Campaign of 1847–1848." *Journal of Modern History* 31 (1959): 1–15.

Bezucha, R. *The Lyon Uprising of 1834*. Cambridge: Harvard University Press, 1974.

– "The Revolution of 1830 and the City of Lyon." In *1830 in France*, edited by J.M. Merriman. New York: New Viewpoints, 1975.

Bouillon, J. "Les démocrates-socialistes aux élections de 1849." *Revue français de science politique* 6 (1956): 70–95.

Buffenoir, M. "Le Fourierisme à Lyon de 1834 à 1848." *Revue d'histoire de Lyon* 12 (1913): 444–55.

– "Les Saint-Simoniens à Lyon, 1831–1834." *Revue bleu*, 14–25 September 1909.

Calman, A.R. *Ledru-Rollin and the Second French Republic*. New York: Columbia University Press, 1922.

"Les Carbonari en France sous la Restauration." *Révolution de 1848* 9–10 (1912–13): 413–20.

Chabaseau, A. "Les Constituantes de 1848." *Révolution de 1848* 7 (1910–11): 287–305, 413–25.

Chalmin, P. "Les crises dans l'armée française, 1848." *Revue historique de l'armée* 18 (1962): 45–62.

Charles, A. *La Révolution de 1848 et la Seconde République à Bordeaux et dans le Département de la Gironde*. Bordeaux: Delmas, 1945.

Charnay, J.P. *Société militaire et suffrage politique en France depuis 1789*. Paris: SEVPEN, 1964).

Chatelain, A. "La formation de la population lyonnaise: L'Apport d'origine montagnard." *Revue de géographie de Lyon* 24 (1954): 91–115.

– "Les migrations temporaires et la propagation des idées révolutionnaires en France au XIXe siècle." *Revue des révolutions contemporaines* 188 (1951): 6–12.

Chazelas, V. "Félix Blanc." *Révolution de 1848* 9–10 (1912–13): 155–64.

Chevalier, L. *Classes laborieuses et classes dangereuses.* Paris: Plon, 1958.

Christofferson, T.R. "The French National Workshops of 1848: The View From the Provinces." *French Historical Studies* 11 (1980): 505–21.

Créveuil, G. "La condition ouvrière et la crise de 1847 à Nantes." *1848, Revue des révolutions contemporaines* 41 (1948): 39–60.

Dautry, J. *1848 et la Seconde République.* Paris: Editions Sociales, 1957.

Davis, N.Z. "The Reasons of Misrule." *Society and Culture in Early Modern France.* Stanford: Stanford University Press, 1975.

De Luna, F.A. *The French Republic under Cavaignac.* Princeton: Princeton University Press, 1969.

Le Département de la Marne et la Révolution en 1848. Chalons-sur-Marne: Archives de la Marne, 1948.

Dessal, M. "Le Complot de Lyon et la résistance au coup d'état dans les départements de Sud-Est." *1848, Revue des révolutions contemporaines* 44 (1951): 83–96.

Dommanget, J. *Auguste Blanqui et la Révolution de 1848.* Paris: Mouton, 1972.

Dufour, C. "L'Assistance à Lyon de 1838 à 1851." *Diplôme des Etudes Supérieures d'Histoire,* Université de Lyon, 1960.

Dupeux, G. *Aspects de l'histoire sociale et politique du Loir-et-Cher, 1848–1914.* Paris: Mouton, 1962.

Dutacq, F. "Le dernier commandement du maréchal Bugeaud." *Révolution de 1848* 23–24 (1925–26): 637–51, 705–16, 829–50.

– "L'Election d'un représentant du Rhône à l'Assemblée Nationale au mois de septembre 1848." *Revue d'histoire de Lyon* 7 (1908).

– "Les elections législatives de 1849 à Lyon et dans la département du Rhône." *Révolution de 1848* 25 (1927): 129–45, 193–205.

– "Un episode de la Révolution de 1848 à Lyon: La dissolution de la Garde nationale mobile." *Revue d'histoire de Lyon* 11 (1912): 103–17.

– *Histoire politique de Lyon pendant la Révolution de 1848.* Paris: n.p., 1910.

– "La police politique et les partis d'opposition à Lyon et dans le Midi en 1852." *Révolution de 1848* 20 (1923): 234–51, 325–34.

Duveau, G. *1848: The Making of a Revolution.* New York: Vintage, 1967.

Fasel, G. "The French Election of April 23, 1848: Suggestions for Revision." *French Historical Studies* 4 (1968): 285–98.

– "Urban Workers in Provincial France, February-June 1848." *International Review of Social History* 17 (1972): 661–74.

Festy, O. "Les deux associations ouvrières lyonnaises encouragées par application du décret du 5 juillet 1848." *Revue d'histoire de Lyon* 11 (1912): 341–67.

Forstenzer, T.R. "Bureaucrats under Stress: French Attorneys General and Prefects and the Fall of the Second Republic." PHD dissertation, Stanford University, 1974.

- *French Provincial Police and the Fall of the Second Republic.* Princeton: Princeton University Press, 1981.

Fortin, H. *Contribution à l'histoire de la Révolution de 1848 dans le Pas de Calais.* Arras: n.p., 1950.

Frambourg, G. "Un Commissaire du Gouvernement provisoire de la République, Guépin." *Annales de Bretagne* 46 (1954): 329–46.

Garden, M. *Lyon et les lyonnais au XVIIIe siècle.* Paris: Les Belles-Lettres, 1970.

Garrier, G. *Paysans de Beaujolais et du Lyonnais, 1800–1970.* Grenoble: Presses Universitaires de Grenoble, 1973.

Gaumont, J. *Le Commerce Veridique et Social (1835–1838) et son fondateur Michel Derrion.* Amiens: Imprimerie Nouvelle, 1935.

- *Le mouvement ouvrier d'association et de coopération à Lyon.* Lyon: n.p., 1921.

Genique, G. *L'Election de l'Assemblée Legislative en 1849.* Paris: Rieder et Cie., 1921.

Girard, L. *La Garde nationale, 1814–1870.* Paris: Plon, 1964.

- *La IIe République.* Paris: Calmin-Lévy, 1968.

Godard, J. *A Lyon, en 1848, les Voraces.* Paris: Presses Universitaires de France, 1948.

- *L'Ouvrier en soie.* Lyon: J. Nicholas, 1890.

Godechot, J., ed. *La Révolution de 1848 à Toulouse et dans la Haute Garonne.* Toulouse: Préfecture de la Haute Garonne, 1948.

Gossez, A.M. *Le Département du Nord sous la Deuxième République.* Lille: Gustave Leleu, 1904.

Gossez, R. *Les ouvriers de Paris.* Vol. 1. *L'Organisation, 1848–1851.* La Roche-sur-Yon: Imprimerie Centrale de l'Ouest, 1967.

- "Presse parisienne à destination des ouvriers, 1848–1851." In *La presse ouvrière, 1819–1850.* Paris: Bibliothèque de la Révolution de 1848, 1966.

Gues, A. "Les expeditions armées de 1848." *Ecrits de Paris* 344 (1975): 82–8.

Haury, P. "Les commissaires de Ledru-Rollin en 1848." *Révolution français* 57 (1909): 438–74.

Hays, D. "Property, Authority and the Criminal Law." In *Albion's Fatal Tree*, edited by E.P. Thompson. New York: Pantheon, 1976.

Johnson, C.H. "Communism and the Working Class before Marx: The Icarian Experience." *American Historical Review* 76 (1971): 642–89.

- "Deux lettres inédites de cinq ouvriers lyonnais à Cabet et à Dézamy." *Revue d'histoire économique et sociale* 47 (1969): 529–39.

- *Utopian Communism in France: Cabet and the Icarians.* Ithaca: Cornell University Press, 1974.

Kaplow, J. *New Perspectives on the French Revolution.* New York: Wiley, 1965.

Kleinclaus, A. *Histoire de Lyon.* 3 vols. Lyon: Librairie Pierre Masson, 1952.

Lacour, R. *La Révolution de 1848 dans la Beaujolais et la campagne lyonnaise.* Lyon: Albums du Crocodile, n.d.

Lacroix, J. *La Deuxième République à Vienne.* Vienne: Ternet-Martin, 1949.

Laferrère, M. *Lyon: Ville industrielle.* Paris: Presses Universitaires de France, 1960.

Latreille, A. *Histoire de Lyon et du lyonnais.* Toulons: Edouard Privat, 1975.

Lecompte, C. "Trois fraternelles dans la région lilloise en 1848 et 1849." *1848, Revue des révolutions contemporaines* 44 (1951): 33–48.

Lentacker, F. "Les ouvriers belges dans le Département du Nord au mileau de XIXe siècle." *Revue du Nord* 38 (1956): 5–14.

Léon, P. *Géographie de fortune et structures sociales à Lyon au XIXe siècle.* Lyon: Centre d'histoire économique et sociale de la région lyonnaise, 1974.

Lequin, Y. *Les ouvriers de la région lyonnaise (1848–1914).* 2 vols. Lyon: Presses Universitaires de Lyon, 1980.

Levy, R. *Le Havre entre trois révolutions.* Paris: Ernest Leroux, 1912.

Levy-Schneider, V. "Correspondance de Martin Bernard, Commissaire général de la République à Lyon, avec sa famille." *Revue d'histoire de Lyon* 12 (1913): 81–115, 179–216.

Loubère, L. "The Emergence of the Extreme Left in Lower Languedoc, 1848–1851: Social and Economic Factors in Politics." *American Historical Review* 73 (1968): 1,019–51.

– *Radicalism in Mediterranean France, 1848–1919.* Albany: State University of New York Press, 1974.

McDougall, M.L. "After the Insurrections: The Workers' Movement of Lyon, 1834–1851." PHD dissertation, Columbia University, 1974.

– "Consciousness and Community: The Workers of Lyon," *Journal of Social History.* 12 (1978): 129–45.

– "Experiments in Organization, Workers Societies in Lyon, 1830–1875." *Proceedings of the Eighth Annual Meeting of the Western Society for French History.* Las Cruces: New Mexico State University Press, 1981.

McKay, D.C. *The National Workshops.* Cambridge: Harvard University Press, 1933.

McPhee, P. "The Crisis of Radical Republicanism in the French Revolution of 1848." *Historical Studies* 16 (1974): 71–88.

Magraw, R.W. "Pierre Joigneux and Socialist Propaganda in the French Countryside, 1849–1851." *French Historical Studies* 10 (1978): 599–640.

Maitron, J., et al. *Dictionnaire biographique du mouvement ouvrier français, première partie: 1789–1864.* 3 vols. Paris: Les Editions Ouvriers, 1964–5.

Margadant, T.W. *French Peasants in Revolt: The Insurrection of 1851.* Princeton: Princeton University Press, 1979.

Maritch, S. *Histoire du mouvement social sous le Second Empire à Lyon.* Paris: Rousseau et Cie., 1930.

Merriman, J. *The Agony of the Republic: The Repression of the Left in Revolutionary France, 1848–1851.* New Haven: Yale University Press, 1978.

- "Social Conflict in France and the Limoges Revolution of April 27, 1848." *Societas* 4 (1974): 21–38.

Moisonnier, M. *La révolte des canuts.* Paris: Editions Sociales, 1958.

Montagne, Captain P. *Le comportement politique de l'armée à Lyon sous la Monarchie de Juillet et la Seconde République.* Paris: E. Pichon et R. Durand-Auzias, 1966.

Payne, H.C. "Preparation of a Coup d'Etat." In *Studies in Modern European History in Honor of Franklin Charles Palm.* New York: Bookman Associates, 1966.

Perreux, G. *Au temps des sociétés secrètes: La propagande républicaine au début de la Monarchie de Juillet, 1830–1835.* Paris: n.p., 1931.

Perrot, M. "Grèves, grévistes et conjoncture." *Le Mouvement Social* 63 (1968): 109–25.

Pouthas, C. *La population française pendant la première moitié du XIXe siècle.* Paris: Presses Universitaires de France, 1956.

Price, R. *The French Second Republic: A Social History.* Ithaca: Cornell University Press, 1972.

- ed. *Revolution and Reaction.* London: Crown Helm, 1975.

Reveil, E. "Notice sur le jeton du Comité provisoire de Lyon en 1848," *Révolution de 1848* 7 (1910–11): 80–3.

La Révolution de 1848 à Moulins et dans le Département de l'Allier. Moulins: Pottier et Cie., 1950.

Reynier, E. *La Seconde République dans l'Ardèche.* n.p.: Maison de l'Enfance, 1948.

Ribe, G. *L'Opinion publique et la vie politique à Lyon lors des premières années de la Seconde Restauration.* In *Annales de l'Université de Lyon,* 3rd ser., Droit, vols. 13–16. Paris: Recueil Sirey, 1957.

Riffaterre, C. *Le mouvement antijacobin et antiparisien à Lyon ... en 1793.* In *Annales de l'Université de Lyon,* n.s., vol. 2. Lyon: A. Rey, 1912.

Rivet, F. *La navigation à vapeur sur la Saône et le Rhône, (1783–1863).* Paris: Presses Universitaires de France, 1962.

- *Le Quartier Perrache, 1766–1946: Etude d'histoire et de géographie urbaine.* Lyon: Audin, 1951.

Rivet, J. *Les œuvres de charité et les établissements d'enseignement libre de 1789 à 1945.* Lyon: Missions Africaines, 1945.

Rude, F. *L'Insurrection lyonnaise de novembre 1831: Le Mouvement ouvrier à Lyon de 1827–1832.* Paris: Editions Anthropos, 1967.

- "Le mouvement ouvrier à Lyon." *Revue de Psychologie des Peuples* 13 (1958): 223–46.

- "Les Saint-Simoniens et Lyon." *Congrès des Sociétés Savantes, Section d'histoire moderne, Actes,* vol. 89, no. 2^1, 1964.

Rudé, G. *The Crowd in History, 1730–1848.* New York: John Wiley and Sons, 1964.

Savey-Casarde. "La criminalité à Lyon de 1830 à 1834." *Revue d'histoire de droit français et étranger* (1962): 248–61.

Schnapper, B. "Les sociétés ouvrières de production pendant la Seconde République: L'exemple girondin." *Revue d'histoire économique et sociale* 43 (1965): 162–91.

Scott, J. *The Glassworkers of Carmoux.* Cambridge: Harvard University Press, 1974.

Sewell, W.H. "La classe ouvrière de Marseille sous la Seconde République: structure sociale et comportement politique." *Le Mouvement Social* 70 (1971): 27–67.

– *Work and Revolution in France: The Language of Labor from the Old Regime to 1848.* Cambridge: Cambridge University Press, 1980.

Sheridan, G.J. "The Political Economy of Artisan Industry: Government and the People in the Silk Trade of Lyon, 1830–1870." *French Historical Studies* 11 (1979): 215–38.

Snyder, D., and Tilly, C. "Hardship and Collective Violence in France, 1830–1960." *American Sociological Review* 37 (1972): 520–32.

Société d'histoire de la Révolution de 1848. *Etudes.* Vol. 19. *Aspects de la crise et de la dépression de l'économie française au milieu de XIXe siècle.* La Roche-sur-Yon: Imprimerie Centrale de l'Ouest, 1956.

Stearns, P. *Paths to Authority.* Urbana: University of Illinois Press, 1978.

– "Patterns of Industrial Strike Activity in France during the July Monarchy." *American Historical Review* 70 (1964–5): 371–94.

Strumingher, L. "The Artisan Family: Traditions and Transition in Nineteenth Century Lyon." *Journal of Family History* 2 (1977): 211–22.

Tchernoff, J. *Associations et sociétés secrètes sous la deuxième République.* Paris: n.p., 1905.

Tenot, E. *La province en décembre 1851.* Paris: A. Le Chevalier, 1868.

Thompson, E.P. "The Moral Economy of the English Crowd in the Eighteenth Century." *Past & Present,* no. 50 (1972) 76–136.

Tilly, C., L., and R. *The Rebellious Century, 1830–1930.* Cambridge: Harvard University Press, 1975.

Tricaud, L. de. *Histoire du Département de l'Aine du 24 février au 20 décembre 1848.* Bourg-en Bresse: Compte-Millier, 1874.

Truchon, P. "La vie ouvrière à Lyon sous la Restauration." *Revue d'histoire de Lyon* 2 (1912): 195–222.

Tudesq, A.J. *Les grands notables en France.* 2 vols. Paris: Presses Universitaires de France, 1964.

– *L'Election présidentielle de Louis-Napoleon Bonaparte.* Paris: Armand Colin, 1965.

Vaucelles, L. de. "La querelle scolaire sous la Seconde République à Guillotière." *Cahiers d'histoire* 4 (1964): 365–88.

Vidalenc, J. "La province et les journées de juin." *Etudes d'histoire moderne et contemporaine* 2 (1948): 83–144.

Vigier, P. *La Seconde République*. Paris: Presses Universitaires de France, 1967.
– *La Seconde République dans la région alpine: Etude politique et sociale*. 2 vols. Paris: Presses Universitaires de France, 1963.
Wasserman, S. "Le club de Raspail de 1848." *Révolution de 1848* 5 (1908–9): 589–605, 655–74, 748–62.
Watkins, J.B. "The Working-Class Deputies of the French Constituent Assembly." PHD dissertation, University of North Carolina, Chapel Hill, 1970.
Weill, G. *Histoire du parti républicain en France*. Paris: Felix Alcan, 1928.
Zaniewicki, W. "L'Armée au lendemain de la Révolution de 1848." *Cahiers d'histoire* 14 (1969): 393–419.
Zastenker, N. "La Montagne en 1849." *Questions d'histoire* 1 (1954): 102–38.

Index